FISHING FOR CHICKENS

FISHING *for* CHICKENS

A SMOKIES FOOD
— MEMOIR —

JIM CASADA

THE UNIVERSITY OF GEORGIA PRESS
ATHENS

Published by the University of Georgia Press
Athens, Georgia 30602
www.ugapress.org
© 2022 by Jim Casada
All rights reserved

Designed by Lindsay Starr
Set in Warnock Pro and Unit Gothic
Printed and bound by IBI

The paper in this book meets the guidelines for
permanence and durability of the Committee on
Production Guidelines for Book Longevity of the
Council on Library Resources.

Most University of Georgia Press titles are
available from popular e-book vendors.

Printed in the United States of America
22 23 24 25 26 P 5 4 3 2 1

Library of Congress Number: 2022932776
ISBN: 9780820362120 (paperback)
ISBN: 9780820362113 (ebook)

Frontispiece: A barefooted young hunter with a long rifle, powder horn, and possibles
bag. Hunting, primarily for bears, wild turkeys, and small game, was an important
part of daily existence and diet for many who lived in the Smokies.
Courtesy of the National Park Service.

Page vi: John Wade prepares to butcher a hog suspended from a gambrel.
Courtesy of Hunter Library, Western Carolina University.

To the memory of the three finest cooks I've ever known, my paternal grandmother, Minnie Casada; my mother, Anna Lou Casada; and my late wife, Ann Casada. All were self-taught culinary wizards, loving souls, and in the case of the first two, wonderful mentors when it came to the mystery and magic of mountain cooking. Both Momma and Grandma had traumatic childhoods—Grandma Minnie was indentured or "bound," something that still existed in the late nineteenth century, while as an infant Momma lost her mother, and her peripatetic father essentially left others in the family to raise her. As a result, Momma's youth was so filled with moves from one place to another that when she and Daddy married, bought a home, and settled down in Bryson City, her heartfelt statement was: "I never want to move again." For well over a half century, until the final weeks of her life, when the ravages of Parkinson's disease forced her into a nursing home, she never did.

For these two women, cooking became an expression of who they were, a means whereby they could simultaneously exercise creativity and convey love to others, and an activity that gave them a great deal of quiet satisfaction. Seldom does a day pass when I don't think of one or both of them, and rarer still are the times when I prepare or eat some traditional mountain dish without them coming to mind. Even after the passage of decades, I miss them terribly, but their influence in the form of mountain fixings and a great deal more remains as powerful and persuasive as ever.

As for Ann, at the point when we married, she was singularly inept in culinary matters, but she was a quick learner and absorbed mountain food wisdom like cornmeal soaking up buttermilk as batter is being prepared for a pone of cornbread. She also read voraciously and within the first decade or so of our marriage had easily surpassed me in terms of actual "in the kitchen" skills, although as a daughter of the Southside Virginia soil, she obviously lacked the deeply rooted link to mountain food folkways I had been exposed to from earliest memory. She was my stellar and skilled partner in a number of cookbooks, and her influence, while largely intangible, permeates these pages just as that of Grandma Minnie and Momma does.

CONTENTS

ACKNOWLEDGMENTS

While this cookbook is dedicated to my grandmother, mother, and wife, I would be remiss if I failed to mention others who have, in varying ways, made a meaningful impact on my long-standing interest in Smokies' foodways.

Foremost among those individuals is my webmaster, distant cousin, and cherished friend, Tipper Pressley. A mountain cook in the finest tradition of the kitchen arts, she occasionally teaches classes in the subject at John C. Campbell Folk School. More significantly, her daily internet dose of Appalachian culture, Blind Pig and the Acorn, regularly features recipes and food lore. For years I've pestered her to put her boundless wisdom into a cookbook, and hopefully someday she will. Anytime I get stuck on something to do with cooking, I know I can turn to her with every expectation of receiving a helpful answer.

A number of friends have assisted me, knowingly and otherwise, with useful information. Larry Proffitt, the owner of famed Ridgewood Barbecue in upper east Tennessee, is not only a cherished friend and good turkey hunting buddy, he is *the* man when it comes to anything connected with hickory-smoked hog. How many little restaurants stuck in the middle of nowhere on a Tennessee back road have been the subject of a book (Fred Sauceman's *The Proffitts of Ridgewood*)? Whenever I talk with or have an email from Craig Stripling, a genial Texan who shares my love of foodlore, my spirits lift perceptibly, and when he comments that some recent dish was "larruping good," I'm reminded of the fact that food talk is not limited to the geographical confines of my beloved Smokies. Delia Watkins, a powerful link to foodways of yesteryear whose culinary skills were well known on the local scene, graciously shared her memories. The influence and recollections of other fine cooks also figure in these pages—my aunt Emma Burnett; venerable Maggie "Aunt Mag" Williams, a beloved Black neighbor from my boyhood; Beulah Sudderth, a Black cook of the next generation after Aunt Mag whose love affair with food and cooking was an inspiration; and extended family members who always had something special for summertime family reunions. Others who shared insights or food memories include Bunny Burnett and her late husband, Bill, along with cookbook author and lifelong friend Sue Hyde and high school class-mate and good friend Maxine Freeman Skelton.

Family ties underlie this entire work, and they extend from those no longer with us—my parents, paternal grandparents, and a bunch of aunts and uncles—to those who still savor mountain fare and food memories, including my siblings, Don Casada (and Don's wife, Susan) and Annette Hensley, along with first cousins James Burnett and Carolyn Healy. My brother and sister reinforced and/or expanded recollections of all sorts of food-related aspects of daily life, and my cousins have been able to shed considerable light on the lives of our paternal grandparents. My daughter, Natasha, has been a steady cheerleader and on more than one occasion has made my day with words such as "it's gratifying to know the old man can still work in a hard and productive fashion."

Finally, at every step of the process from initial inquiry about the manuscript forward, staff at the University of Georgia Press have been gracious, helpful, and prompt (something that is not always the case with academic publishers). I owe them a genuine debt of gratitude, and special praise is due to Nate Holly, the acquisitions editor with whom I've worked closely throughout the project. His enthusiasm, prompt responses to any and all questions, and willingness to deal patiently with a technological troglodyte have been gratifying indeed. Similarly, Jon Davies, managing editor at the Press, has been timely in his responses and admirably pro-fessional every step of the way. Courtney Denney, the copyeditor who handled my manuscript, not only did a stellar job in righting my literary wrongs but was a distinct pleasure to work with as well.

FISHING FOR CHICKENS

Minnie Price Casada (Grandma Minnie) holding me as an infant (circa 1943) at the side of her home, where I spent so many wonderful days and enjoyed so much fine food.

Courtesy of the Casada family.

INTRODUCTION

These words are being written in December, and decreasing daylight associated with this time of year can be depressing and bring on that miserable malady variously known by mountain folks as cabin fever, the miseries, or mullygrubs. It seems that even on sunny days, deep down in a mountain hollow or on a north-facing slope, brightness never penetrates. Such times somehow seem made for the resurrection of memories and the comfort of filling and fulfilling foodstuffs. Short of dining on sumptuous dishes redolent of Smokies cooking at its finest, I know of no better way to drive away the blues than through food memories. There's a great deal of delight to be had from indulgence in such daydreaming. While they obviously form an integral part of such excursions into the past, this material isn't just a collection of traditional family recipes. It's a history of how my family lived, an exercise in social commentary, and a reflection of time and place. Join me in a loving trip back to a gustatory world we have to some degree lost. It has much to tell us about the Smokies and indeed all of southern Appalachia as they once were.

All the reminiscences touch, in some fashion or other, on traditional foods. As such, they are intended to sharpen memory, whet appetites, and serve as an introduction to a wide-ranging assortment of food memories, food folkways, and recipes, many of them treasured hand-me-downs, from an individual who proudly styles himself a son of the Smokies. I grew up in Bryson City, North Carolina, a small town set squarely in the heart of the Great Smokies, and from the earliest reaches of my memory onward mountain foodways have held immense appeal for me.

Among the clearest of my early recollections, ones that reach back to a time when my growing mind and body were at that point when humans start assembling the mental collectibles that will accompany them all their years, are those directly related to food. My first regular assigned household chore as a small boy involved splitting kindling for the wood stove on which Momma prepared our meals. During the warmer months of the year its use would be limited to preparation of breakfast and dinner (the midday meal), and it would be allowed to die down during the heat of the day. Sometime before I went to bed I would be responsible for laying the next day's fire. That involved stacking some rich pine kindling atop crumpled newspaper. The bigger sticks of wood were kept in a box beside the stove and Momma or Daddy would add those when they lit the stove to begin breakfast preparations.

I took the job seriously, at least in part because I loved going down in the basement and chopping up kindling with a small hatchet. That didn't seem like real work, and Daddy's stern stipulations about exercising due care not to chop off a finger and stressing the importance of the job gave me a case of the "big head," which had precisely the end result he intended. I was careful, took pride in my work, and derived quiet satisfaction from being part of the household's overall approach to food preparation.

The wood-burning stove was replaced when I was still just a splinter of a boy—maybe seven or eight years of age—with the marvel of an electric stove. For a time Momma had decidedly mixed feelings about having gone upscale. She reckoned the oven didn't bake bread the way her old wood burner had, moaned about not having a "warmer" in which to keep bread, and no doubt had to make some adjustments in terms of how fast things cooked and heat control. But she liked being able to turn a burner on and be in business immediately, and certainly the comparative absence of heat during the summer months was a blessing.

While the wood-burning stove left our household in my tender youth, it didn't go far and I didn't lose touch with it. Daddy gave it to Aunt Mag Williams, a wonderful old Black lady (yes, "Aunt" was the standard way of describing venerable and particularly honored African Americans in that time and place, and it was in no way meant in disrespect—our entire family loved Aunt Mag) who lived only a couple hundred yards down the road. There, thanks to Aunt Mag's generosity and the fact that I regularly gave her fish in return for worm-digging privileges in her chicken lot, along with selling her the carcasses of muskrats I had trapped, I had a standing invitation to drop by for a bite to eat.

One bitterly cold winter day I had been out rabbit hunting by myself for a number of hours. For some reason, perhaps suspecting there might be a piece of pie or a batch of cookies just beckoning a greedy-gut lad, I knocked on the door and was, as always, welcomed in the little frame house. Aunt Mag was, as usual, knitting in her living room rocking chair, but my primary impression was that the aroma coming out of the adjacent kitchen was enough to set salivary glands into overflow mode.

I commented on the wonderful smell and asked what was cooking. "Oh, I made me a stew this morning," she said, "and it's sitting on the stove just keeping warm. Get you a bowl off the shelf over there, you know where they are [that was a certainty—I had plenty of prior experience when it came to eating her fixings], and spoon you out some. There's some cornbread too if you want a piece."

That was exactly what I had hoped to hear and no second invitation was required. There was in due course, however, a second helping. It was a rich, savory stew, liberally laced with carrots, potatoes, green peas, and gravy, but the key ingredient was chunks of meat I didn't recognize. Not that it really mattered for the moment. The meat and vegetables had melded in a delightful fashion, and it seemed to me as fine as anything I'd ever eaten. Finally, after two whopping bowls, I belatedly remembered my manners and thanked Aunt Mag while politely inquiring what it was I'd been enjoying.

It was the moment for which she had waited. Cackling with pure delight, she said: "You been eating muskrat. Ain't it fine? Now you see why I been paying you a quarter for every one you bring me." Once again the old wood-burning stove and Aunt Mag's genius had worked wonders. The pair presumably continued their partnership until her death, not much short of the century mark. By then I was off at college, but the marvels she and that old stove wrought remain entrenched in my mind until this day.

Aunt Mag and that ancient stove belong to a world we have long since lost, but through traditional recipes and methods of preparing them we can at least retain tenuous links to tastes from the past. One such link comes through cookbooks, but therein lies something of a conundrum. Unquestionably the Smokies region is an area with rich and rewarding culinary history. Yet most cookbooks dealing with food from the region treat it as merely being a part of southern Appalachia. They define "southern Appalachia" as a region encompassing parts of West Virginia, Virginia, Tennessee, Kentucky, the Carolinas, Georgia, and Alabama. Some even include Ohio and Mississippi. Unquestionably the hill-and-hollow folks of that wide swath of America share many culinary traditions in common, and you'll find foodstuffs such as cornbread and streaked meat, wild game and chicken, as bright aspects anywhere you go in the lower reaches and extensions of that ancient spine of time known as the Appalachian chain.

I would staunchly maintain, however, that the Smokies area is distinctive and different in a host of subtle yet ultimately significant ways. Accordingly this book is far more limited in geographical scope than the wide-ranging and somewhat amorphous southern Appalachia. It deals strictly with the Great Smokies of western North Carolina and east Tennessee along with the immediately contiguous chains of mountains—those such as the Blacks, Nantahalas, Alarkas, Snowbirds, and Unakas. The precise geographical boundaries of the Smokies can vary somewhat according to individuals, and interestingly many folks who, strictly speaking, did not grow up within the Great Smokies claim them as their homeland. That's a testament to the aura of mystique, one that at times approaches reverence, associated with the region. A poet who called Bryson City home for much of his life, Leroy Sossamon, once described the Smokies in the title for one of his books as the *Backside of Heaven*. That's about as fine an assessment of the bewitching appeal of these hills and hollows as anyone could desire.

As far as specific geographical boundaries for the Great Smokies, there's arguably no better qualified authority than an early explorer of the region, Arnold Guyot. In a map of what he labeled the "Great Smoky Mounts," the range covers the area from the Little Tennessee River northwards to where it meets the Newfound Mountains at Max Patch, including the peaks to the east of the Pigeon River up to the Newfound Mountains. That embraces portions of today's counties of Swain and Haywood in North Carolina and Blount, Cocke, and Sevier in Tennessee. The immediately adjacent counties of Cherokee, Graham, Macon, and Jackson in North Carolina sometimes claim to lie within the Smokies, but this is a bit of a stretch. They actually embrace mountain chains linked to the Smokies.

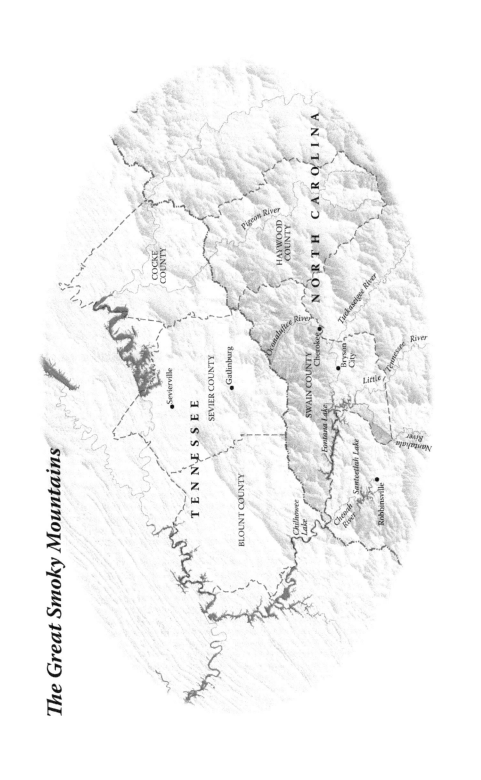

The Great Smoky Mountains

It's where I grew up, where the roots of not only my food knowledge but the essence of my being belong. This book offers one individual's perspective on what might be called a subculture or subregion of Appalachia as a whole. It involves dishes I've cooked and eaten, recipes handed down through family or close friends, food memories of an intensely personal nature, and an abiding love for a fast-fading way of life. Fancy-dancy food magazines and self-ordained cuisine cognoscenti regularly rave about gustatory delights reflecting the Appalachian cooking tradition. Yet they focus on restaurants in regional cities such as Asheville and Nashville, Chattanooga and Cleveland, or even the bustling metropolis of Atlanta. Simply put, they are missing the boat, at least in my eyes.

Real mountain cooking involves instinct as much as it does precise ingredients, experience rather than the expertise of formal training. I'll give one specific example to make my point. In recent years ramps have been all the rage in high-dollar restaurants in the region and beyond. More than once I've had waitstaff mention during menu discussions some item or the other garnished with ramps or featuring ramps as a side dish. I simply ask whether they have been cooked, and without exception, the answer is yes. That's understandable, because the aftereffects of raw ramps redefine halitosis and make garlic seem a pantywaist poseur. When I was a youngster, anyone coming to school after having eaten a "bait" of ramps earned an automatic three-day pass. You simply couldn't stand to be in the same room with the offender.

Yet raw ramps as part of a salad of branch lettuce "kilt" with grease from hot bacon or fried streaked meat, dosed with a few drops of vinegar, and dusted with salt and black pepper will, to use an old mountain description, "make you slap your granny." So will finely chopped ramps atop a dish of scrambled eggs cooked with real butter and partnered with a cathead biscuit or two slathered in butter. It's just that everyone present or who will be around those dining on this delicacy need to partake of the dish. Doing so means no worry about odiferous matters. That won't work for a public eatery. But this book is about home cooking, not an excursion into the higher realms of culinary wonders as defined through restaurant fare and all too many contemporary eyes.

I now realize that my family was, if you looked at matters from a national perspective rather than that of the Smokies in the 1940s and 1950s, comparatively poor. We weren't impoverished by any means, and the word a good friend and high school classmate uses to describe her family's circumstances at the time, destitute, was not applicable. We always had plenty of food on the table, never worried about where the next meal was coming from, and my siblings and I got some new clothing at the beginning of each school year. It was only when I went off to college and saw others who had folding money in their pockets and didn't give a second thought to eating out or spending several dollars on a date that reality dawned about the true nature of our circumstances.

Maybe the best way to describe the situation is through a story my father, who lived to the age of 101 and was keen as a properly sharpened Case knife right to the end, loved to tell. I was in the first grade, and as was frequently the case over the course of the school year, the class was asked to contribute money for some project or the other. Most students volunteered a few cents or maybe even a nickel or dime. Not me. In a classic example of a little shaver getting a bad case of the big britches, I spoke up and said: "My daddy will give five dollars!"

When I got home and told Mom and Dad what I had promised, the world seemed to cave in. That amount of money represented a good start toward the monthly payment on their mortgage (they had bought the house and land for $2,500 on a long-term note) and would have taken care of most of our store-bought food needs for a week. Daddy honored my commitment but only after the kind of parental input that left no doubt whatsoever that there would be no future pledges, no matter how small, from his oldest child. He did, however, garner some long-term benefit. Over the years he must have told that tale fifty times, always doing so when I was present, for a renewed round of well-deserved humiliation.

I now know that my family, and to an even greater extent many of the families of my contemporaries, lived an existence that in some ways was not all that distant from pioneer times. That was particularly true when it came to self-sufficiency. Virtually everyone was poor, at least if you measured personal wealth on the basis of money in the bank, but we were rich in knowing how to grow, raise, catch, kill, trap, or find in nature essentials for life. We had a keen sense of community, an even stronger one of family ties, and most of all a deeply embedded love of place. It was a way of life, and of all the familial ties binding us together, food was the strongest. Our life may have been simple and our sustenance marked by cornbread, not crêpes suzette, but it was a good one. We not only had an adequate amount to eat. We ate wonderfully well.

With that in mind, it seems fitting to start with a sort of preliminary quiz—mental food prep if you will. Here, in the form of a lengthy list of culinary experiences, is your opportunity to take this little examination on mountain cuisine. If you can honestly answer "yes" to a goodly number of the questions, then it is probable this line of discourse has found your salivary glands kicking into involuntary overdrive and that you are already familiar with the joy provided by traveling in the fast lane to the loftier southern regions of culinary paradise. Conversely, if most of what for me are winsome food memories seem strange to you, let not your pea-picking heart be troubled. A brave new world of tastes and treats lies ahead. In other words, this is a quiz where no one fails and where everyone has the opportunity to open the door to what my Grandpa Joe would have described as "some mighty fine fixings." With each point below I am simply asking: HAVE YOU EVER?

- Eaten a supper consisting of nothing but cornbread and milk (either sweet or buttermilk). Those who haven't enjoyed this culinary pleasure might think it constitutes slim pickings. In truth, a big chunk of cornbread made from stone-ground meal and crumbled in a glass of cold milk is a taste treat of great delight.

- Enjoyed home-churned butter, nicely salted and pressed in an old-time wooden mold.

- Eaten fried pies with filling made from dried apples or peaches folded into a round piece of dough folded like a half moon to hold the fruit. Slathered with butter, such fare is fit for a king or any son or daughter of the Smokies.

- Dined on baked chicken when the featured dish came from a free-range flock. The beautifully browned hen will have lots of little eggs in the making inside the body cavity, and those are a real delicacy.

- Poured molasses over soft butter and mashed it all up before applying the resultant mix to a cathead biscuit. The trick is to get just the right amount of molasses and butter for the biscuit, although missing your measurement isn't a tragedy. It's just an excuse to eat another biscuit.

- Enjoyed the cane syrup known as Dixie Dew. I'm not at all sure Dixie Dew even exists anymore, but it was a staple on our family table. While it was undeniably tasty, I liked both molasses and honey better than it. Nonetheless, this sweetening from the 1950s had an absolutely irresistible advertising slogan. It read:

"Covers Dixie like the dew and gives a biscuit a college education." Some public relations genius had to be behind that piece
of wordsmithing.

• Eaten fresh-made pork sausage for breakfast. If you have partaken of fresh sausage, chances are pretty good that you've
also had the even greater pleasure of eating tenderloin from a
recently butchered hog.

• Been part of the rendering process that produces cracklings or,
better still, chomped down on a big chunk of crackling cornbread. It's a treat that will make you shed worries about cholesterol simply because of the pure pleasure it produces.

• Had hamburger or sausage made into milk gravy, and with cornbread, served as a main dish. That was one of Mom's favorite
ways of making a relatively small amount of meat go a long way.

• Eaten old-fashioned stick candy in flavors such as horehound.

• Taken a hefty dose of sulfur and molasses, or maybe a cup of
sassafras tea, as a "spring tonic."

• Gathered poke sallet and eaten it as a welcome fresh vegetable after a long run of those that kept well—such as cabbage,
turnips, carrots, and potatoes—but lacked the spring taste of
earth's rebirth.

• Drunk syllabub at Christmastime.

• Prepared chicken for the family table the old-fashioned way—
catching the live chicken, either wringing its neck or chopping
off its head, removing the entrails while being careful to save
the giblets, plunging the fowl into scalding water, then plucking
the feathers. To go through this arduous background work,
which was standard stuff for our forebears, will give you a fuller
appreciation of just how they worked as they went about their
daily lives.

• Slopped hogs.

• Fed scratch feed to chickens.

• Shelled corn you had raised to feed fattening hogs you
would eventually eat.

- "Plugged" a watermelon to check its ripeness. I never really understood this process; once the melon was plugged it had to be used.

- Eaten sauce or pies made from some of the winter squash that were widely grown, along with pumpkins, in the mountains. Among them were candy roasters and cushaws.

- Feasted on country ham your family had cured, with the obligatory side dishes of redeye gravy and biscuits.

- Eaten sawmill gravy (a milk and cornmeal gravy, usually made with drippings from sausage or bacon with plenty of meat bits left in for good measure).

- Savored a properly made stack cake, with at least seven thin layers of cake, each one separated by spiced sauce made from dried apples or maybe blackberry jam.

- Attended an all-day singing with dinner on the grounds.

- Participated in an old-fashioned homecoming or family reunion with dishes such as cold fried chicken, ham biscuits, deviled eggs, and potato salad.

- Saved the rinds from a feast of watermelon to be "put up" as watermelon pickles.

- Prepared homemade peach pickles.

- Drunk water straight from a mountain spring that was so icy cold it set your teeth on edge.

- Participated in a watermelon seed-spitting contest.

- Picked up ripe honey locust pods from the ground and eaten the meat that surrounds the seeds.

- Found a prime patch of hazelnut bushes and gathered the delicious nuts.

- Gathered fox grapes to make jelly.

- Dined on small game—squirrel, rabbit, quail, or grouse—you had killed and cleaned.

- Enjoyed freshly caught trout wearing dinner jackets of stone-ground cornmeal fried to a golden turn and served with fried taters and onions.

- Located a hollow filled with pawpaw bushes (they never quite attain tree status) laden with ripe fruit and enjoyed a woodland feast.

- Eaten the sweet-sour flesh surrounding the seeds of yellowed maypop fruit.

- Sampled liver mush, liver pudding, scrapple, headcheese, or other foods made from the parts of pigs that frugal "waste not, want not" mountain folks put to good and tasty use.

- Eaten a cobbler made from berries you picked.

If you haven't done any of these things, you have lived what I genuinely consider a life of culinary deprivation and almost certainly don't have deep mountain roots. Fortunately, there's no time like the present to change the deprivation part of the equation. On the other hand, if you share many of these food memories, consider yourself blessed as well as being someone pretty well immersed in mountain culinary traditions. Even so, however, I think you'll find the wide-ranging sampling of food memories and recipes that follows worthy of your attention and a resource for recollection.

Two young boys dig into a meal at a mountain
table set with the standard condiments.
Courtesy of Hunter Library, Western Carolina University.

Plowing ground in preparation for spring planting.
Courtesy of the National Park Service.

PART I

STAPLES OF LIFE

Come stroll with me down memory lane
To happenings in days of yore
When we lived a good life in the Smokies
In spite of our being "pore."

GLADYS TRENTHAM RUSSELL,
It Happened in the Smokies

Until fairly modern times (post–World War II) mountain diet involved, to a considerable degree, living off the land. Rural folks raised their own livestock, grew their own fruits and vegetables, and supplemented these with game, fish, berries, fruits, nuts, and greens from nature's abundant larder. Only a few necessities, such as salt, spices, and perhaps sugar, came from stores. The primary form of sweetening was often provided by molasses from cane the family grew, sometimes supplemented by honey, or less frequently, maple syrup. Through drying, canning, pickling, smoking, storage in root cellars or canneries, use of spring houses for perseveration, and other means, hardy high-country residents were self-sufficient. Even when it came to things like flour and cornmeal, they either had a small tub mill of their own, or more frequently, took grain—corn, wheat, and even rye, along with buckwheat (which is technically not a grain)—to the local mill to be ground. The miller was usually paid in a barter system, keeping a portion of what he ground.

Virtually every family had chickens, hogs, and a milk cow. Sometimes turkeys or guineas figured in the mix of domestic fowl. Until the sad demise of the American chestnut, hogs ranged wild for a portion of the year, with distinctive ear markings enabling owners to identify what pigs belonged to them. Beef rarely figured in mountain diet, but milk, buttermilk, and butter were staples. A country family without a milk cow was in effect destitute.

The coverage in this section focuses on the dietary items that formed the heart of what sons and daughters of the Smokies ate on a daily basis. Almost all the recipes belong to what might be described as traditional foodstuffs. That means you won't find Italian, Tex-Mex, Asian, or French fare. Dishes from the British Isles, on the other hand, do appear. This recognizes the Scots-Irish roots of most of those who resided in southern Appalachia in general and the Smokies in particular. With relatively few exceptions, the recipes come from my family or that of my wife, and in every instance, they involve dishes that have actually been prepared in Casada kitchens. Taken in their entirety, what you will find in these opening nine chapters represents a solid cross-section of both daily fare and delicacies from mountain life in yesteryear.

CHAPTER 1

CORN

Long before the first white settlers made their way down the ancient spine of the Appalachians into the highlands, corn was a staple of mountain life. As part of the "three sisters" approach to agriculture practiced by the Cherokees, corn, beans, and pumpkins and other winter squash figured prominently in American Indian diet. Pioneering Europeans learned of its uses and methods of cultivation from Indians, for the grain was foreign to their experience. Originally known as turkey wheat, corn was consumed in an amazing variety of ways.

These included standard Indian approaches such as "samp" (ground corn soaked in milk until it reached a porridgelike consistency), bread made from grains that had been pounded with homemade mortars carved from especially dense woods such as dogwood or persimmon, and hominy. Soon settlers expanded the uses of corn in dramatic fashion. It was used not only as a human foodstuff but as fodder for farm animals: corn shocks dotted farm fields and were fed to cattle as needed during the lean months of winter; the grain finished fattening hogs after they had been browsing on chestnut mast; and cracked grain and inferior ears called "nubbins"

An elderly man "grits" corn using a homemade device. This was a common way of readying corn for cooking at the point when it was just past the "milk" or roasting ear stage and beginning to harden and become starchy.

Courtesy of Hunter Library, Western Carolina University.

became scratch feed for chickens. Crude mattresses were sometimes stuffed with husks, and cobs soaked in kerosene furnished a sure, swift way to get a fire started in cook stoves or hearths. Husks became works of primitive art when fashioned into dolls. Even cobs had uses. Corncob jelly and corncob dumplings were considered delicacies. Cobs could be shaped into bowls for homemade pipes used to smoke homegrown burley tobacco. Insertion of a slender peg of hickory, dogwood, or other dense wood turned a portion of a cob into a "striker" for slate turkey calls. While the use of cobs as a substitute for toilet paper is likely more myth than reality, rough humor often attributed this use to cobs.

A section of corncob, whittled to shape, made a fine stopper for a jug, and that brings us to the most notorious and controversial use of corn—for production of moonshine. This is unquestionably a notorious and infamous aspect of corn's role in mountain life. Variously described with terms such as white lightning, squeezings, golden moonbeam, stump water, tanglefoot, mountain dew, peartning juice, and snakebite medicine, liquid corn became a standard if illicit adjunct to life on many homesteads in the Smokies.

Call liquid corn what you will, and duly recognizing it was less prevalent than many would have you believe, the making of it was a widespread cottage industry in the mountains, although it was not practiced to anywhere near the degree reading of books such as Horace Kephart's *Our Southern Highlanders* would lead one to believe. Kephart was given to sensational stereotyping, and the book suffers considerably from that fact (a full 40 percent of it is devoted to various aspects of moonshining). He was also a noted consumer of squeezings, and he died in an automobile wreck after a visit to a local moonshiner.

The corn of choice for production of moonshine was Hickory Cane. It contains higher sugar content than a rival type of field corn, Hickory King, and that extra sweetness meant a bit less store-bought sugar was required in the distillation process. The late Popcorn Sutton, a legend among modern moonshiners who lived over Maggie Valley way, once told me that there was "no finer corn for making a run of likker than Hickory Cane grown in mountain soil." I'll leave it to others to judge the accuracy of Popcorn's statement, but you have to give some credence to a noted practitioner of the moonshiner's art who was also the author of a book on the subject, *Me and My Likker* (almost certainly ghostwritten), and who achieved cult status in his later years and following his death by suicide.

Carefully constructed corn shocks were a standard feature in winter fields of yesteryear. In addition to furnishing food for livestock, those shocks often did double duty as protection for other foodstuffs such as pumpkins, cabbage, and turnips. Buried in straw beneath the base of a sizeable corn shock, they were nicely protected from the elements until such time as they were needed in the family kitchen.

Corn was a crop that could be raised almost anywhere—from rich bottomlands along the region's larger streams to steep hillsides in remote hardwood coves where girdled trees let in enough sun to grow a patch for a few years until the thin soil was exhausted. The grain figured prominently in mountain diet at all seasons. A line from a traditional folk tune, "Jimmy cracked corn and I don't care," was suggestive in that regard. Family farming practices revolved around corn and where it was to be planted, because it was the most essential of all agricultural crops and figured in diet throughout the year.

Once danger of frost was past, spring planting would find families sowing row upon row, using seed carefully selected and saved from the previous year's crop. There would be field corn such as Hickory King for animal food and cornmeal, decorative Indian corn with its seeds of many colors, "sweet" corn to be eaten fresh throughout much of the summer, and possibly even a few rows or a small patch of popcorn. Successive plantings, spaced two weeks apart, could produce fresh sweet corn from the first roasting ears of the year well into late summer's dog days.

Some interesting sidelights to growing corn merely added to its appeal. Thanks to standing tall and strong, field corn was tailor-made for its symbiotic relationship with beans, another plant in the traditional "three sisters" crop system. The stalks provided ideal support for October beans or other climbers, as they did for field peas if those legumes happened to be preferred. While planting pumpkins (or perhaps candy roasters) to complete the interstices of the three sisters was commonplace, many mountain farm corn patches would also have volunteer ground cherries come up among the rows. A knowing hand with a hoe made sure not to chop these providers of tasty treats.

While "garden truck" corn was harvested with the ears still green and the kernels in the milk stage for the table and for canning by itself or as the base ingredient in soup mix, field corn with its lower sugar content and higher starch content took up far more cultivated space on mountain farms. The explanation was simple—for most homes, especially outside the region's towns, it produced the meal from which the majority of their bread was baked, from which grits were ground, hominy processed, livestock fed, and daily life lived.

My youth included a great deal of experience with field corn at Grandpa Joe's place, because he always grew enough to take care of fattening hogs and feeding chickens as well as providing corn to be ground into meal. Once on a lovely Saturday in early October we were working our way through a patch close to the pig pen pulling up armfuls of the plentiful "hog weed" (purslane) to slop the hogs. The swine loved that vegetable, which was also a favorite with humans, and it was available in great abundance on Grandpa's place.

He lived on the banks of the Tuckaseigee River near Bryson City, and one of my great boyhood ambitions was to throw a rock across what is, by mountain standards, a major stream. On the fateful fall day that I happened to mention that unfulfilled dream, Grandpa chuckled then said: "Why, I can throw a rock across the river." This came from a man well into his seventies, crippled and bent with arthritis, and to me the very thought of him making such a throw was ridiculous.

Accordingly I responded: "Why, Grandpa, if you throw a rock across the river, I'll pull weeds and slop the hogs for a week all by myself." It never occurred to me to get a quid pro quo should he fail—the whole concept was so preposterous I deemed it an impossible task.

Grandpa replied with one of his favorite expressions. "Well, I reckon I'll just have to show you." He then took out his razor-sharp Barlow knife, looked around a bit, and selected a particularly tall stalk of corn. He cut it off close to the ground, stripped the fodder, then cut the upper end a ways from the top. He was left with a stalk about seven or eight feet long.

His next step, undertaken with meticulous care, was to cut out a notch in the stalk a few inches from its smaller end. At that point I suddenly began to get an inkling of what he had in mind and realized that a major mechanical advantage just might enter into his "throwing." Sure enough, we walked down to the riverbank, where after kicking around in the rocks a bit, he selected a donnick that suited his fancy. He fitted it into the notch and with an over-the-shoulder heave launched the rock from the cornstalk in a fashion somewhat reminiscent of an atlatl. It was still going up when it got to the other side of the river.

He turned to me, a grin splitting the wrinkles that lined his face like so many waterways on a topographical map, and said: "Son, things ain't always what they seem. I reckon you better get busy pulling weeds for those hogs." Then, still bemused by the manifest misery of his crestfallen sidekick, he added, "But I'll help you. By the time we finish I reckon your Grandma will have dinner ready." Rest assured that corn in at least two forms, one of them being cornbread, was part of that meal and every other summer and early fall midday meal at Grandma's. I have no idea what else we ate at that particular dinner, but I never think of corn without remembering that Indian summer day.

The ingenuity of mountain cooks when it came to the use of corn was little short of incredible. Fresh sweet corn could be roasted, boiled on the cob, or as it matured and became increasingly starchy, cut from the cob and prepared cream-style or stewed with other vegetables such as tomatoes. Another use for the slightly starchy but still soft kernels was gritted cakes, made by mixing corn freshly cut from the cob with cornmeal and cooked on a griddle. Cornmeal, perhaps ground in a small tub mill owned by a family or taken to a mill and ground on shares, could be used in numerous ways—pones baked in a cast-iron skillet greased with fatback, hoecakes, muffins, fritters, corn dodgers, and the like. Often, especially in the case of pones, bread was made more delectable through the addition of cracklings (savory bits left when hog fat was rendered into lard), bits of bacon, chopped ramps in the springtime, or flakes of hot pepper. Almost always, when served hot, cornbread was accompanied by a hefty slathering of home-churned butter.

While biscuits or buckwheat cakes might form featured items on the breakfast menu, the main meal of the day, dinner (and in the mountain lexicon this is the midday repast) almost always offered hot cornbread accompanied by whatever the season and family circumstances allowed—fresh vegetables in the summer; canned or dried vegetables from late fall until the first wild greens of spring; long-keeping items such as pumpkin, winter squash, turnips, and onions; and the primary meat in mountain diet, pork, served as fried fatback, in sawmill gravy, as sausage with milk gravy, or less frequently, cured ham. Any wild game the menfolk happened to trap or kill, along with fish caught from rivers and streams, offered variety and formed a welcome bonus. Add dried fruit such as peaches or apples reconstituted into "sauce," or perhaps that fruit made into fried pies as dessert, and you had mighty tasty eating.

Always though, no matter what the supplemental fare, there were items based on that staff of mountain life, corn. Often supper would be nothing more than a hefty chunk of cold cornbread, perhaps accompanied by slices of raw onion or some streaked meat fried until it was crisp, with a big glass of sweet milk or buttermilk from the springhouse.

The meal ground to make cornbread, whether baked as a pone or prepared in any of its many other manifestations, came from a patch or patches set aside for that purpose. The ears would be allowed to dry in the sun of late summer and early fall before being pulled from the stalks and stored. One of the important characteristics of corn, in days before electricity, freezers, and all sorts of modern conveniences, was how it lent itself to storage. Weevils and flour moths could wreak havoc with ground meal, but corn still on the cob and with husks intact was much more resistant to insect depredations.

Every farm of any size had a corncrib, and a "friendly" king snake or black snake, perhaps ably aided by a cat that had proved to be a good "mouser," kept rats and mice at bay. Beyond that, a roof to keep out rain and snow was about all corn required until such time as it was to be shucked and shelled for chicken or hog feed, toted to a nearby mill for a run of cornmeal, made into hominy, or put to some other use.

Whenever the cornmeal supply ran low, whether the family had its own tub mill or carried it to a miller, it was time to visit the crib. Ears of corn would be shucked, perhaps of an evening before a warming fire, and hands already rough and hardened from hoeing and constant work would shell kernels from the cob. With the whole family involved in the shelling, getting enough grain for a run of meal—usually at least a half bushel of grain—could be accomplished in short order.

Along with cornmeal, some of the dry grain from field corn would be turning into grits or hominy. In the case of grits, which have never enjoyed quite the same level of popularity in the mountains as elsewhere in the South (gritted corn is another matter entirely), background preparation was a fairly straightforward undertaking. It involved little more than a different, coarser setting for grinding stones at the local mill. In the high country, grits were sometimes styled "little hominy," and to confuse matters further, elsewhere in the region they were referred to as "hominy grits."

Real hominy, however, was not ground at all, though it required considerable effort of a different sort. Ashes from wood cooking stoves and open hearths were regularly saved, because they had numerous uses in the "make do" ways of the high country. Ashes helped offset the typical acidity of mountain soil, provided lye for the production of soap, and were used to make hominy. The lye, formed by mixing wood ashes and water, softened the tough hull of individual kernels of corn. The grain swelled and shed the hull while soaking in lye, and after repeated rinsing with fresh water, the ultimate result was hominy. It could be eaten immediately or canned, and one of its advantages was that small "runs" could be made whenever needed.

Corn no longer figures anywhere nearly as prominently in mountain diet as was once the case. From the standpoint of health, that is probably just as well, but it must be remembered that folks who lived close to the land and worked hard from first light to coming night seldom worried about being overweight or having elevated cholesterol levels. Even today, changed lifestyles notwithstanding, those of us who are mountain born and bred consider corn in all its culinary forms a tasty and tangible part of life capable of bringing added pleasure to any meal. The next time a slice of buttered cornbread graces your plate, you happen to espy the increasingly anomalous sight of corn in shocks, or maybe notice some folk art such as corn-shuck dolls, pause and ponder for a moment. Your eyes are beholding things associated with corn that once were an integral and vitally important part of the mountain way of life.

As a foodstuff and in other ways, corn lay at the heart of mountain culture, and in culinary matters, it was ubiquitous. Corn in some form, and maybe several, would be consumed every day throughout the year. Cornbread graced tables as a matter of course, many a mountain lad and lass carried their lunch to school in a bucket that contained a chunk of cornbread and molasses, but those are merely two examples of the most common of usages. The ingenuity of those who went before us found a myriad of ways to enjoy this culinary pillar of high-country life.

As good a spot to begin as any is with corn fresh from the garden. Sometimes called roasting ears, at others corn on the cob or sweet corn, this is simple yet scrumptious fare at its finest. Boiled for a couple of minutes, cooked over charcoal with the shuck still in place (or with tinfoil covering the ear), or even eaten raw, freshly harvested new corn in the milky stage is fit to grace the tables of any five-star restaurant. Maybe you won't find it in such establishments, but mountain folks know fine vittles when they are put before them. As Grandpa Joe used to say at the conclusion of every mealtime prayer blessing food: "You'uns see what's before you. Eat hearty." Rest assured that with fresh corn eating hearty takes precious little encouragement. An ear (or maybe a couple of them) of piping-hot corn slathered in butter and seasoned with salt and pepper is something sure to bring tears of joy to the eyes of a country boy.

Yet this is but one of many ways to enjoy fresh corn. As the ears mature and begin to make the transition from sugar to starch, though still not hard, other methods of preparation come into play. They include creamed corn, fried corn (cooked in a frying pan with a bit of grease from a couple of pieces of streaked meat, this is a personal favorite), or gritted bread. All involve cutting or grating the corn from the cob, a somewhat arduous process but one worth every bit of the effort.

Gritted bread, which I haven't had in many a year, finds the grated corn being mixed with some flour or cornmeal, salt, a bit of baking soda, and some bacon or streaked meat grease and cooked in a cast-iron pan. It can be baked in the oven or cooked atop the stove. Either way it is delicious. When it's hot, adorn it with butter for a true treat, while cold gritted bread may grace a glass of sweet milk or buttermilk in a heavenly fashion.

Speaking of bread, cornbread appeared daily (usually twice or even three times a day) on menus, while biscuits or any type of bread made with wheat flour were reserved primarily for breakfast and special occasions. Still, there was enough variety to remove any danger that cornbread would become so commonplace as to be unwelcome. It might be served as dodgers, muffins, hoecakes, batter cakes cooked on a griddle like pancakes, or most commonly, a pone (a cake of cornbread baked in an iron skillet).

Every little mountain community had a grist mill of some kind, and one of the great virtues of the small, somewhat primitive mills that were so widespread in the mountains was that they were slow. Slow grinding meant less heat and tastier meal. Usually it would be sifted at least once before use in baking. This was to remove larger pieces of hull and chaff. Even the leavings weren't wasted. They became scratch feed for family chickens.

Two memorable experiences from my boyhood center on cornbread. The first one was, I must admit, a bit traumatic. I was away from home for a week to stay with my maternal grandparents in their home in Winston-Salem. It was a big city in my eyes, and it didn't take but a few hours for me to begin to get homesick. There were houses everywhere and no woods or branches where a boy could escape to play.

The real shocker, however, came at suppertime the first night. Grandma Ledford put out a big glass of milk, a cold chunk of cornbread, and nothing else in front of me. Mind you, I was accustomed to crumbling cornbread up in milk for a hearty snack, but the thought of this being *all* my supper was quite troubling. Yet I now know that such a meal was standard fare in mountain homes for many decades, and my grandmother, who grew up in Clay County just outside the Smokies, was being true to her culinary roots.

The other memory is quite different, because it is one that even after the passage of well over a half century can, as Grandpa Joe might have put it, "set a fellow to slobbering." Until I was in my teens, we raised our own hogs; or rather, Grandpa Joe raised hogs for the extended family after his children, including my father, bought piglets. Nothing went to waste, and that meant when the lard was rendered there were cracklings aplenty. Mom and Grandma Minnie canned them by stuffing jars full of the crisp, tasty, and cholesterol-laced tidbits before covering them with hot grease. The lard served as a sort of second seal.

A pone of cornbread with a liberal lacing of cracklings was as tasty as anything I've ever eaten in the bread line. Never mind that it is today deemed decidedly unhealthy, Grandpa Joe and Grandma Minnie ate crackling cornbread all their years. Both lived well over eight decades. I like to think they worked hard enough to counteract any and all fat and cholesterol, as was true for countless other mountain folks who led similar root-hog-or-die lives. Besides, anything that tastes as good as crackling cornbread can't be all bad.

Most mountain folks produced their own hominy, saving wood ashes for that purpose (and also to use in production of lye soap). It was an exacting process, but the end result was a dish of pure delight. Some folks turn away from hominy in disdain, but for me a hot bowl of it, nicely buttered and sprinkled with black pepper, makes mighty fine and filling fare.

The same thing seems to hold true with grits. Let folks from outside the South, pantywaist connoisseurs of cream of wheat, see a bowl of grits and they shake their heads in dismay or derision. Yet it is a dish, much like the corn from which it is produced, of incredible versatility and delectability. Buttered grits, grits and gravy, cheese grits, fried grits cakes, grilled grits (yes, you can grill leftover grits, and they are scrumptious) and various other uses come immediately to mind. The recipes that follow touch on a number of possibilities for using corn, but they are but a mere sampling of scrumptious eating that corn and creativity have produced.

Traditional Mountain Cornbread

The keys to making really good cornbread are: (1) Cook it in a well-seasoned cast-iron skillet, (2) Grease the skillet with streaked meat or bacon, (3) Use stone-ground cornmeal, and (4) Include the right ingredients. Most store-bought cornmeal has been ground at too high a temperature and this does something to the flavor. Often it also contains additives, such as salt or preservatives, which mitigate again a true traditional pone. Also, stone-ground cornmeal, even if it is sifted, has more body or "crunch" to it than other grocery shelf offerings. Buttermilk, eggs, and lard are essential if you want really moist cornbread. This simple recipe has served my family well for as far back as my memory stretches, and I know Grandma Minnie was preparing it this way, though she never measured anything, before the turn of the twentieth century.

Streaked meat or bacon, enough to render
3 tablespoons grease, plus more to grease pan

1 cup buttermilk

1 skimpy teaspoon salt

½ teaspoon baking soda

1 egg, beaten

2 cups slow-ground cornmeal (white or yellow corn,
although I think the best meal comes from a
white field corn such as Hickory King)

Preheat oven to 425°F. Prepare skillet and grease by frying the streaked meat to render grease. In a large bowl, mix the buttermilk, salt, baking soda, and egg with cornmeal and stir thoroughly. Pour 3 tablespoons of the grease into the batter and stir in well. Pour batter into hot skillet and bake for a half hour or until the top crust is golden brown. The bottom crust should be dark brown and the whole pone perfect for slicing or crumbling pieces up in a bowl of pot likker. You can sop with cornbread if you wish, but for the ideal marriage of pot likker and corn pone, a big soup bowl is the way to go.

Crackling Cornbread

1 pint cracklings

1 quart slow-ground cornmeal

1 pint buttermilk

1 egg, beaten

1 teaspoon baking soda

Generous pinch of salt

Preheat oven to 375°F. Use a rolling pin to crush the cracklings into small bits. Make batter of cornmeal, buttermilk, egg, baking soda, and salt. Heat the cracklings in a frying pan and then stir them into the batter, which should be fairly stiff. Shape into small cakes or bake the entire batch of batter in a well-greased pan until golden brown.

TIP: Heat the cracklings in the pan you plan to use to bake the bread. They will ensure it is nicely greased.

Cornbread Salad

I have to give a tip of the hat to my staunch friend Tipper Pressley for this simple and scrumptious idea. When she mentioned cornbread salad, it was one of those "How in the world have I managed to miss that all these years?" moments. Grandpa regularly would crumble cornbread in field peas, creamed corn, or pot likker of several kinds (he was especially partial to that from turnip greens and cabbage), not to mention in a glass of milk, and in a sense cornbread salad is just another way of using leftover cornbread in a fashion somewhat similar to what he was doing.

To prepare cornbread salad, take leftover cornbread, crumble it up, and mix with whatever fresh vegetables you happen to have available or particularly enjoy. My personal top choices include tomatoes chopped up fine, onions prepared the same way, diced cucumbers, cooked crowder peas (drain them), and raw corn cut straight from the cob. Bell pepper is another possibility, although my stomach unfortunately allows me to "enjoy" bell pepper more than once anytime I consume it. If you want a bit of "heat," crumble in a few flakes of dried hot pepper or chop one or two fresh ones and add to the mix. Stir and top with ranch dressing, buttermilk, or oil and vinegar. Alternatively, mix in some sour cream. Once it is gently stirred, I find it best to let the bowl sit in the refrigerator for a few hours so the ingredients can mix, mingle, and marry.

Cornbread Dressing

Make Traditional Mountain Cornbread using the recipe on page 25. Save broth from a baked turkey or chicken (or use purchased broth) and to it add finely chopped celery and onions, chopped pecans or chopped, boiled chestnuts (the latter have long been traditional in my family), and your choice of spices. (I like a lot of black pepper and do not use sage, but many folks like the special taste sage imparts.) Use a blender to turn your cornbread into crumbs. Add enough of the broth mixture to make a batter of about the same consistency as cornbread batter. As a friend of mine aptly puts it, your mixture needs to be "sloppy" when it goes in the oven. Pour batter into a baking pan and bake at 350°F until the top browns and a toothpick inserted in the dressing comes away clean. The dressing should still be moist, although if it gets a bit dry you can always adorn it with gravy.

Momma's Fried Corn

What Momma called fried corn wasn't really fried at all, although it was prepared in a frying pan. Cut three or four thick slices of streaked meat (you can call it streak o' lean, side meat, middling meat, salt pork, or any of a number of other names, but to me it has always been streaked meat for the simple reason that is what folks called it in my boyhood) into a large skillet. Fry the streaked meat until crisp and brown. Set the meat aside on paper towels to drain and retain the hot grease in the pan. If you have too much grease pour some off and save for use in cooking and seasoning other dishes, such as green beans, crowder peas, or butterbeans. Pour corn that has been cut or grated from the cob into the hot grease. Stir steadily until the corn is cooked, and serve piping hot. A piece of the streaked meat crumbled atop a serving of corn is right tasty, while a big slice of a garden-grown tomato is this dish's equivalent of a cherry atop a sundae.

Creamed Corn

Creamed corn is the essence of simplicity, although as is so often the case with mountain cooks and recipes, I can't offer specific measurements when it comes to the ingredients. Place freshly grated or cut from the cob corn in a pot of suitable size. Add whole milk or half-and-half, along with butter, then simmer on low heat, stirring to make sure it doesn't stick, until done. Salt and pepper to taste. You can eat it hot from the pot or freeze. If you slip up and let corn mature a little too long so that it loses milkiness and becomes starchy, this is a good way to enjoy it. The half-and-half and butter make up for some of the sweetness and moist texture you have lost. Corn in this stage is much better fixed this way than served on the cob.

Corn Chowder

Second only to corn, potatoes topped the vegetable list for mountain folks. They kept well, were easy to grow, and were filling. In this recipe, a hearty one that could, particularly when served with corn dodgers, make a fine meatless meal, two staples of high-country life unite in a marriage of culinary wonder.

2 medium-sized potatoes

2 cups water

1 large or 2 small onions, diced

2 cups milk (or for extra rich soup, 1 cup whole milk and
1 cup half-and-half)

8 teaspoons chicken bouillon grains or 4 teaspoons bouillon
grains and 2 chunks streaked meat

3 cups corn cut from the cob

Peel the potatoes and dice into half-inch pieces. In a saucepan, bring the water to a boil and add the potatoes and onions, simmering until the potatoes are tender (about 20 minutes). Transfer two-thirds of the cooked potatoes and onions to a bowl and mash until smooth (or transfer to a blender). Add a bit of the milk if the mix is too thick. Return smoothed potato mixture to the remaining chunks of potatoes and onions. Gradually stir in milk. Add the bouillon and the creamed corn, and return to a boil while stirring constantly. The finished consistency should be that of a thick cream soup with the chunkiness associated with chowder. *Makes 8 large servings*

Corncob Jelly

12 corncobs with kernels removed

4 cups water

1 box powdered fruit pectin

Yellow or red food coloring

Jelly jars and lids

Place corncobs and water in a large stew pot and bring to a rolling boil, allow to continue for 10 minutes. Remove and discard the cobs, then strain the liquid through cheesecloth. You should have about 3 cups of liquid (add enough water to make 3 cups if not). Return to the pot and stir in the pectin, and return again to a rolling boil. Skim off the foam and add a few drops of food coloring. Pour into hot, sterilized jars. Cool and refrigerate until use. While essentially a novelty item, the jelly is delicious.

Cheese Grits

Prepare grits according to instructions (stone-ground are best), but if the directions call for water, use milk instead. Adding a small amount of half-and-half makes the grits extra creamy. Then add shredded Cheddar cheese, salt, and pepper to taste. Stir until the cheese is melted and well blended. Meanwhile chop several slices of bacon in small bits and fry until crisp. Remove bacon bits and save drippings in the pan for future use. Sprinkle bacon liberally atop the grits and serve immediately.

Baked Hominy and Cheese

The distinct flavor of hominy isn't appealing to all palates, but it suits mine just fine and was popular with some, but not all, of my family. This is a way to prepare hominy with a twist, and much in the same fashion that cheese takes grits to a different dimension, so is the case here.

Preheat oven to 325°F. In a mixing bowl blend two cups of prepared hominy (cooled) and one and a quarter cups whole milk. Mix with a sturdy whisk or stirring spoon until completely smooth. At that point add three-quarters cup grated sharp Cheddar cheese, a teaspoon of salt, and five egg yolks (set aside the whites). Mix well. Next beat the separated egg whites and fold them into the mixture. Place in a well-buttered casserole dish. Bake for forty to fifty minutes or until golden on top and completely firm. Serve piping hot.

NOTE: Leftovers can be stored in refrigerator and, for another meal, cut into squares and fried.

Fried Grits

When allowed to cool after having been cooked, grits readily congeal. To enjoy fried grits, cook an extra batch when you are having them as a breakfast dish, and place the surplus, while still warm enough to flow, in a baking dish or rectangular cake pan. Keep in refrigerator until ready to use, then cut into serving-size sections. Lightly oil a skillet and fry the grits cakes, turning once. Easy and scrumptious. Grits cakes can also be grilled, although it takes a deft touch to keep them from crumbling.

CHAPTER 2

PORK

Food memories and folkways have always been so important to me that they almost seem to sear my soul. Maybe that's because so many things from boyhood that I cherish revolved around food—family feasts at Thanksgiving and Christmas; those countless times when we partook of nature's abundant bounty in the form of wild game such as squirrel, rabbit, and grouse; trout on the table times without number; Grandma Minnie's scrumptious stack cakes and cathead biscuits; Aunt Emma's wonderful ambrosia; and all those dishes Momma cooked so lovingly and so well.

Yet were I forced to give pride of place to a single recollection of wonderful eating, it would be associated with hog-killing time in November. Let me make it perfectly clear that I'm no expert on the subject. Although I've been involved in cleaning, butchering, and freezing a few wild hogs during my adult years, my acquaintance with hog killing when it involved domestic pigs ended somewhere around the time I reached my teens. Up to that point though, hog killing was an important annual occurrence, and in the fond vaults of memory it remains a big deal.

John Beech with a sow and her shoats. Our extended family bought shoats
of about this size each year, and Grandpa Joe would fatten and care for them
from the time they were acquired until hog-killing time in November.
Courtesy of Hunter Library, Western Carolina University.

Grandpa Joe raised hogs for the whole clan. All of his children who lived locally—Daddy, Uncle Hall, and Aunt Emma—would pool monetary resources and buy a number of shoats early in the year. Normally there would be one or two for each family, along with a couple for my grandparents. Grandpa took care of feeding and fattening them in a hog lot at the lower end of his property. Pigs are veritable eating machines, and with the notable exception of cucumbers, they are omnivores not only willing but eager to consume anything. The oft-used phrase "eat like a hog" reflects simple reality.

At Grandpa Joe's, they enjoyed a decidedly varied diet. Almost all table scraps and leftovers went straight from the house to the hog lot, with leftover bread and eggshells being exceptions. The chickens got those. Inferior garden produce, surplus vegetables, and even weeds were likewise part of the diet that eventually produced pork. Grandpa's pigs ate mighty well, and that was especially true in late summer and early fall as the "fattening up" process got into high gear.

I often helped with feeding, and Grandpa could almost make a game out of pulling red-rooted pigweed for feed, carrying inferior pumpkins to fill troughs, and of course offering plenty of corn. As a most welcome sidelight to the fattening up process, Grandpa could always be counted on for tales of the glorious days when the American chestnut had not yet been devastated by blight. He told of earmarking hogs to identify their owners and then turning them loose, in late summer, to forage on their own. As mast began to fall, those free-roaming pigs dined sumptuously. According to Grandpa, while acorns were important, it was chestnuts that gave the meat delightful taste and "rounded them off" in inimitable fashion. About the time chestnut mast was gone, it would be time to catch the pigs, feed them plenty of corn for a short time, and take advantage of the first cold spell to butcher the coming year's primary meat supply.

This usually happened in late October or more likely November. Grandpa had an uncanny ability to read signs and predict when the weather was going to be right. At that point a Saturday would be set aside for hog killing. It all began with a hearty breakfast well before daylight, and soon thereafter Grandpa personally executed the hogs. It was a somewhat gruesome but quick, efficient process, and he made a point of never letting hogs see one of their brethren die. Whether it was true or not, he firmly believed that doing so would taint the meat of the rest of the pigs. He would funnel each victim to a boarded off section of the lot where it was invisible to the other pigs and kill it with a point-blank range shot to the brain from his .22 rimfire rifle. Perhaps because mountain boys of my age and that generation were one part poacher, two parts bloodthirsty, and completely educated in the realities of the cycle of life, I found the process fascinating.

Once all the hogs had been killed, a whole succession of steps, with everyone pitching in to fill their assigned roles, followed in rapid-fire order. The first steps involved gutting the hogs (they were hoisted aloft on a gambrel with the aid of block and tackle) and scraping the hair from the hides after serious applications of boiling water, which had been heated in a massive cast-iron container. Once those preliminaries were completed, the hogs were skinned. From that point forward it was an assembly line–like process. Meat from one pig after another filled up numerous wash tubs, dish pans, and other receptacles with organs, fat, prime cuts, skin, and the like. A second cast-iron pot, atop a separate fire, then came into play. I don't recall Grandma using the cauldrons any other time of the year, although before my time they had diverse uses such as making hominy, preparing homemade soap, or for washing clothes. At hog-killing time though, the second pot was for rendering fat into lard.

Meanwhile, there were other things going on as well. These included grinding of meat for sausage; setting aside hams for curing; cutting up the tastier portions for fresh tenderloin, backbones and ribs, or canning; and other activities. Virtually no part of the hog was wasted. It was a messy, smelly undertaking, but there was a great deal of attention placed on cleanliness.

It lasted from daylight until well after dark, and in all honesty I'm sure there were many details I don't recall. I do, however, vividly remember what counted most in the mind of a greedy-gut boy—the end food products. There may be finer meat than pan-fried fresh tenderloin served with biscuits and milk gravy, but if so I've never eaten it. As I've heard mountain folks say, "Anything better God must have reserved for use in heaven." Mind you, I wouldn't turn aside from a mess of fresh backbones and ribs stewed until the ribs are so tender you can chew the marrow out. Likewise, cholesterol considerations notwithstanding, anyone who has never eaten crackling cornbread made with slow-ground cornmeal using fresh cracklings or those that have been canned in lard has lived a life of culinary deprivation.

When the hog killing and butchering process finally wrapped up, with everyone bone tired but quietly satisfied with knowledge of a day's work well done, you would have rows of quart jars of sausage that had been ground, fried, then canned by pouring hot lard over the contents to seal them. Cracklings were put up in much the same fashion, while better cuts (excluding the hams) that were not eaten at the time were also canned. Each family had its own distinctive approach to handling hams and side meat, and I can remember Daddy rubbing in salt, brown sugar, and black pepper in a big wooden container he had made for precisely that purpose. Once the salt mix began to be absorbed, he hung the hams from rafters and had a homemade device beneath them to catch the drippings. Grandpa had a separate building for the process, but none of our family used a smokehouse. Our meat was strictly salt cured.

Those were grand days, a time when pork was a staple of mountain life for folks as it had been for generations. Anyone who has given much thought to the area's traditional foodways, consumed their share of Smokies victuals, or researched traditional regional fare, realizes that historically pork has been the high-country meat of choice. Hog killing was as much a part of the annual farm calendar as laying by time or Christmas. Performed the old way, raising and butchering your own pigs increasingly belongs to a world in which we no longer reside. Yet I have to believe that anyone who was an integral part of the process gained a fuller understanding of precisely what was involved in the transition from live animal to food on the table. I know I did, and the resultant insight and appreciation for the good earth and the entire nature of the human food cycle was something you won't gain from a grocery store shelf or a meat section display.

My recollections associated with pork are wide ranging and filled with fondness. They include, for example, the occasional special treats of delicate pink slices of cured ham, fried to a perfect turn and served with biscuits and redeye gravy. Any leftover country ham was ideal for a cold meat biscuit to carry afield when hunting or simply enjoy as a snack. From time to time Momma would open up a jar of canned pork, and that made for mighty enjoyable eating with side dishes such as baked or fried potatoes and green beans.

As much as I loved country ham and the finer cuts, I had an even greater affection for portions of the hog that went by varying descriptions. As has already been alluded to in the preceding chapter's coverage of corn recipes, these cuts included side meat, middling meat, streaked meat, fatback, streak o' lean, thick bacon, and more. It didn't all come from the same spot on a hog, as some of the names suggest, but everything was cured and salted and considered less desirable than the luxury cuts.

You lived "high on the hog" when you ate tenderloin or ham, but it was the "low on the hog" portions that loomed largest in day-to-day mountain diet as I knew it.

I think both Mom and Grandma Minnie would have been lost without streaked meat to use as seasoning when cooking all sorts of dishes. Various types of dried beans, when soaked overnight, simmered for most of the day with some streaked meat, and served with cornbread, were front and center in family diet. For that matter, a slice of streaked meat fried until it was crunchy crisp throughout made for mighty fine eating when placed in a wedge of cornbread sliced open in the middle.

A typical mountain breakfast might feature cathead biscuits with eggs, streaked meat fried until it was crisp, and milk gravy made from the fat cooked out of the meat. Dinner would almost certainly feature one or more vegetable dishes employing streaked meat for flavor—dishes as varied as creasy greens, poke sallet, or maybe a bait of ramps in the spring; fresh green beans, corn, cabbage, and squash in summer's time of bounty; field peas, mustard greens, and turnips in the fall; and leather britches and dried beans in the winter. Supper throughout the year likely involved crackling cornbread or regular cornbread with a few slices of streaked meat having been cooked in the iron skillet to season it before the batter was introduced as a side. Sawmill gravy, which had its beginnings with grease from streaked meat, was a mainstay likely to be offered with any meal. In short, for taste, seasoning, and savory eating, streaked meat came right at the top of the list of must-have ingredients for mountain cooks.

In addition to its versatility, already suggested by the uses mentioned above, streaked meat enjoyed the undoubted advantage of making a little meat go a long way. What were in essence meatless meals were commonplace in the kitchens of my mother and grandmother, the places where almost all of my eating experiences while growing up took place. Other than one or two "sit down" meals connected with some school activity, I can't remember ever "eating out" at a restaurant during my boyhood, although there were plenty of church suppers, family reunions, dinner-on-the-grounds events, and holiday gatherings where we ate somewhere other than at home.

Momma and Grandma Minnie, two wonderful and completely self-trained cooks, may not have had platters of beef or chicken to grace the table with regularity, but they always had the toothsome flavor of meat in gravy and the vegetables they cooked with streaked meat. Presumably we got the necessary protein in our diet from eggs along with plenty of pinto, navy, October, and other dried beans. Those staples, nicely matched with cornbread or biscuits and perhaps rounded off with a single piece of fried streaked meat providing three or four special bites, were filling and tasty.

One of my favorite mountain scribes, John Parris, mentions the thoughts of his great-grandfather on this subject in a piece entitled "Mighty Peart Woman with a Skillet." Looking back fondly to the cooking talents of his deceased wife, the old man opined: "To give boiled beans or boiled cabbage or boiled potatoes taste you've got to boil 'em with a piece of fatback. They ain't got no taste if they're not fixed that way. Might as well eat a piece of rawhide as to eat beans that ain't cooked with fatback." All I can add to the thought process of that sage of the Smokies is a heartfelt "Amen!"

In today's dietary world, streaked meat has a bad name—too much fat, laden with cholesterol and salt, and plain unhealthy are what you'll likely hear. That's probably true in contemporary, sedentary society, but our forebears needed a hearty diet. They performed hard physical labor from dawn to dusk. Changing times notwithstanding, you can include me among the ranks of those who still think a pot of turnip greens or pinto beans tastes far better when cooked with streaked meat. If you share my joy in this staple of mountain cooking, here are some simple recipes using streaked meat.

Streaked Meat Milk Gravy

Fry several pieces of streaked meat until they are crisp and brown. Remove the slices of meat from the frying pan and set aside. With the grease still hot, gradually add a half cup of flour and stir steadily, reducing heat if necessary to ensure the flour does not scorch, until brown. Once your flour is brown (Cajuns and others call this a roux, but I have never heard the term used in connection with making mountain gravy), add milk (a cup will generally be enough, although use more if necessary) and stir until the desired thickness is reached, keeping mind that the gravy will continue to thicken after you remove it from the pan. You can, if desired, crumble the fried streaked meat and add it to the gravy just before removing it from the pan. Serve piping hot with cornbread or biscuits.

Streaked Meat Dutch Oven Potatoes

Thoroughly scrub five or six good-sized baking potatoes and then quarter them. Place in a well-seasoned Dutch oven and sprinkle black pepper to taste over the potatoes. Cover with strips of streaked meat and cook at 400°F for about an hour. Check while cooking to be sure they aren't over-heating and use a fork to make sure the potatoes are done. The tines of the fork will readily pierce the potatoes when they are done. You may need to add salt but do not do this until after the potatoes are cooked. The streaked meat will usually contain sufficient salt to season them, and the grease released from the meat will prevent any sticking or scorching. Serve as a main dish with sides such as greens, green beans, and stewed fruit.

Fried Streaked Meat and Cornbread

If you can't fry streaked meat you best not fool with something complicated like boiling eggs. The key to frying streaked meat is the essence of simplic-ity—fry it until the fat streaks are fully cooked and crispy. At that point it's a sinful, salt-laden, cholesterol-laced slab of pure delight. A big piece fried until it's so crisp you could crumble it with your hands will, when placed in a piece of cornbread, flat-out bring tears of joy to a glass eye.

Streaked Meat and Hominy

Streaked meat works wonders with the somewhat bland taste of hominy. Instead of butter and black pepper, the seasonings most commonly asso-ciated with hominy (and for that matter, hominy grits), just fry a few thin slices of streaked meat until crispy brown, then crumble and add to hot hominy. If desired, add a bit of salt to taste and sprinkle with black pepper.

Cabbage Pot Likker

Another way in which pork is used for seasoning, as opposed to being a meat-on-the-platter main dish in a meal, is pot likker. In a sense, pot likker's kind of like barbecue sauce. Everyone seems to have a different opinion on precisely how it should be made and which recipe results in the best taste. The only difference is that pot likker, while not as widely known or consumed as barbecue with its endless array of sauces, is if anything more confusing. Some misguided souls seem to think it is watery leavings in a pot fit only for dogs to eat or to be added to the slop bucket for hogs. Others are under the misimpression that pot likker is the liquid left behind after a mess of greens or something similar has been cooked. While those vitamin-infused byproducts of preparing vegetables merit serious attention and can be delicious, it is something of a misnomer to call them pot likker. My Grandpa Joe sometimes used that terminology, but he more frequently described what was left after all the beans had been scooped from a bowl or all the poke sallet transferred to his plate as "leavings." That's probably a pretty apt choice of words.

Properly prepared pot likker is an entirely different matter, a dish that no five-star chef, no fancy city restaurant, can aspire to imitate. Aficionados will sometimes wax so eloquent as to suggest that true pot likker is so closely akin to another kind of likker, that made from corn, and so delectable as to make a fellow disinclined to share it with anyone other than close family or special friends. I'm somewhat of this persuasion, for when served with a pone of cornbread it is nectar of the culinary gods. Pot likker offers a spark of culinary brightness lighting up the dead of winter and is sho nuff sustenance of the sort to fill the inner soul. The delicacy is, in short, a dish fitting to make anyone in their right mind hasten to the table to sit and take nourishment.

For reasons I don't really understand, Momma never made true pot likker. She'd sometimes refer to the last bit of liquid remaining from a big bowl of greens or boiled cabbage as pot likker, but her cooking repertoire, and she was masterful, did not extend to the real McCoy. Grandma Minnie, on the other hand, frequently made pot likker, and my, oh my, was it ever fine. Anytime I happened to be at the home of my grandparents when she served cornbread and pot likker was a moment of gustatory glory.

While there are likely as many ways of preparing pot likker as there are recipes for fruitcake or apple pie, all have certain basic ingredients and approaches. The one offered here comes from memory as well as some reading, but I know firsthand it is scrumptious. If you want to vary it a bit—say substituting dried flakes from homegrown hot red peppers for store-bought black pepper (which Grandma Minnie did), or seasoning with streaked meat rather than ham shoulders—that's fine. You can even make pot likker using turnips rather than cabbage, and turnips enjoy the advantage of cooking quicker.

Put a ham shoulder, backbones and ribs, or maybe the bone left over from a Thanksgiving or Christmas feast (you will want to be sure there's a good bit of meat on the bone) in a big pot of water and let it simmer for a couple of hours. Then wash and core a head of cabbage. Cut it into quarters and add them to the pot. If you started with hambone from a cured ham, you will not need salt; otherwise, add a tablespoon of salt. Sprinkle in black pepper, red pepper, or both to taste. Let simmer for two hours, being sure to keep the level of liquid up by adding water as needed.

When cooked you can pour off the pot likker and serve it separately, or as Grandma Minnie always did, leave the cabbage, meat, and juice together. When served with a pone of cornbread or maybe hoecakes, along with a bowl of stewed apples, this makes a hearty and exceptionally satisfying meal.

Fried Tenderloin

Were it somehow possible to go back to the halcyon days of my youth and choose a single meal featuring pork that exceeded all others in excellence and enduring appeal, I would probably, after considerable mental debate, select fried fresh tenderloin. Before coming to that conclusion, however, the merits of backbones and ribs, country ham, and shoulder meat would have to be duly pondered and accorded their richly deserved praise.

Recently I asked the meat market manager at my local grocery store whether he had any tenderloin or backbones and ribs. He asked me to repeat my question and gave me a quizzical look, which strongly suggested he felt I had taken leave of my senses. Realization dawned that he didn't have a clue about the cuts I had mentioned. That's a matter of terminology, insufficient knowledge, and an indication of the stark differences between processing procedures as I knew them and what comes from today's massive hog farms. He tried to sell me pork loin, a fine piece of meat but not tenderloin. As for backbones and ribs, you would have thought that today's slaughterhouse swine came without a spine.

I just thanked him and walked away, thinking as I did so that somehow two of my all-time favorite cuts had for all practical purposes disappeared from the world of commercial meat sales. Of course, there are multiple solutions—find someone who does custom butchering, buy a whole hog and give them directions on the cuts you want, find a farmer who might be willing to go "halfers" with you along mutually agreeable lines, or raise and butcher your own.

In my lexicon, tenderloins are two rather small pieces of meat tucked away under a hog's backbone. Tender as your mother's heart, they are the Kobe beef of the pork world. To my way of thinking, there's only one way to enjoy tenderloin should you be so fortunate as to have access to this delectable portion of pig meat. It should be sliced about three-quarters of an inch thick, dusted in flour, and pan fried just to the point where it is cooked all the way through. Sprinkled with a bit of salt and black pepper and eaten by itself, or gracing a homemade biscuit, it's a small chunk of heaven on earth.

Feeding time for chickens. Although free-range chickens managed pretty well on their own in the warmer months, they always welcomed supplemental scratch feed along with table scraps, and this type of feeding practice improved egg production.

Courtesy of Hunter Library, Western Carolina University.

CHAPTER 3

YARD BIRDS

Three generations or more ago chickens were, for all practical purposes, as much a part of the normal mountain homestead as bedsteads or corncribs. Look at vintage black-and-white photos of homeplaces and it is surprising how often the image will show some free-range chickens scratching in the yard. Chickens had a myriad of virtues. They were to a remarkable degree self-sufficient—capable of getting a goodly portion of their living on their own in the form of insects, worms, seeds, and in season, garden vegetables. As long as they were free range, and most were, their menu was wonderfully varied, and grit for grinding gizzards took nothing but pecking. Moreover, one of their favorite foods was "scratch feed," which in yesteryear essentially translated to various versions of corn—leavings from winnowing or sifting, leftover cornbread, grains rubbed from cobs, and the like. Provide supplementary food as needed, make sure that water was available, offer them the shells of their own eggs or ground oyster shells for needed calcium, and chickens pretty well looked after themselves.

Along with occasional cleaning of the chicken house (and that produced super-rich fertilizer) and some supplements to their diet during the period between the first killing frost and spring's greening-up time with its abundance of tender shoots and sprouts on which to feed, the biggest needs of a flock of chickens in terms of human support focused on two things. Chickens sometimes needed protection from a host of potential enemies, and they required provision of housing basics in the form of cover, roosting areas, and nesting places. In the latter case though, I remember many of Grandpa's flock roosting in trees, and particularly during spring nesting season there was always an obstreperous old hen or two that wanted to wander off and lay her eggs in some hidden spot on the ground as opposed to one of the perfectly good boxes provided in the henhouse.

Vigilance on the part of the farm family took care of enemies. Never mind that raptors are federally protected in today's world, there was a time when every hawk was a "chicken hawk." Grandpa Joe would have had my hide if a hawk showed up and, should I have happened to be carrying a gun, failed to take a shot at it. In truth though, I don't remember any problems in that regard. I strongly suspect that the little bolt-action .22 rimfire he owned took care of avian predators in short order.

Mammalian predators were a bigger, more frequent threat. Rats, weasels, coons, skunks, foxes, minks, and possums could go after both chickens and eggs. Egg-sucking dogs and egg-eating snakes could likewise wreak havoc. For every adversary though, there was an answer. It only took one moment of interaction with an egg that had been "blown" (had its contents removed without breaking the shell and filled with hot pepper sauce) to cure dogs and snakes of any future interest whatsoever in eggs. Traps or, more commonly, the family shotgun, dealt with other attacks on chickens. Since they raised an unholy ruckus anytime a predator showed up, the flock in effect had a built-in alarm system to provide intruder alerts.

Of course, they could in no way match guineas in this regard. A flock of guineas makes a finer guard dog, at least in terms of alerting the household to visitors (welcome or otherwise), than the most vocal fice ever known to man. They create an unholy ruckus and don't seem to know the word *stop*. Many mountain households raised guineas with that aspect of their behavior in mind. They in no way match chicken when it comes to table fare, and their eggs are inferior as well. However, if you wanted a hard-shelled egg for use in "egg fights" at Easter time (a contest where the pointed ends of two boiled eggs were knocked against one another, with the winner getting to keep the broken egg of the loser), a guinea egg was a sure winner.

Like chickens, guineas for the most part ranged free, and both could make a fine living, at least in the warmer months of the year, simply by roaming about a mountain homeplace. Still, you had to keep an eye on them, and daily gathering of eggs was a part of this ongoing human vigilance. They also required some human guidance for their own well-being. For example, chickens absolutely love tomatoes, and I fondly recall Grandpa Joe allowing them unimpeded passage to his patch of mixed varieties such as Brandywine, Rutgers, and Marglobe, along with both the prolific red tommytoes and the little pear-shaped yellow ones he grew. That didn't happen until Grandma Minnie had canned and made all the soup mix she needed, but by late August that would have been accomplished and tomatoes would be in gradual decline. Grandpa would have quit tying them to stakes or else the plants would have grown out the top of their supports. It was time to give yard birds their turn, and there would still be enough tomatoes high on the stalk to meet slicing needs for dinner and supper.

More than once I heard Grandpa say: "You've got to pay close attention to yard birds when they get on maters. They'll eat 'em to the point of half starving to death while doing so. They'll also go off their egg-laying duties." There isn't a great deal of protein or food value in tomatoes. Of course, no matter what the diet, laying activity dropped dramatically during the dog days of late August and early September. Where during the morning a few months earlier the chicken lot sounded like a cackling Tower of Babel as dozens of proud hens celebrated their laying accomplishments, now there might be no more than four or five hens out of the entire flock proclaiming to the world how proud they were of having laid an egg.

As long as access to tomatoes was reasonably controlled and they weren't damaging other garden truck, chickens were allowed to roam pretty much where they wished. Their menu was wonderfully varied, and like Grandpa I enjoyed watching them going about their daily business. At times the chickens could be flat-out comical. Such was certainly the case when Grandpa and I enjoyed one of our grand summertime pleasures—getting down to business on a cold watermelon in midafternoon after an arduous session of work. We would devour the brilliant red, juicy goodness and compete on who was the most accurate or had the greatest range in seed-spitting contests. Watching the chickens scramble for each shiny black tidbit at such times would often find both of us laughing out loud.

Eating the seeds was nothing more than a clean-up operation, but the overall dining preferences of free-ranging yard birds had significant benefits. They kept unwelcome insects such as potato beetles, grasshoppers, bean beetles, crickets, and packsaddles under control without any need to resort to spray, dust, or use other chemical agents of control. To get the grit chickens needed for grinding gizzards took nothing but pecking; I know of nowhere in the mountain soil where grit of a suitable size, whether rocks or sand, isn't immediately available.

Most mountain yards a few generations back were completely bare, and there were reasons for this. It kept ticks, fleas, chiggers, and other unwelcome insects at bay, and frequently there would be stately black walnut trees to help in that regard. The roots of walnuts are a bit toxic, and as a result, plants don't grow particularly well under them. Add a busy housewife wielding a broom from time to time and the passage of a regiment of chickens marching through on a regular basis—time and effort involved in mowing grass simply didn't come into play.

Chickens serving as a sort of ever-alert Orkin employee when it came to insect control were highly useful, and another ancillary benefit they provided came in the form of manure. In that regard, along with literally being capable of scratching out a goodly portion of their living, chickens were multipurpose recycling machines. You have to be careful with chicken droppings—they are so high in nitrogen that overly generous applications will burn a plant up—but properly used they make wonderfully effective fertilizer. I hated that aspect of dealing with yard birds, because shoveling up the manure in roost areas and around coops was smelly, nasty business. Still, it had to be done and somehow it seemed I was the worker of choice whenever it came time to clean out the chicken lot.

Chicken on the table was an important part of Smokies life, but that was normally a luxury reserved for holidays, guests, church suppers, and Sunday dinner. No dinner on the grounds or meal associated with a revival or other special religious event would have been complete without chicken aplenty, and I love Rick McDaniel's description in *An Irresistible History of Southern Food* in which he describes barnyard fowls as "the Gospel Bird." Sunday was most likely when chicken was served, and another colloquial name, preacher bird, suggests as much. Certainly it was the case throughout my boyhood and beyond, and mere thoughts of Momma's fried chicken awaiting our return home after church services can set my appetite into drooling overdrive to this day.

Of course, chicken was front and center at special gatherings such as homecoming or Decoration Day, and a visit from a seldom seen family member was likely to put chicken on the table. Verses from the old folk classic "She'll Be Coming Round the Mountain," which mention "we'll kill the old red rooster when she comes" or "we'll all have chicken and dumplings when she comes," are suggestive in that regard.

The preliminaries to episodes of kitchen legerdemain such as those Momma performed on a weekly basis didn't involve going to the meat market and selecting your bird. Instead, the chicken was already on the property awaiting the not-so-tender attention of those residing there. Typically, procuring a bird for the table involved one of two approaches. Either you waited until after fly up time and lifted a bird from the roost or else you cornered a bunch of chickens against a fence and seized one of them. In both cases, in the immediate aftermath of apprehension came execution. That was accomplished by wringing the bird's neck (the way Grandpa killed them) or by a swift stroke of an axe or hatchet while the bird's neck lay atop the chopping block where kindling was split.

About as mad as I ever saw Daddy was an occasion when I somehow talked Momma into letting me do the chopping. She held the intended victim by the legs with its neck across a section of apple log, and I attempted to whack its neck with a hatchet, which had been a Christmas gift a few weeks earlier. I don't know whether Momma turned the chicken loose too soon or I hit a mislick (each of us accused the other when explaining the scenario to Daddy). You frequently hear the phrase "running around like a chicken with its head cut off" used to describe weird or untoward behavior, but in this instance the situation involved a hen running around with its head only partially cut off. Daddy expended a great deal of energy in apprehending the maimed hen, and that ended my chicken-killing career for a couple of years.

Although it took the better part of a half day, from the failed execution until Daddy came home from work and captured the chicken, in the end its fate was like that of every other yard bird destined for the family table. Whatever the means of the bird's demise, once it had stopped flopping, it was time to prepare the carcass for cooking. The bird would be immersed in a bucket of scalding hot water, plucked and gutted, then readied for the kitchen. If it was a pullet or frying-size chicken this would mean the additional step of cutting it up into legs, thighs, wings, breast (in halves), and back complete with the "pope's nose," or in Grandpa Joe's colorful description, "the south end of a chicken headed north." Baking hens, of course, remained whole.

The daily routines and behavioral patterns of yard birds fascinated me as a kid. At times their singular lack of intelligence astounded me, although old chestnuts about them being so lacking in brainpower that they will drown looking up at a heavy rain are just that—old chestnuts, and rotten ones in the bargain. But I was captivated by the way some slight change in their humdrum routine could result in a tremendous racket, the manner in which a hen would defend her chicks with astounding aggressiveness, and a seemingly complete inability to recognize certain types of danger while going bonkers when faced with other threats.

The finest example of their seeming obliviousness to peril revolved around the manner in which Grandpa Joe caught chickens for table use. His method always garnered my rapt attention, and whenever possible I liked to accompany him "to get a chicken." He wanted no part of lifting them from the roost or chasing them down. "That'll put 'em off their egg-laying duties," he'd say, "and you know we can't have that." Instead, he had worked out a method of capturing chickens that was ingenious in its simplicity and almost unbelievable inasmuch as yard birds never learned of the imminent jeopardy connected with an old man carrying a lengthy cane pole.

Grandpa observed his chickens, which might range in number up to forty or fifty during the spring growing season when peeps were making the transition to adulthood, with astuteness. Cockerels would, once they reached full growth, immediately become candidates for the family table. Pullets, on the other hand, were left unmolested in order to move into their predestined duties as egg producers. This gave them a stay of execution, but once the time of year rolled around for baked chicken (Thanksgiving and Christmas) their gender and activities as laying hens no longer offered guaranteed security. Thanks to daily observation, Grandpa knew exactly which hens had become lethargic layers. They would be the object of his interest when it came time to bring Grandma Minnie a hen (maybe two or three if a big family gathering was in the works).

Carrying a handful of scratch feed along with his "chicken fishing pole," as he styled it, he would scatter the feed on the ground, step back, and carefully observe the resultant scramble to peck up every bit of grain. He had his pole at the ready when the right moment arrived. It was a cane pole of precisely the same sort he used to fish in the Tuckaseigee River, which ran by the house, chicken lot, and hog pen. It was somewhat longer—maybe fifteen to eighteen feet—and equipped quite simply with two or three feet of the black nylon line used on casting outfits of the day tied to the pole's tip. The other end of the line had a small fish hook (size 10 or 12) affixed to it.

Grandpa would "bait" the hook by pinching a small piece of bread onto it. He then held the pole aloft at a forty-five-degree angle, well above the hens, and waited until his target was off alone, far enough away from the other hens to make sure she would be the only one able to grab his "bait."

He then adroitly dropped the baited hook on the ground right in front of the intended victim. Invariably there would be a quick peck of the sort that gives rise to the description "like a chicken on a June bug," and the hen would be hooked. Grandpa then began pulling her toward him with a hand-over-hand motion as he moved down the cane pole from its base to the end holding the chicken. Once the hen was within reach, he grabbed her neck, gave it a quick twist, and that was that. He would remove the hook after the flopping was over.

The amazing thing about this rather gruesome but eminently practical scenario is that the other hens never learned. If he needed two hens for the kitchen, Grandpa could repeat the performance without so much as a sign of angst from the feathered congregation brought together by his dispensation of scratch feed. It probably says something about my psyche and certainly does nothing to endear me to organizations such as People for the Ethical Treatment of Animals, but I thoroughly enjoyed the entire process. Its effectiveness was undeniable, and Grandpa's chickens lived far better lives than those eaten by anyone who purchases their meat at grocery stores or dines on fare from places such as KFC or Bojangles. If you eat chicken and are somehow dismayed by the way it got from the coop to the family table in days gone by, you really are at a rather distant remove from understanding the cycle of life.

For all that they brought dining delight when served on mountain tables, in the grander scheme of overall dietary practices, it wasn't really chickens that took primacy of place. It was the eggs they produced. Eggs were a key component of diet, standard fare at breakfast, vital for all sorts of baking, useful for a boiled egg snack, available for pickling in times of real surplus, a possible source of a bit of welcome cash money or for use in bartering for essentials such as salt or sugar, and regularly used for deviled eggs when any reunion or community feast was in the offing.

Some of the peepers of spring, whether raised by setting hens or purchased from the local cooperative, were destined to be fryers. But most of the hens enjoyed protection when they reached adulthood, so long as they kept up with expectations when it came to egg-producing duties. Invariably when our family enjoyed baked hen, the chickens that ended up on the table had been derelict as layers. For meat on special occasions and eggs on a daily basis, yard birds formed an integral part of farm life and livestock in the Smokies. Here are some of the many examples of how they figured in my family's diet.

Momma's Fried Chicken

I'll acknowledge at the outset that try as I might I've never quite been able to match Momma's fried chicken, and I don't think anyone else has either. Grandma Minnie was a wizard in the kitchen, but when it came to frying chicken, Mom had her beat. My brother, Don, fries first-rate chicken as well, but somehow it's never quite as succulent or melt-in-your-mouth tender as Momma's was. Quite simply, she had the touch.

**1 or 2 whole chickens, cut into pieces
(legs, thighs, wings, and breasts) with skin left intact**

1 or 2 eggs, beaten

Salt and pepper

All-purpose flour

Cooking oil

Drench each piece of chicken in the egg wash and then coat thoroughly with flour that is seasoned with salt and pepper before placing in piping hot oil in a cast-iron pan (I think cooking in cast iron makes a difference, but don't ask me to prove it). Then lower the heat to medium and cook, turning to brown evenly, until thoroughly brown.

All of this seems normal enough, but it was Mom's final step that made all the difference. Once she had all the chicken fried and placed atop paper towels to drain a bit, she would wipe the cast-iron skillet clean with a dish rag and put the fried chicken back in it. She then turned the oven on at low heat (175°F or maybe a bit less) and put the skillet in the oven. She normally did this just before heading off to church on Sunday. After church and once she'd readied the rest of the meal, she would pop the skillet out of the oven. I don't recommend leaving it for a couple of hours the way she did, or at least not until you figure out the right timing and temperature of the oven, but for her it worked wonderfully well. Being in the oven seemed to do two things—cook away some of the surplus grease and make the chicken so tender it almost fell from the bones and melted in your mouth. Mercy was it fine!

After the Feast Soup

STOCK

1 baked hen carcass with some saved chicken scraps
(or a wild turkey carcass)

1 large onion, peeled and quartered

4 ribs celery with leaves, chopped

1 large carrot, scrubbed and cut into chunks

2 garlic cloves

1 bay leaf

Remove any remaining skin from the carcass and discard. Place carcass in a stock pot and surround with onion, celery, carrot, garlic cloves, and bay leaf. Cover with water and bring to a boil. Reduce heat and simmer, covered, for 2 hours. Refrigerate stock and fat that accumulates on the top. Remove all meat from bones and set aside. Discard bones.

SOUP

8 cups prepared stock (supplement with canned
chicken broth to get 8 cups if needed)

2 cups milk

4 medium potatoes, peeled and diced

3 carrots, peeled and diced

3 ribs celery, diced

1 cup frozen or canned lima beans

2 ounces small shell pasta

2 cups fresh, chopped spinach

1 cup frozen green peas

Meat from carcass

¼ cup fresh parsley

½ teaspoon dried basil

1 teaspoon fresh black pepper

Salt to taste

1 cup evaporated milk

2 tablespoons all-purpose flour mixed with
4 tablespoons water (optional)

Cook stock, milk, potatoes, carrots, and celery for a half hour. Add lima beans, pasta, spinach, peas, chicken meat, parsley, basil, and pepper to the soup and cook an additional 20 minutes. Remove from heat, season with salt if necessary, and stir in evaporated milk. Return to low heat, stirring often. Do not let soup boil. Thicken with flour paste if desired. *Makes 12 hearty servings*

Chicken Pie

6 tablespoons butter

6 tablespoons all-purpose flour

¼ teaspoon (or slightly more) black pepper

2 cups homemade chicken broth (make your own stock,
save broth from stewing a chicken, or you can
use store-bought chicken broth)

⅔ cup half-and-half or cream

2 cups cooked chicken

Prepared pastry for 2-crust pie (or,
preferably, make your own)

Preheat oven to 400°F. Melt butter in a small saucepan; add flour and pepper. Cook about a minute, stirring constantly. Add broth and half-and-half and cook slowly until thickened. Add chicken and pour into pastry-lined pan. Top with rest of pastry and pinch edges together. Bake for 30 to 45 minutes or until pastry is browned. An alternative is to add cooked vegetables, such as corn, green peas, and carrots, to the cooked chicken and make a pot pie.

Chicken Pâté

More often than not, giblets from the hens we ate went into gravy, but occasionally the organ meats would be set aside and saved for use on their own. I love the rich taste of the giblets, and here is a simple way of enjoying them as an appetizer, snack, or spread for crackers or toast wedges. I personally prefer it to liver mush from pork (and that's a treat I thoroughly enjoy).

Giblets (heart, liver, gizzard) from several chickens

1 sweet onion, chopped

3 to 4 garlic cloves

3 or 4 tablespoons butter or olive oil

2 eggs

Salt and pepper

Clean and chop the giblets into small pieces and sauté in a large frying pan with the onion and garlic using butter (my preference) or olive oil. Then mince thoroughly in a food processor and allow to cool. Boil eggs then peel and chop them finely. Add salt and black pepper to taste (I like lots of black pepper). Mix minced giblets and eggs thoroughly and press into a bowl or mold and chill until solid.

Chicken and Dumplings

1 large (mature hen or rooster) chicken cut into pieces
(legs, thighs, wings, halved breast, neck, back)

4 to 5 large carrots, scraped and cut into 2-inch sections

1 large sweet onion, diced

4 stalks celery cut into sections

Salt and black pepper

¾ cup green peas or double handful of spinach

1 cup all-purpose flour

2 teaspoons baking powder

½ teaspoon salt

½ cup milk

Cornstarch (optional)

Place the chicken pieces, carrots, onion, and celery in a large stew pot, season with salt and pepper, and cover with water. Bring to a boil, then cook over medium heat for an hour. Add green peas and cook for an additional 15 minutes. You should have about 8 cups of broth; supplement with additional chicken stock if necessary and return to low boil. You can, if desired, cool and remove the bones from the chicken, but it is simpler and less time consuming to leave the bones and, as Grandpa Joe used to say, "eat around them."

To make the dumplings, mix the flour, baking powder, and salt in a small bowl, and slowly add milk and stir until mixed. Drop this dough by teaspoons into the boiling soup. Cook for 15 to 20 minutes or until dumplings are done in the center.

If desired, you can thicken the broth with a bit of cornstarch. I personally like the broth somewhat "runny" because it seems to mix best with the dumplings. Serve piping hot.

Garden Omelet

I somehow associate springtime with eggs, although properly fed and cared for hens will lay reasonably well throughout the year. Beyond the fact that greening up time is when some ancient switch of procreation is triggered in not only chickens but most birds, part of my line of thinking unquestionably goes back to boyhood days of gathering eggs with Grandpa Joe. The hens always laid well at this season, although Grandpa had to stay alert to keep up with wayward ones bent on raising a brood in secret hideaways rather than the henhouse. That meant two or three headstrong hens that eschewed the convenient nests he provided sought hidden places elsewhere. I loved to accompany him on his daily mission to gather eggs, and when a search for outlier nests was included in the mix, it almost became a scavenger hunt.

During the springtime abundance of eggs, extras came in handy in a variety of ways. Some of the hens would be allowed to continue their setting to hatch and raise a brood, but mostly we just gathered the eggs. Some were given to family members, some were sold (by Grandma, an arrangement I never quite figured out since Grandpa did all the work but she kept the income as her own private stash), and that period of the year saw a bounty of cake baking thanks to the plentiful supply of eggs. There were also the extra demands posed by children (like yours truly) wanting a bunch of Easter eggs for their baskets.

In short, a superabundance of eggs didn't pose any problems. Eggs are sometimes described as the perfect food, and Grandma Minnie certainly knew how to put them to mighty tasty use in a wide variety of ways. However, I don't recall either Grandma or Momma ever making omelets, and mention of something like a frittata would have brought perplexed headshaking.

For my part, I love them, and a favorite supper of mine is a two- or three-egg omelet incorporating whatever is available in the way of vegetables from my garden or that of nature. Choices might involve asparagus, spring onions, ramps, spinach, Swiss chard, morel mushrooms, watercress, or other items. Add salt and pepper to taste, some sharp cheese, a bit of butter, or maybe crumble in a couple of slices of bacon fried to a crisp, cook the omelet so the outside edges show a hint of brown, and you have some mighty fine eating. I normally use an omelet pan, but you can make an omelet in a large frying pan. Just empty the beaten eggs and other ingredients into a well-greased skillet, and once the bottom is firmly cooked, flip half over to make a half-moon shape and complete cooking.

HINT: Adding a tablespoon or so of water to the mix when you beat the eggs up produces a fluffier end product.

Chicken and Egg Salad

This is a fine way to use leftover stewed or baked chicken and/or a surplus of eggs. It's good whether eaten atop a lettuce base, stuffed inside a large tomato, with soda crackers, or in a sandwich.

> **2 cups chopped chicken (or use blender to pulse it to a coarse but not overly minced state)**
>
> **4 large eggs, boiled, peeled, and coarsely chopped**
>
> **¼ cup chopped sweet pickles**
>
> **2 to 3 tablespoons mayonnaise (more if needed for right consistency)**
>
> **1 to 2 tablespoons prepared mustard (amount will depend on how much you like the tang of mustard)**
>
> **Salt and black pepper**
>
> **Paprika (optional)**

Prepare the chicken, eggs, and pickles, then place together in a large mixing bowl. Add the mayonnaise, mustard, and salt and pepper to taste. Add a generous sprinkling of paprika, if desired. Stir thoroughly with a large wooden spoon. Refrigerate until ready to eat.

HINT: One of my favorite kitchen tools, and it's one I must admit I've never seen in a Smokies kitchen, is the Inuit knife known as an ulu. Its handle and rounded blade make it faster, safer, and more functional than any butcher knife, and it works wonders with tasks such as chopping up boiled eggs.

CHAPTER 4

———

DOMESTIC FRUITS

Almost every mountain homestead had fruit trees. Whether these rose to the status of meriting the term orchard or not, there would be a goodly variety of trees that provided welcome, indeed needful, additions to the family's diet. Among them likely would be several varieties of apples, both soft and "cooking" (hard) pears, plums, cherries (sweet and sour types), and clingstone (early) and freestone (later) peaches. They might be right in the yard or alongside a garden. I have a grand photograph of a cabin in the Bryson Place area of Deep Creek, taken early in the twentieth century, and for the knowing eye one of its most intriguing features is a row of large, stately apple trees in the foreground.

More often though, fruit trees, especially if there were enough of them to constitute an orchard or maybe provide a surplus for things such as cider, vinegar, brandy, or sale in town, would be in a carefully selected spot that might lie an appreciable distance from the house. The location would depend on the lay of the land. Ideally a slope, which was never a major problem in the Smokies, was involved. This meant good drainage, suitable air flow to help with threats of frost in blooming time, and the

Apples drying on a rack. Apples, peaches, green beans, and other foodstuffs were commonly dried for use through the late fall and winter.

Courtesy of the National Park Service.

direction the slope faced was also a critical factor. Sunny south faces had a tendency, especially at lower elevations, to bring bloom on prematurely and thus risk a late frost killing the year's crop.

For reasons lying beyond my ken, old-timers didn't worry much about disease, blight, and insects affecting fruit trees, and they really didn't need to be concerned. Daddy often talked about the fact that when he was growing up they never sprayed any of their trees and didn't need to do so. "We had worm-free fruit, even with the Indian peaches, and no matter what variety of apple was involved, they'd be sound." He marveled at those memories from a boyhood spent on Juney Whank Branch in what now is an area of the Deep Creek drainage encompassed by the Great Smoky Mountains National Park (GSMNP), at least in part because the little orchard we had at our own homeplace just a few decades later required (and received) a great deal of attention when it came to spraying. Daddy did recall doing some pruning during his youth, although even that basic aspect of caring for fruit trees, and it is particularly important with apples and peaches, did not draw an inordinate amount of attention.

Some areas in the Smokies were especially well suited to tree culture, and residents of those areas grew apples and other tree fruits not only for home use but for the market. Cataloochee Valley, deep in the heart of Haywood County, was especially well known in this regard. Today it lies within the GSMNP, but apples continue to be an agricultural crop of some note in other portions of Haywood County.

Those who are intimately familiar with Horace Kephart's *Our Southern Highlanders* may recall a situation where apples loomed large. This was his chapter entitled "The Killing of Hol Rose." Here, as in countless other instances, many of Kephart's details cannot be trusted, but there is no doubt about the defense offered by the accused murderer, Babe Burnett. A resident of Swain County's Brush Creek area, Burnett had several barrels of apple pomace in a state of fermentation when Rose, a confrontational character who was not particularly well liked on the local scene, attempted to arrest him for illegal moonshining.

Burnett claimed he was making vinegar, although later there would be some suggestion he was producing brandy, which sort of skirted the edges of what was and was not legal when it came to distillation. Whatever the exact nature of the situation, no one denied that Burnett had a fine apple orchard, a surplus crop that year (1920), and was using the fruit in a way that lay outside the normal drying / canning / apple butter methods of preservation.

One of the most compelling extant accounts of the trauma wrought by creation of the GSMNP comes from an early 1970s recording in the oral history collection of the GSMNP Archives. Winfred Cagle lived on Toms Branch, a feeder of Deep Creek situated only a mile or two from the place where my father spent the most meaningful days of his youth. Interviewed in old age, Cagle recounted how his family had worked unceasingly to clear the woods, remove rocks, ditch the land, plow the fields, build a cellar, and eventually, plant fruit trees. "Now we had grapes and we had pears, we had plums, we had peaches and just about any brand that you'd grow. Elbertas and the Indian peach—the red one for picklin' and all of this. We had the open stones and clings and ever'thing. Then we had . . . apples of all brands just about. I guess we had twenty-five or thirty different varieties. . . . Then somebody come along and say, 'You got to git out. Got to move. We're going to take this land and put it into a park.' Well, at that time people didn't know anything 'bout parks. They just knew the people [who] lived on Deep Creek. They didn't care what was goin' on out on Larkey [Alarka, in another part of Swain County] an' down in Georgie and Mexico an' all them places. They let them people tend to their business and live and be happy, and we done the same thing."

Bitterness flows through Cagle's words in a powerful, plaintive fashion, and the manner in which he highlights fruits gives an accurate reflection of just how large orchards loomed in Smokies life. Some of the finest orchards in the entire southern Appalachian region vanished, gone just as surely as the blight had taken the American chestnut, with the coming of the GSMNP. Even today though, more than four score years after the park's creation, it is still possible for the wise wayfarer who knows where to look and what to look for to find survivors of those trees that once were a staff of life in the Smokies. They stand as sentinels, lonely and largely forgotten, to a vanished way of life.

— APPLE TIME —

When I was a boy, we had a small apple orchard. It amounted to only a half acre or perhaps a bit more but the trees were highly productive. That was thanks in large measure to Dad's meticulous care of them—judicious annual pruning, multiple sprayings, and attention to every detail at picking time. Of course, he was meticulous about most everything, a characteristic of his I wish I had emulated in greater degree. Daddy tended his small orchard, which featured Stayman, Red Delicious, and Golden Delicious varieties along with a single volunteer tree that produced a tart, bright red apple with exceptional keeping qualities, with almost loving care.

That included careful pruning in late winter, keeping the ground beneath the trees clean, applying a treatment to the trunk called an "oil spray" once a year to discourage any worms from boring into the wood, and a succession of sprays over the course of several months from immediately prior to blooming time right through to just a few weeks before harvest. The spraying was done using a cumbersome device that featured a hand-pumped tank attached to a frame that somewhat resembled that of a wheelbarrow. With the tank full, it was difficult enough to maneuver on flat ground. On the steep hillside that was home to our orchard, moving the sprayer about without spillage was a demanding chore.

Not that anyone asked, but I found little joy in the pruning and spraying operations. They were just work expected from me, and later, my younger brother, as we helped Daddy with this in the same way we performed so many other chores. While keeping the trees in fine shape and treating them to ensure production of sound fruit was burdensome, I absolutely loved harvesttime. By the middle of September, I could pluck a couple of prime Red Delicious apples off a tree on the way to school—one for me and one for the teacher. With some rubbing on my pants leg, they took on a shiny scarlet brightness lovely to behold. Not long afterward, usually when the first windfalls showed up on the ground as a signal the fruit had reached full ripeness, it would be harvesttime.

Year after year, with rare exceptions when a late frost killed most of the blooms (the trees weren't ideally situated at all, being on a south-facing slope, but somehow they survived frost virtually every year), we had an abundance of apples. How I relished, starting somewhere around mid-September, picking one still wet with dew as I headed off to school and eating it. I'd pick another one or two in the afternoon when I got home to snack on as I headed to the woods to hunt squirrels. Of course, apples figured prominently indeed in our family diet.

Throughout my boyhood years, Momma had a stated goal of canning two hundred quarts of apples each autumn. We would eat them almost daily through the late fall, winter, and as far into spring as the supply lasted. The "sauce" (it was really more like stewed apples, with big chunks still intact) was sometimes eaten hot with a pat of butter added but most often as a cold fruit dish. In addition to a succession of canning runs, some apples would be worked up and dried.

The remainder of the crop was carefully stored in an earth-floored basement that was, for the most part, dug out by Daddy with some help from me. Along with bushel baskets, there were a couple of capacious homemade bins in the basement where he stored apples. One of my chores was to go through them weekly to remove any that showed signs of going bad. The Golden and Red Delicious weren't particularly good keepers—they'd begin to shrivel up and lose both juiciness and taste—but the Staymans and those from the volunteer tree kept extremely well. They were what my parents and others called "cooking apples." That meant they were somewhat tart and tasted best when cooked with the addition of some sugar, in contrast to sweeter "eating apples" such as the Delicious varieties. Cooking apples were especially tasty in cobblers or pies. Most years we would still have fresh apples, although long since mellowed to the point where the chin-drenching juice each bite provided in September was no more, well into December.

Getting apples prepared for canning or drying was an "all hands on deck" chore, often performed on the porch of an evening if it wasn't too chilly. If memory serves, my sister didn't care for peeling, quartering, cutting out the core, and putting the pieces in a big dishpan full of slightly salty water to keep them from turning brown until they were ready to be cooked and canned. She had a pronounced tendency toward temporary deafness at such times. On the other hand, it was a chore I enjoyed. After all, I've always found it comforting to be putting food by for times to come, and in this instance, whenever you peeled a particularly promising Red Delicious you could, if the spirit moved you, eat a quarter of it and put the other three pieces in the dish pan.

Momma usually dried a couple of bushels for use in fried pies, but Grandma Minnie, perhaps harkening back to precanning days, dried far more. Grandpa Joe also had apple trees, so like our immediate family they had the joy of "apple time" come early fall. Grandma was always a great one for making stack cakes, and that delicacy, along with fried pies, claimed the bulk of the apples she dried each fall. These delights form some of my fondest memories of her variegated culinary wizardry, but rest assured her cooking skills were at a high level of excellence no matter what she prepared.

Fresh Apple Cake

4 eggs

3 cups sugar

3 cups self-rising flour

1 cup raisins

1 cup cooking oil

3 cups apples, diced small

1 cup black walnuts

2 teaspoons vanilla

Preheat oven to 350°F. Beat the eggs and add remaining ingredients and mix together. Batter will be stiff. Bake for 1 hour in a cake pan or large loaf pan.

FROSTING

1 (13-ounce) package cream cheese

4 tablespoons (½ stick) butter or margarine

2 cups powdered sugar

1 teaspoon vanilla

Mix frosting with a blender on low speed and allow cake to cool before applying the frosting to it.

Fried Pies

Every summer both Momma and Grandma Minnie, like countless other mountain women, carefully peeled, sliced, and dried apples and peaches. They were sometimes blanched by burning "just a tetch" of sulfur to keep them from turning brown, but more often than not, the fruit was dried just as it was after being worked up. In the case of its use in fried pies, that made perfectly good sense. The reconstituted fruit would turn brown anyway, and once it found the perfect nestling place inside a half moon of crust to form the pie, the cooking process left the filling, if anything, even browner.

Forget color though. A fried pie, whether hot off the griddle or eaten cold for a snack as leftovers, was perfectly suited to the needs of a purt nigh permanently peckish boy. They were sheer bliss and a grand example of how something simple in conception and easily prepared could be a dessert to rival the most delicate crème brûlée or some devilishly difficult cake. At any rate fried pies found great favor in my family.

Also known by such delightful colloquial names as "half moons" and "mule ears," fried pies were standard dessert fare throughout my youth, and they remain something I regard as toothsome to the nth degree. The only forms I have ever eaten featured fillings of reconstituted apples, peaches, or apricots, although there's no reason they couldn't be prepared out of other dried fruits. In every case the fruit to be used for filling was dried until time came to cook it for immediate use, and in my experience apples were far and away the most common.

Grandma Minnie never measured much of anything, and other than regular kitchen spoons and possibly a cup with markings, I don't think she even owned measuring utensils. But as nearly as I can approximate her ingredients (and this is what Momma wrote down), here's Grandma's recipe. Although she was a masterful baker, this was the dessert she produced most frequently, and whenever it came straight from her griddle to my plate, I had a pat of butter waiting to adorn it before introducing the finished product to what was, in this case, my aptly named "piehole."

FRUIT FILLING

1 pound dried fruit

¾ cup brown sugar

2 teaspoons ground cinnamon (or to taste)

2 tablespoons butter

Cover the dried fruit with water and allow to soak overnight. Drain any extra water and cook slowly until completely tender, mashing the fruit as it cooks. Then stir in the other ingredients, perhaps cutting back on the sugar a bit depending on personal tastes and factors such as whether the dried apples, if that is the fruit being used, are sweet or tart. Allow to cool while making the crust.

CRUST

3 cups all-purpose flour

1 tablespoon sugar

1 teaspoon salt

4 tablespoons (½ stick) butter

¾ cup solidified lard or chilled vegetable shortening
(Grandma used home-rendered lard from
hogs we had butchered)

½ cup ice water

Pulse flour, sugar, and salt in a food processor, and then add the butter and lard (Grandma owned no processor so all mixing and blending was done by hand). You will need only a dozen or so pulses before you add ice water. Continue pulsing until you have a solid clump of dough. Empty onto a well-floured cutting board and roll into a ball. Refrigerate for a half hour or so and then you are ready to roll out and cut dough pieces for each individual pie. Be sure to keep your cutting board and rolling pin well floured to avoid sticking.

Roll dough out thin with a rolling pin and then cut in circles. Grandma always got perfect circles by using a large saucer to make an imprint then cutting around the resultant image with a handy little gadget with a cutting edge that rolled as she pushed it. It was homemade and I suspect Grandpa Joe had cobbled it together, one of countless examples, in the kitchen as elsewhere, of necessity being the mother of mountain invention. Using a small knife, pizza cutter, or the edge of a ulu works fine for this process.

PIES

Prepared fruit

Prepared crust

Cinnamon or cinnamon sugar (optional)

Once the crust is ready, add enough prepared fruit to half of a circle of crust, fold the other half over on the fruit, and use a fork to crimp and seal the edges. Repeat with remaining circles of crust and fruit. Heat a frying pan on the stove top and add enough lard to prevent sticking. When the lard is piping hot, pop the pies into the pan. (You may also cook these atop a griddle.) Fry pies, turning once the bottom is brown (you can lift gently with a spatula to check). Make only a single turn. Drain on paper towels and serve while still warm. If desired, you can sprinkle each pie with cinnamon or cinnamon sugar. Fried pies warm over quite nicely and they also make a wonderful dessert for a hunter's field lunch.

We ate stacks of these delicacies, and they are almost as good left over, whether rewarmed or eaten cold, as when just out of the frying pan. On days when I hurried home to set out on a "mixed bag" hunt in late fall or early winter, I would tuck two or three fried pies carefully wrapped in wax paper into a pocket of my Duxbak jacket. Munching on one while meditating and waiting quietly for a bushytail to appear was pure heaven, and if I happened to hit a rabbit I had jumped or a grouse I had flushed, consuming a celebratory pie was just the ticket. I washed the delicacies down with water directly from mountain springs without a second thought about contamination and never suffered any harm. They were also most welcome during midday breaks when on wintertime, all-day rabbit hunts with my father and some buddies. For me, at least, those truly were banner days of fried pie fun and fond memories.

⸺ PEACHES ⸺

Although peaches, especially the red-fleshed clingstones old-timers referred to as "Indian" or "Cherokee" peaches, had once done wonderfully well in the Smokies, by the time of my youth virtually no one locally grew peaches for personal use, and to my knowledge there were no commercial operations involving the fruit. Instead, everyone got their peaches, mostly trucked in from South Carolina or Georgia, at roadside markets or impromptu setups on pickup tailgates.

Momma had an understanding with the proprietor of the largest local produce market. Whenever he had peaches going bad, she would get a call (or maybe she just checked periodically, I don't recall which) to let her know that a bushel or two of culled, bruised, or unsalable fruit was available. For a pittance in payment—perhaps ten cents on the dollar—those peaches became hers. It was a good deal for all involved. The vendor got a bit of return for what otherwise would have been thrown away, and Momma had the makings of pies, dried peaches, and especially what she called peach butter.

She would get the peaches home and set to work almost immediately, knowing that even minimal delay meant further deterioration of overripe or rotting fruit. She would peel the peaches, carefully cutting out the bad spots, and then work them up according to what suited her fancy or future family needs. Mostly she made large runs of peach butter (just a type of preserves that adorned a cathead biscuit in mighty fine fashion) but there would also be some drying done in order to have fruit for dried peach pies in the winter. Maybe once or twice a summer there would also be a churn of homemade peach ice cream, although I think this became more common later, after I was grown and married and we had an electric ice cream churn. There would also be container after container of peaches treated with some type of fruit freshener to prevent browning that went into the chest freezer once we got that symbol of modernity. Finally, anytime she got fruit from "the peach man," as she called the produce stand owner, there would be either a peach cobbler or peach pie.

Peach Cobbler

In our family we ate far more fruit and berry cobblers than we did pies. I suspect the reason was that cobblers were less trouble and didn't require as much prep time. Also, Momma had a fail-safe recipe she had made so many times using so many different basic ingredients—apples, peaches, cherries, raspberries, blackberries, strawberries, and blueberries—that she didn't even have to check one of her carefully maintained wooden boxes stuffed with recipes to make certain of the ingredients. The recipe is offered for peaches, but it will work equally well with almost any of the fruits and berries covered in these pages.

1 cup all-purpose flour

1 cup sugar

2 teaspoons baking powder

1 cup whole milk

¼ pound (1 stick) butter or margarine, melted

2 to 4 cups sliced fresh peaches

Preheat oven to 350°F. Combine flour, sugar, baking powder, and milk in a large mixing bowl; stir with a wire whisk until smooth. Add melted butter and blend. Pour batter into a 9-by-13-inch baking dish. Pour peaches (amount depends on personal preference) evenly over batter. Do not stir. Bake for 30 to 40 minutes or until golden brown. Serve hot with milk, cream, whipped topping, or vanilla ice cream.

Spiced Peaches

Peaches rank as one of my favorite fruits, and I enjoy them in a whole bunch of ways—fresh, in a cobbler, sliced atop a bowl of cereal, golden nuggets in a churn of homemade ice cream, baked halves with a bit of brown sugar and honey in the seed cavity, and in other fashions. A recipe I really enjoy is spiced peaches. In keeping with my general approach to cooking, which is the KISS method ("keep it simple, stupid"), here's how I prepare spiced peaches. It is modeled on my grandmother's approach as I recall it.

Peel fresh peaches and cut into slices, thaw sliced frozen peaches, or use canned peach slices. Place in a large saucepan with a bit of water added if you don't have sufficient juice or syrup. Sprinkle liberally with brown sugar and cinnamon (or cinnamon sugar). Heat until just simmering and add two or three tablespoons of honey. If you want curried fruit, add a light pinch of curry powder at this point as well. Reduce heat and stir gently until well mixed and serve immediately. Peaches prepared this way are suitable either as a side dish with the main meal or as a dessert. I particularly like them with fried quail or wild turkey tenders.

— PEARS —

Mountain folks grew two basic kinds of pears—eating pears and cooking pears. The former turned soft when ripe and did not keep well. Once they were ready to be picked, and the first windfalls sent a clear signal in that regard, they needed to be worked up quickly. The standard approach for those that were eaten raw or cooked for immediate table use was to peel, core, and slice them and then can the halves in sugar syrup. On the other hand, cooking pears, or hard pears as they were commonly known, kept quite well. They were nothing special when eaten raw but did nicely when it came to preparing pear butter or marmalade.

Pear and Hazelnut Salad

4 to 6 cups lettuce (old-timers often used a fall planting of black-seeded Simpson lettuce)

2 large fresh eating pears, cored and chopped

1 cup toasted, coarsely chopped hazelnuts

3 to 4 tablespoons mild blue cheese

Salad dressing

Arrange greens on salad plates. Sprinkle pears, nuts, and blue cheese atop them. Drizzle with a mild Italian dressing or homemade raspberry vinaigrette. *Serves 4*

TIP: Nuts of almost any kind except black walnuts work well in green salads. Try hickory nuts, butternuts, or pecans as well as hazelnuts. Black walnuts work nicely in fruit salads such as Waldorf salad.

Cherries

Much like the situation with pears, there were two distinct types of cherries grown in the Smokies—sour or "cooking" cherries and sweet or "eating" ones. We had a wonderful sour cherry tree, a Montmorency, at our home. Competition with the birds for the ripe fruit, never mind that it was tart enough to produce a persimmonlike pucker, was keen. However, between tin pie plates dangling from limbs and jangling in the breeze, the tree being quite close to the house, and my noble guard duties with a BB gun, we usually managed to get at least a decent share of the harvest.

Momma made them into pies, canned them for the same purpose so they could be used in winter, and always put up a run of cherry jam, which offered tanginess instead of cloying sweetness. I loved to put a hefty dollop of the jam between halves of a hot, buttered biscuit that had been nestled in the oven not more than sixty seconds before. Usually it went down so well that repeating the performance seemed the logical thing to do. Or, as Grandpa Joe liked to put it, "the only thing better than a biscuit with cherry jam is two biscuits with cherry jam."

Mine was a teetotaling family, possibly influenced in part by an uncle who, by family accounts, "drank himself to death" while still in his twenties. At any rate, there was no consumption, much less production, of alcohol in any form. However, mention of cherries demands at least passing reference to a famed Smokies toddy known as "cherry bounce" or "cherry jump." The means of its manufacture varied somewhat, from pouring white lightning over ripe, pitted cherries jam-packed in quart jars to carrying the cherries through the distillation process to produce something more closely akin to brandy. Cherry bounce was a favorite at George Washington's Mount Vernon, so it shouldn't come as a surprise that the drink made its way on down the Appalachians. As for the name, I have no idea of its origins, but I did once hear a mountain wit suggest, "Drink enough of it and you'll feel like you are capable of jumping off walls; next morning though, you'll think something got loose in your skull and is bouncing from ear to ear."

Watermelon Salad

Most of this book's recipes trace back for generations, but this one is my own invention. Cube a portion of a good watermelon and remove the seeds (a "good" watermelon, to me, is going to have seeds and not be one of the modern sissy philistines, mere seedless pretenders that sacrifice taste in order to get rid of seeds). Add some torn spinach, lettuce, or arugula along with a chopped mint leaf or two and some sunflower seeds. Dress with just a bit of oil and vinegar and dig in for a summer's day treat.

Gardens surrounded by a split rail fence. Split rail fences, usually
made from locust or chestnut, were often used to protect gardens.
Courtesy of Hunter Library, Western Carolina University.

CHAPTER 5

GARDEN VEGETABLES

As someone who has long been keenly interested in the history of the Smokies, I've looked at thousands of vintage photographs of the region. Where those images embrace a setting showing a home or maybe a grouping of homes, a common feature involves gardens. For example, thanks to descendants of I. K. Stearns, a businessman and local figure of some note in Swain County, I have copies of scores of images he took in the early 1940s. Stearns was a skilled photographer and ahead of his time in many ways, inasmuch as these are color slides when that medium was in its infancy. Although his subject matter was normally something else, many of these slides show flourishing gardens along with adjacent expanses of pasture.

What those vintage images convey to anyone who is interested in or pays attention to such matters is that gardens were commonplace at the time, as were individual families owning a milk cow. You didn't have to own a great deal of land to grow a fine garden and pasture a cow for milk and butter. These were simply a part of daily existence in the Smokies, and they applied to town dwellers as well as those living out in the country. A decent-sized garden, properly tended, could provide an impressive amount of food, and a half acre to an acre could mean cannery shelves groaning with quart jars and a wealth of produce to keep grocery bills to a minimum. Add a milk cow, with a steady supply of milk, buttermilk, and butter, along with a flock of chickens for eggs and the occasional special meat treat, and you took a fairly substantial step in the direction of self-sufficiency.

Raising a garden, even a modest one, involved plenty of hard work. Folks lacking a plow horse could make arrangements to get their patch plowed and harrowed each spring for a reasonable cost (that was what both Daddy and Grandpa did in my youth), but there was still extensive labor to be performed with push plows (sometimes called wheel plows), hoes, garden rakes, potato forks, pitchforks, hand trowels, and other tools. Gas-powered tillers didn't exist, much less weed eaters. Except for initially preparing the ground for spring planting, and possibly a second plowing after everything had been harvested and the garden cleared off in late fall, gardening was done entirely with hand tools or literally by hand.

In addition to loving and laboring hands—there's no tool yet invented to match a knowing pair of hands when it comes to removing weeds from tight places while protecting the plants on which they are encroaching—much of what went into the soil had a degree of immediacy that is unusual today. Folks grew their own tomato, green pepper, hot pepper, and other plants from saved seeds and transplanted them once they reached the right size. Sweet potato slips came from a few tubers carefully saved from the fall crop and nurtured in a protected bed. Many types of seeds—beans, peas, butterbeans, October beans, corn, pumpkins, and more—were saved from year to year and done so with a degree of selectivity that would have done Gregor Mendel proud. What wasn't raised in beds or from saved seeds was usually available at the local feed and seed store or Farmers Federation.

A fine garden was a matter of pride, and Daddy would shake his head in dismay anytime he saw "gone to weeds" plots planted in springtime with good intentions and then semiabandoned when the heat of summer laid hot hands on the land. Most folks, however, worked mightily to keep weeds at bay, enjoyed talking about well how a particular crop was doing, did a bit of bragging about a "fine harvest" of some item, or boasted of how many quarts of a given crop their wife had already put up. Gardens had been a way of life for generations, and planting them provided benefits not only in the form of substantial savings but a sense of continuity and connectedness to the land in which many found quiet comfort. Most of all, a flourishing garden meant healthy, tasty food, whether fresh, canned, or dried, on the family table throughout the year. And it cost only sweat equity, not cash money.

The Goodness of Greens

Thanks to the nature of climate in the Smokies a surprising number of fast-maturing vegetables could be grown in both spring and fall. That included various types of lettuce, with leafy types such as black-seeded Simpson being favorites, cabbage, and what mountain folks have always described with the simple term "greens." Swiss chard, collards, and kale would have also worked well, but I have found little evidence of them being widely grown prior to the last two or three generations. When it came to the catch-all generic term "greens," they fell into distinct categories, with mustard and turnips leading the way. In years when winter was mild, occasionally greens left in the garden would even make it through the coldest months and put out harvestable new growth in early spring. While some folks grew turnips strictly as a root crop, it is important to remember turnip greens are just as delectable as the roots.

Greens have always been a staple of mountain diet in the cooler seasons (and even in the dead of winter, for plenty of folks canned them), and they were standard fare on our family table when I was a boy. We probably ate them at least two or three times a week in season, and the way both Momma and Grandma Minnie prepared them remains my favorite. They began by cutting several thin slices of streaked meat and frying it in a cast-iron skillet. The grease thereby produced served as seasoning for the greens as they cooked in a pot of water. Sometimes, instead of frying, the slices would be cooked directly with the greens, but the crispy fried slices were so enjoyed by our family that was rarely the case. One of those scrumptious slices of fried streaked meat placed inside a piece of cornbread made the perfect accompaniment for a mess of greens. Indeed, often that would be the only meat we had in a meal that featured greens, cornbread, pinto or October beans, and fruit sauce (canned apples).

Momma liked to mix mustard and turnip greens when she cooked them, and she had two distinct approaches when it came to using the root portion of the turnip. Sometimes she sliced or even diced roots quite thin and cooked them with the greens; on other occasions she stewed the turnips separately, and once they were done, topped them with a bit of butter along with salt and pepper to serve as another vegetable dish. My, oh my, was that ever fine eating.

Grandpa Joe loved greens, and he had an interesting way of eating them. He would get a hefty helping of the greens and place them on his plate, but that was only part of the culinary attention he devoted to greens. Once he had a satisfactory-sized helping (which meant a whopping one, because he was flat-out a first-rate trencherman, never mind being slender and tough as a seasoned hickory stick), there remained a second dish associated with the greens. He crumbled cornbread up in a bowl and poured a liberal splashing of the liquid in which the greens had been cooked over it. Although it never occurred to me at the time, I suspect he was getting the best of the vitamins and nutrition from the greens in those leavings.

I've relived that simple, satisfying feast from boyhood times without number through the ensuing years, although I'll confess to often skimping a bit when it comes to the pork seasoning. That translates to using lean, low-sodium bacon instead of fatback. While fancified bacon isn't fatback, no matter how you look at it, I have to acknowledge it's better for those of us who lead a comparatively sedentary life. That was never a concern for Grandpa Joe. Until well into his seventies he performed manual labor from dawn to dusk six days a week. That hard work more than offset any negatives associated with the kind of foodstuffs he liked to have on the family table.

Stewed Turnips

When I first visited Scotland many years ago, folks kept talking about "neeps." I had no idea what the dish was until it was served and I had the first taste. It's just their colloquial word for turnips. Call 'em what you will, stewed turnips are dandy in my book. Wash and then peel (if you wish, although peeling isn't essential) several turnips. Cut into fairly thin slices and place in a suitably sized saucepan with enough water to cover. Cook until tender (it won't take long—they cook appreciably faster than potatoes, for example). Drain, salt and pepper to taste, and top with a good chunk of butter. Or you can mash them up like potatoes.

Baked Sweet Potatoes

Sweet potatoes can be prepared in a wide variety of ways that touch both the vegetable and dessert portions of a meal, and whipped sweet potatoes with a bit of blackstrap molasses blended in sort of straddles the boundary between those two types of offerings. Yet in Smokies fare, the most common way of serving sweet potatoes, by far, was baked in their own skin. When cooking was done over an open hearth or fireplace, nestling a few sweet potatoes beneath coals and ashes and leaving them for several hours was the essence of simplicity. With stoves, all that was required was to put them in an oven (in a baking dish to catch the syruplike sweetness they exuded so as not to dirty the oven) and allow time and heat to work their magic.

When cooked through, with bits of juice oozing out of the skin and caramelizing as if a trickle of molasses had magically appeared, they could adorn a big, inviting platter on the dinner table. Split open and decorated with a hefty chunk of butter, they were as tasty as they were filling. Moreover, any potatoes that were left could be set aside to be enjoyed later.

My father often talked of carrying a sweet potato along with a chunk of cornbread to school in his lunch bucket. He wasn't overly fond of them, but for my part any day where a sweet potato was featured on the menu was a special one. I particularly loved coming home from school in squirrel season, quickly changing clothes, and grabbing my gun before heading to the woods. My last bit of preparation was to grab a cold sweet potato or two in the kitchen for a woodland snack. If it so happened Momma had cooked the waxy, white type of sweet potatoes, so much the better.

Walnut Crunch Sweet Potatoes

¼ pound (1 stick) butter or margarine, softened

2 eggs

2 teaspoons vanilla

1 cup sugar

3 cups baked, peeled, and mashed sweet potatoes
(you can also use pumpkin or cushaw)

Combine butter, eggs, vanilla, and sugar. Add to mashed sweet potatoes and stir until fully mixed. Place in a baking dish.

TOPPING

⅓ stick butter, melted

1 cup packed brown sugar

2 tablespoons all-purpose flour

1 cup finely chopped black walnut meats

Preheat oven to 350°F. Mix topping ingredients and crumble over potatoes. Bake for 25 to 30 minutes or until bubbly and golden brown.

TIP: Pecans or English walnuts can be substituted for black walnuts.

"New" Potato Salad

I enjoy potato salad at any time of the year, but my favorite way is to make it with new potatoes. There's something particularly appealing about their texture and taste, and the first potatoes of spring nicely coincide with the peak period of egg laying, so in this season both basic ingredients are available in abundance. Here's how I make it, although there are no precise measurements, for the simple reason that I don't use them.

Hard-boil three to six eggs (depending on how much you want to make), then set aside to cool. Cook three times the volume of eggs in new potatoes. Cut the potatoes into chunks and boil until just tender. Drain and set aside while you peel the eggs. Chop or cut the eggs into pieces in a large bowl and then add the boiled potatoes. Cut up sweet pickles to taste (I like a lot of pickles in my salad) and add to the eggs and potatoes. If you like raw onion, chop up a large Vidalia onion and add to the bowl. Add mustard and mayonnaise to taste—I just squeeze mustard out of a container until it looks like enough, add several tablespoons of mayonnaise, and stir everything up. If I need more mayo or mustard, I add it. Salt and pepper to taste and top the finished potato salad with a really hefty sprinkling of paprika. Stir the paprika in and place the bowl in the fridge to chill.

Rich Potato Soup

A hearty bowl of potato soup on a cold day has long been a family favorite when someone is under the weather. It was Momma's equivalent of chicken noodle soup when one of the children felt poorly, but I find it comfort food at most any season. Here's how she prepared it.

Peel several potatoes, cut into chunks, and place in a saucepan or Dutch oven. Cover with water and boil until the pieces are tender and almost ready to break apart when tested with a fork. Remove from the stove top and pour off some of the water. Then use a large spoon to mix and break the potato chunks a bit, stirring just enough to separate them to the point where there are still pieces of potato. Add a goodly bit of butter (use the real McCoy) and milk. If you want extra-rich soup, use whole milk. Salt and pepper to taste. Return to the stove top and heat, stirring steadily to be sure the soup doesn't scald. While the soup is heating, fry several slices of bacon to a crisp brown in a pan atop another burner. Set the bacon aside, atop a paper towel, to drain.

When satisfied with the consistency of your soup, pour into bowls, crumble bacon atop each serving, and eat immediately. This can also be made using diced celery and/or onion in the soup. It's filling, nourishing, and mighty tasty.

Potato Cakes

As a family we ate plenty of leftovers. In the summer in particular, Momma would prepare the main meal at dinner. More often than not supper would be a cold one, using whatever was left from the midday meal along with tomatoes, cucumbers, and maybe a jar of apples that had been opened. There was a major exception to that with one member of the family. Daddy would not take a bite of cucumber, adamantly declaring, "I'm not going to eat anything a pig won't touch" (hogs will eat almost anything, but for them cucumbers are evidently not on the menu—both Daddy and Grandpa Joe vouched this was the case, although I've never personally tested swine tastes in this regard). Another exception, this time involving the general theme of cold leftovers for supper, came with fried potato cakes.

Whenever Momma fixed mashed potatoes—and spuds in this form or others, including roasted, baked, boiled, and fried, were almost as much of a menu fixture as biscuits and cornbread—she always made enough to have plenty of leftovers. Potato cakes were simple to prepare and oh so tasty. It involved nothing more than shaping the leftover mashed potatoes into round, flattened cakes about twice the width of a biscuit, dusting them with flour, and frying them in a thin coating of fat from streaked meat. Browned on each side and served straight off the griddle or out of the frying pan, potato cakes were always a welcome treat.

Fried Okra

While frying okra isn't the healthiest way to eat it, I can't get enough of it. Okra and August go together like heat and humidity, but from the first cuttings until frost finally puts the quietus on a crop that bears as few others do (just keep it cut and it will keep producing—it's that simple) it's there for the frying, drying, stewing, mixing in soup, broiling, roasting, or even deep frying. For old-timey fried okra, the kind I enjoyed as a boy and still love today, chop the pods into pieces about one-half to three-quarters of an inch in width. Dip in an egg batter, coat with cornmeal, and fry in oil until crisp. The oil needs to be quite hot when the okra is put in the pan; otherwise too much of it is soaked up. I like to fry okra until it is crispy and not too far removed from burning. Drain briefly on paper towels and serve piping hot.

Deep-Fried Okra Pods

This idea comes from a good friend and hunting buddy, Darrin Dawkins, and is not one tracing back to my Smokies roots. Yet it harkens to Smokies ways and I like it so much I've included this approach. Darrin and his wife, Robin, have been regular recipients of my okra bounty over the years, and I suspect that at times they may have tired of my delivering a big mess a couple of times a week. Be that as it may, they periodically host me for a fish fry. Standard accompaniments on such occasions include hush puppies, French fries, onion rings, and slaw, but on one occasion, since he already had the oil in the deep fryer at a rolling level of heat, Darrin decided to try a big batch of whole okra pods. They were crunchy crisp, not at all greasy, and flat-out delicious. They now make a regular appearance on the menu for his summertime fish fries.

Stuffed Summer Squash

1 or 2 yellow crookneck squash or 1 small zucchini
per person

Cornbread

Sharp Cheddar cheese, shredded or sliced

Fried bacon or streaked meat bits

Cook squash in oven or microwave just long enough to get them done completely through. Remove and allow to cool before scooping out the small seeds and interior flesh. Mix the scooped material with crumbled cornbread, meat bits, and maybe a spoonful of grease from the fried pork. Stuff the squash with the cornbread mix and top with Cheddar cheese. Bake briefly in oven until the cheese melts and maybe just begins to brown. Serve piping hot. This is my favorite way to eat squash and our family liked it so much that Momma prepared the dish at least twice a week as long as squash plants in the garden bore.

Squash Pie

If you have squash (or zucchini) in such abundance that the neighbors hide when they see you coming with a bag full, here's one more option for using it.

2 cups grated raw squash or zucchini

1½ cups sugar

3 eggs, beaten

4 tablespoons (½ stick) butter, melted

1 tablespoon all-purpose flour

1 teaspoon lemon flavoring

1 teaspoon coconut flavoring

2 pie shells, unbaked

Preheat oven to 350°F. Mix squash, sugar, eggs, butter, flour, and flavorings well and pour into the 2 pie shells. Bake for 45 minutes.

Makings from Maters

Since a passel of tomato recipes appears below, in part because I consider tomatoes, along with corn, the quintessential items from a mountain garden, maybe some thoughts on the keys to producing successful tomatoes seem merited. They are an accumulation from Grandpa Joe, Daddy, various gardeners of my acquaintance, and more than a half century of planting and working my own garden.

- Rotate where you plant tomatoes from year to year. That helps keep various problems with blight at bay.

- Leave ample room between the plants. That lets the plants breathe and works against too much moisture buildup and resultant progression of various tomato diseases.

- Stake plants religiously (I use eight-foot metal fence posts) and prune the indeterminate varieties (which includes most heirloom types) relentlessly. Leave the sucker below the first bloom cluster and thus have two main stems, but remove all other suckers. Exceptions are Roma-type tomatoes and tommytoes—don't prune them at all, and in the case of the latter, keeping them supported is a real problem. They'll run out the top of an eight-foot stake in no time at all.

- To avoid using Sevin or other pesticides, try planting marigolds between the tomato vines, spraying plants with soapy water when aphids appear, and applying *Bacillus thuringiensis* as soon there is any sign of tomato hornworms. When I see the telltale signs of their depredations the search is on (fresh droppings help in locating these masters of camouflage). When I locate the hornworm there's a good squishing, with green juice a-flying, to send the pest to insect paradise, and treatment follows in case any of his kinfolk have been missed and are still around.

- Perhaps the best tip I can offer is to remove leaf stems as soon as they show any sign of yellowing, black spots, or disease. They will usually tear or break away from the main vine fairly easily. By midsummer, the lower reaches of plants look naked, but the precaution not only keeps the spread of disease at bay but lets the plant put its energy into producing more tomatoes as the season advances. Don't throw the diseased vegetation on the ground. I carry a five-gallon bucket with me and put the leaves in it as I move down the rows. They then go straight to my burn pile at a good distance from the garden.

- Keep the ground beneath the plants clean and free of weeds. I think mulch is a mistake because it makes a perfect home for disease. If it gets really dry and you need to water the plants, do so early in the day so that moisture on the plant will dry before nightfall.

- The varieties you plant are largely a matter of personal choice, and no two seasons find me with exactly the same types. That being said, I always have some Cherokee Purples, Lemon Boys, Sweet 100s (or just volunteer tommytoes), Romas, Black Krims, Mr. Stripeys, and Beefmasters. Beyond that, additional heirlooms are most likely, although in my experience they aren't as productive as many of the hybrids. They more than offset that with taste. I normally plant a total of at least three dozen of the above-mentioned varieties, always trying to grow at least one previously untried heirloom. For "late" tomatoes, you can root suckers in potting soil (you can use a bit of rooting hormone, although it isn't essential as long as you make sure the soil in which you place the "cuttings" has adequate moisture). Obviously, I grow a lot of tomatoes, and in good years I've given away bushels after putting up all I need. But between drying, freezing, and canning, not to mention use in soup mix, a lot of the tomatoes never "leave home." Here are some of the countless ways you can enjoy them.

Tomato Pie

Prebake individual phyllo shells according to directions. Sauté a small, diced onion in cooking oil. Slice four to six tomatoes fairly thin and lay them atop paper towels. Salt the tops and let sit ten minutes before patting them dry.

For the topping, shred two cups of sharp Cheddar cheese (Cabot Seriously Sharp is a good choice). Mix with three-quarters cup of mayonnaise, adding salt and pepper to taste (remember that the tomatoes have been salted, and even though the patting will remove some of it, a salty tang will remain).

In each phyllo shell layer tomatoes, then onion and fresh basil, then another tomato layer, and spread topping to fill to the tops. Bake at 375°F for thirty or so minutes or until done.

Tomato Dill Soup

¼ pound (1 stick) butter

1½ large onions pureed in a food processor

¼ cup fresh minced garlic

1½ teaspoons dried dill

¼ tablespoon kosher salt

⅛ tablespoon black pepper

9 cups tomatoes, crushed or diced—that is 2 (28-ounce) cans plus 1 (14.5-ounce) can, or use a comparable amount of ones you have canned or frozen

3 cups water

2 cups heavy cream (a pint of half-and-half with
some whole milk added will also work)

Place butter, onions, garlic, dill, salt, and black pepper in a large covered pot. Sauté on low heat until onions are translucent. Add tomatoes and water. Simmer for 1 to 2 hours. Remove from heat and blend in cream.

Juice Tomatoes

For rich, intense, and extra juicy tomato preparations (think vegetable soup, venison vegetable soup, or cream of tomato soup), tommytoes are the way to go. They are filled with flavor and literally burst in your mouth with just a bit of pressure. I save them by freezing the whole tommytoes in ziplock bags until I have enough for a big run of juice. Then it's into the pot, cook until bubbling, and put them up by canning, or as I prefer, in heavy-duty freezer bags. If desired, you can remove the peels by pressing the juice through a colander after cooking. I also find that Cherokee Purples work fine for juice, although I like them so much sliced or on sandwiches that it's hard to get enough ahead to have a sufficient quantity for making juice.

Stewed Tomatoes and Okra

Cut a small cross or plus sign at the bottom of several dead-ripe tomatoes and then dip in hot water for fifteen to thirty seconds. This will loosen the skin and allow you to peel it away with ease. Core and quarter the peeled tomatoes. Set aside briefly while you prepare okra pods by cutting away the stem area. Pods can be cut into one-inch slices or left whole. Combine with the previously prepared tomatoes in a large cooking pot, add salt to taste along with a couple of slices of fried streaked meat (if desired), and simmer slowly (do not overcook, because everything will turn to mush). This dish does not look particularly appealing, and for some folks the slick or slimy nature of stewed okra is a turnoff. Visual aesthetics aside though, this as a grand vegetable dish. Leftovers can be used as the beginning of a big pot of vegetable or vegetable-beef soup.

Tomatoes and Eggs

Preheat oven to 350°F. Slice away the bottom quarter (stem end) of a large tomato and carefully remove any core that remains in the large section, which needs to have a cavity large enough to hold an egg. Place the tomato "container" atop a greased baking sheet or pan, cavity end up, and carefully break a small or medium egg into the opening at the top. Bake until the egg sets to a point just short of the consistency you desire. Remove from the oven, sprinkle liberally with shredded sharp Cheddar cheese, then place back in the oven until the cheese melts. Eat piping hot.

Baked Cheesy Tomatoes

Preheat oven to at 375°F. Slice away the bottom of tomatoes and discard. Place tomatoes on a baking sheet and then sprinkle tomatoes liberally with a mixture of Parmesan cheese and bread crumbs. You can buy crumbs, but heels from a loaf of bread given a quick whirl in a processor are cheaper and work just as well. Bake until the cheese/bread topping begins to turn brown, and eat hot from the oven. If you have them, try leftover biscuits or crumbled cornbread as an alternative crumb base.

Simple Summer Tomato Salad

When my wife was still alive and able to work her wonders in the kitchen, seldom did a summer meal pass that we didn't have either a tomato salad or sliced tomatoes to accompany other vegetables. Her salads were the essence of simplicity—just cubes or chunks of tomato mixed with cucumbers (and sometimes with raw corn cut straight from the cob), anointed with a bit of olive oil and vinegar, and served as a side dish. Early in our marriage the salad would also include diced onions, but increasingly our aging and no doubt jaded digestive systems rebelled at raw onions.

Topped Tomatoes

I can take two hefty slices of a dead-ripe tomato (and to me a hefty slice is a half inch thick) and have the base for a meal. Top those slices with various offerings such as stewed corn cooked with a bit of bacon grease, hamburger gravy, crowder peas hot from the stove, or slip the slices between a sho nuff cathead biscuit and you are knocking on the gates of culinary heaven.

Traditional Green Beans

String and break a good mess of green beans fresh from the garden (a "mess" depends on how many folks you have to feed) and then rinse them thoroughly in cold water. Brown two or three slices of streaked meat in a skillet and save the grease that cooks out. Place beans, pork, grease from browning the meat, and enough water to cover the beans completely in a large stew pot or Dutch oven. Cover and simmer for at least two hours, adding more water as needed. You don't want to drown the beans—just keep them completely covered. When removed from the stove they are ready to eat. Some salt may be needed but don't add it during the cooking process because it's likely the streaked meat will provide salt enough. Serve piping hot, maybe with some chopped raw onion or a few red pepper flakes sprinkled atop the helping of beans.

Onions and Milk Gravy

This recipe may seem a bit strange but in truth it's just another choice of wording for what in effect are creamed onions. This was a vegetable that made a regular appearance on mountain tables but is little heralded, mainly because it, in effect, played a supporting role in most dishes. Yet you could count on an onion or two being sliced up when soup mix was prepared, small chunks of onion were cooked with almost all kinds of dried beans and greens, it appeared in chowchow and other relishes, and a big slice of raw onion wedged in a slice of cornbread was a favorite snack. Most mountain gardens included multiplying onions almost as a matter of course, and the fact that larger onions kept well when properly cured, usually by drying in the sun and then hanging in bunches in some well-aerated space such as the attic or by dangling from a rafter in the room holding the fireplace, was another of the vegetable's virtues.

Cut three or four onions into thin slices. Fry a couple of pieces of streaked meat and save the grease (or else heat lard). Add three or four tablespoons of flour to the hot grease and stir rapidly as it browns, then add a cup of milk. At this point put the onions in the gravy and simmer until translucent. Season with salt and black pepper and eat the onions by themselves or in a bowl atop crumbled cornbread.

Candied Carrots

Much like onions, carrots were another common Smokies vegetable more frequently used as a secondary or supporting ingredient than by themselves. They figured regularly in soups and hearty stews, and eating one raw in the heart of winter was a treat. Carrots stored exceptionally well and could be left in the row right where they had grown in the garden if mounded over with enough leaves, straw, or pine needles to keep the ground from freezing solidly around them. More frequently though they were dug and "toed in" beneath a corn shock, stored in a root cellar, or placed in a specially dug hole, where they were covered with straw and the top protected with sawmill slabs or old pieces of tin in order to keep rain out.

For candied carrots, chop into one-inch sections. For thicker sections, cut each one-inch portion in half. Cook in a saucepan with butter and molasses, honey, or sugar (which was seldom used in early days, when anything store-bought was hoarded or replaced by substitutes) until tender.

Fried Cabbage

Cabbage does exceptionally well in the Smokies, and at lower elevations down in the river valleys it can sometimes be grown twice—spring and fall. For the most part though, this cool-weather crop was planted at about the end of dog days for late fall harvest. A fine keeper, whether stored in root cellars, underground, or with the protection of a shock of corn, it was a "green" vegetable for winter meals. In truth, storage blanched cabbage until it was almost white, but it was fresh and could be eaten raw in slaw or cooked. Fried cabbage, often prepared with streaked meat and sometimes cooked down to pot likker, was a staple dish.

Shred or chop a head of cabbage. Cook several pieces of streaked meat in a large cast-iron skillet or Dutch oven and set the cooked meat aside.

Place the cabbage in the hot grease, stirring in some red pepper flakes if desired. (Grandpa Joe loved this dish with hot pepper, but he wanted it so peppered up no one else would have been able to eat the end result. Accordingly, he just crumbled a dry pod atop his serving.) Cook on fairly high heat until the cabbage wilts completely and begins to turn shiny, then lower the heat and continue cooking until it is fall-apart tender.

Smokies-Style Slaw

In the sense that both use piping-hot grease from bacon or streaked meat, this dish is similar to a springtime favorite, kilt lettuce. Cook several slices of bacon or streaked meat, and when done, remove the meat from the pan, leaving the hot grease. As the meat fries, chop or dice a head of cabbage and place in a large bowl. Add a tablespoon of sugar and 2 or 3 tablespoons of vinegar (more if you enjoy a vinegary slaw). Stir thoroughly. Then pour the hot grease over the cabbage and mix quickly to spread the oil evenly. Add salt and black or red pepper to taste. The hot grease, something readily available in mountain homes, took the place of mayonnaise. Of course, the bacon or streaked meat that produced the grease was always welcome as something to accompany cornbread, be crumbled atop beans, or eaten alone.

NOTE: For variety or a slightly different taste, sometimes a diced raw turnip would be mixed with the cabbage.

Buttered Beets

To a far greater extent than any other vegetable I can think of, although in the meat line chitterlings and headcheese would fall into pretty much the same category, beets reside in the realm of extremes. You either love them or feel they are dirt disguised as a red, fleshy root crop. Grandpa Joe was passing fond of beets, but that's not surprising. He was a trencherman whose taste buds were completely nondiscriminatory. He could and would eat—and enjoy—pretty much anything he could grow, catch, or kill. In fact, the only foodstuff I ever heard him mention with disdain was possum. "I've seen possums eat stuff that will turn a man's appetite," he'd say, "and no amount of trapping 'em and feeding 'em a diet to clean 'em out will change my mind."

For her part, I assume Grandma Minnie liked beets as well. She certainly cooked and pickled plenty of them, but I pretty much draw a blank when it comes to remembrances of what she ate (in sharp contrast to vivid recollections of what she cooked). A tiny woman, she ate like a bird yet somehow had boundless energy to carry through daily tasks.

In my immediate family, beets were sort of an iffy proposition. Daddy raised them and I enjoyed young, tender ones stewed with a good dollop of butter, and later I would discover an affinity for the tops, which taste much like chard or spinach. I certainly don't remember anyone raving about them, and other than possum (I'm in Grandpa's corner there), pickled beets are one of very few foods I dislike. If you like the hearty, earthy taste of beets, this is a fine way to enjoy them.

Clean and scrape beets, being sure to remove the entire outer layer. A scraper of the type used on carrots works well. Once clean, slice ovals from the beets of a thickness less than a quarter inch. Place in a saucepan with just enough water to cover, add butter, and simmer until the beet slices are completely tender.

CHAPTER 6

WINTER SQUASH

Winter squash figured prominently in Smokies agriculture. Pumpkins and other "keeping" squash such as cushaws; candy roasters; and acorn, butternut, and blue Hubbard varieties were grown in both fields and gardens. Although pumpkins usually got top billing in that regard, almost all types of squash worked perfectly well in the tried-and-true "three sisters" arrangement. If some began to go bad in autumn because of a bit too much shade or unusually moist conditions, that posed no problems. They simply became hog feed.

The pumpkins were a far cry from the highly decorative ones most frequently seen today, invariably around Halloween or in connection with colorful displays of fall flowers such as chrysanthemums. All of the pumpkins sown and grown were what folks variously called eating, cooking, or sweet pumpkins. Multiple characteristics stood out when it came to selection of pumpkins and saving seeds from year to year. One was taste, and the greater the sugar content, the closer the flesh came to resembling a sweet potato, the better. Another was the ease with which a pumpkin could be "worked up." If the stringy part of the interior holding the seeds came away readily, and if the pumpkin cut up easily so it could be baked

Grace Laney with a giant winter squash and a pumpkin. "Keeper"
members of the squash family were important in winter diet.
Courtesy of Hunter Library, Western Carolina University.

or otherwise cooked for removal of the rind, that was a real plus. Finally, keeping qualities entered into the picture in significant fashion. A pumpkin that, when properly stored, would last right through the winter until the cusp of spring was a desirable variety.

Over time folks figured this out. For example, I grow a variety called Chambers Creek pumpkins. The name comes from the fact that their origin traces back to Chambers Creek, a small stream now deep within the GSMNP that empties into the north shore of Fontana Lake. Prior to the creation of the park, however, a thriving little community flourished along the drainage.

This variety of pumpkin I plant each spring and dutifully save seeds from come fall's gathering time has a long, appealing history. Years ago, I enjoyed the blessing of coming into some heirloom seeds Christine Proctor, a woman who was born in the area, had preserved, sown, and saved for the entire time period since the park came into being in 1934. They have all the characteristics you want in an eating pumpkin. They had been in her family for decades before that, so the lineage of my pumpkins dates back to Smokies days well over a century ago.

I've always had a real hankering for pumpkin dishes. It comes from youth. Momma made varied and scrumptious use of the pumpkins Daddy and Grandpa Joe raised every year, and there are few vegetables that are easier to grow. Plant them with your corn and keep weeds at bay long enough to let the vines get a start. From that point on, right up until frost, they will look after themselves. Incidentally, a few pumpkins go a long way, they store well for months, and if one starts to go bad in a root cellar or similar place of storage, it's easy enough to throw it in the compost pile or, if you are lucky enough to be raising them, feed it to pigs or chickens.

Momma prepared pumpkin a number of ways, including as a vegetable dish, but primarily it went into desserts. Before I share some of her favorite recipes, it might be helpful to give the basics of how she worked up a pumpkin. I've tried various ways of processing pumpkin, but after due trial-and-error, I think the way Momma and Grandma Minnie did it works best.

Begin by washing the outside of the pumpkin and then cutting it in half top to bottom before using a large, sturdy spoon to remove the seeds and loose fiber holding them together. Save the seeds for use in next year's garden or to eat. Next cut the halves into more workable sections (four or six pieces). Place the sections, rind side down, in a large roasting pan. Insert in a 350°F oven and cook until the rind readily pulls away with a fork. You will find quite a bit of moisture accumulates in the pan. Just pour it off once you remove the pan from the oven, or if you want to make pumpkin soup, save some of it for that purpose.

Allow the baked flesh to cool until you can use your hands to work with the pumpkin. Then pull or peel away the rind, which is easily removable if the pumpkin has been cooked thoroughly. Throw the rinds away, till them into the garden, put them in your compost pile, or if you have hogs, add them to the slop bucket. The pumpkin flesh can be placed in a blender and mixed just like you would prepare your morning smoothie (I can only imagine what Grandma Minnie would have had to say about contraptions such as blenders, much the less about a concoction known as a smoothie. She likely would have shaken her head in abject dismay in much the same fashion she did when Grandpa Joe and I managed to test her patience a bit too much). The pumpkin is then ready for cooking or freezing in appropriate portions.

Pumpkin Cake

This recipe requires considerable effort, but rest assured, the end result is worth the labor. Moist, tasty, and redolent of all fall's comforting flavors, it will be a hit even with folks who insist they don't like pumpkin.

2 cups all-purpose flour

2 cups sugar

2 teaspoons baking powder

Large pinch of salt

Small pinch (perhaps ¼ teaspoon) ground cinnamon

1 teaspoon ground cloves

½ teaspoon ground nutmeg

1 cup canola oil

4 large eggs

2 cups pumpkin (if possible, use the real McCoy, not pumpkin pie filling from a store-bought can)

Cream cheese frosting or caramel frosting; or applesauce, whipped cream, and molasses (optional)

Black walnut pieces (optional)

Preheat your oven to 350°F and grease and flour 2 nine-inch cake pans. In a mixing bowl whisk together the flour, sugar, baking powder, salt, cinnamon, cloves, and nutmeg. Form a hollow in the center of these dry ingredients and into it pour the oil and eggs. Whisk this together and then add the pumpkin, stirring until thoroughly mixed. Pour into the cake pans and bake for 30 minutes or until a toothpick comes away from the center clean. Let the baked cakes cool on rack for 10 minutes, and then, with the aid of a spatula if needed, slip around the edges of the pans and remove the cakes. Let set for an hour.

When this period is over, add cream cheese icing or, if you prefer, caramel icing, using your favorite recipe for either one. Yet another alternative is to serve it without icing using applesauce, whipped cream, or even warmed molasses as an "adornment." If desired (and I always desire) sprinkle black walnut meats atop the cake and press some into the side as well.

Pumpkin Bread

I don't recall ever having pumpkin bread in my boyhood, but I've eaten more pumpkin prepared this way in the last three or four decades than any other. As a snack, a breakfast food topped with cream cheese, or dessert, it's delightful. I also like slices toasted in the oven just long enough to make them slightly crispy on the edges and to melt the dab of butter placed on top.

3 cups sugar

1 cup canola oil

3 large or 4 small eggs

1 (15-ounce) can pumpkin or the home-prepared equivalent
(pumpkin cans and freezes quite well)

3 cups all-purpose flour

1 teaspoon ground cloves

1 teaspoon ground cinnamon

1 teaspoon ground nutmeg

1 teaspoon baking soda

½ teaspoon baking powder

½ teaspoon salt

1 cup chopped black walnuts (or substitute English walnuts
or pecans, though they aren't as tasty)

Preheat your oven to 350°F. Butter and flour two (9-by-5-by-3-inch) loaf pans. Pour sugar and oil in a large bowl and blend before mixing in eggs and pumpkin. Sift flour, cloves, cinnamon, nutmeg, baking soda, baking powder, and salt in a separate bowl. Gradually and thoroughly stir into the pumpkin mixture while adding the walnuts.

Divide the batter equally between the two pans and bake 60 to 70 minutes or until a tester inserted into the center of the loaves comes away clean. Transfer to cooling racks, and after allowing the loaves to cool for 10 to 15 minutes, use a knife to cut around the edges and turn loaves out onto the racks to cool completely.

Roasted Pumpkin Seeds

Having been raised by parents who reached early adulthood in the depths of the Depression and for whom frugality was a byword, I've always been a staunch adherent to the "waste not, want not" school of thinking where food is involved. That certainly applies to saving seeds rather than buying them and to using garden bounty to the fullest possible extent. The material above deals with pumpkin flesh, but it's a mistake to overlook the tasty seeds inside these members of the winter squash family. Seeds are tasty, nutritious, and make a fine snack.

To prepare pumpkin seeds, put them aside when you work up the pumpkin, then while the pumpkin flesh is roasting in the oven, separate the seeds from the stringy fiber to which they are attached. Save plenty for pumpkin planting in the next garden cycle (putting them in a small bag and storing them in the freezer assures viability) and toast the rest. To do this, lightly coat the cleaned seeds in cooking oil, spread them out atop a cookie sheet, sprinkle with salt, and place in a 375°F oven. Toast until they begin to show a hint of brown, and remove. The seeds can be eaten whole, or if you have the patience, cracked and the kernel removed. I eat them whole and figure that along with the fine taste I'm getting some fiber.

NOTE: You can roast smaller quantities of seeds in a frying pan atop a burner.

A Craving for Candy Roasters

Some years back I had the great pleasure of being involved in what is known as a "writer fam trip" in Haywood County, North Carolina. The idea behind such outings is to expose writers to an area and familiarize them with various aspects likely to have visitor appeal. While I made known the fact that I already had considerable familiarity with Haywood County, thanks to my mountain roots, the fact that it is set squarely in the Smokies, and as the result of varied sporting and other experiences in the county over the years, folks hosting the trip still graciously insisted I join them. That proved a great blessing. I had numerous joyous experiences, among them trips to various farm-to-market and pick-your-own agricultural operations, a visit to local microbreweries, sampling the fare at some fine restaurants, a cook-and-serve-it demonstration from folks at a trout farm, show-and-tell by a lady involved in all sorts of neat gourmet canning and pickling, and a stop at a farmers market.

The writers stayed at historic Cataloochee Ranch, and that's where, in most welcome fashion, I took a grand and totally unexpected trip back to various aspects of my youth. Awaiting me in my room at check-in was a little gift bag, which included a small jar of candy roaster butter. That immediately resurrected food experiences I had not known for decades.

Grandpa Joe regularly raised candy roasters, along with pumpkins and other types of winter squash, in his corn patches. In early autumn, with the corn crop made and ears hanging down awaiting pulling and placement in the corncrib, his corn patch would be dotted with colorful pumpkins, cushaws, candy roasters, and the like. They were usually left to cure and sweeten in the sunny Indian summer days of late September and early October before being gathered and stored prior to the first frost.

Grandpa stored the finest of his winter squash beneath corn shocks, always being careful to keep them protected from the ground with a layer of straw, as well as making certain they didn't touch one another. Additional pumpkins and candy roasters, perhaps showing slight imperfections or looking like they wouldn't keep well, might be put in the smokehouse/cannery just outside Grandma Minnie's kitchen. The rest of the crop went to the hogs in a perfectly timed relationship between garden clean up and hog-killing time. Armageddon day for the pigs lay not far distant, but in the meantime they were able to eat like—well, like pigs.

The tasty treats both Grandma and Momma produced with candy roasters and pumpkins were a source of pure wonder. They liked both types of winter squash but had a particular affinity for candy roasters because their flesh wasn't as stringy as that of pumpkins. Today efforts of these two wonderful cooks run through corridors of my mind like a sweet, ever-unfolding dream, and the Cataloochee experience set that recurrent return to the past once more in delightful motion.

Candy Roaster Sauce

The uses for candy roasters varied appreciably. One personal favorite involved mashing up the cooked candy roaster, with the addition of "just a tetch" of brown sugar or molasses, along with cinnamon, to make a nondessert dish somewhat similar to applesauce. It was actually, as the "candy" part of the name suggests, sweet enough to have been a dessert. Or the golden flesh could be used to make pies quite similar to those prepared with pumpkin, in candy roaster bread or muffins, in cakes, or as candy roaster butter. The latter, slathered across a cathead biscuit that had already received a generous application of regular butter, gave that particular biscuit a taste sure to please the pickiest of gourmets.

Candy Roaster Butter

This particular recipe does not come from my family, although I feel fairly comfortable in stating it was quite similar to one Grandma used (with possibly the exception of the lemon juice), but rather from a grand cookbook, *Cataloochee Cooking*, written by Alice Alexander Aumen, one of the daughters of Cataloochee Ranch founders Tom and Judy Alexander. This cookbook is, it might be noted, first-rate when it comes to coverage of high-country culinary recipes and traditions.

1 gallon candy roaster flesh, cooked and mashed

3 cups sugar

¼ cup lemon juice

¼ cup ground cinnamon

1 tablespoon ground cloves

1 tablespoon ground nutmeg

1 tablespoon ground ginger

2 cups apple cider

1 box Sure-Jell

Mix all of the ingredients except the Sure-Jell. Bring to a boil and cook for a minute. Remove from heat and blend in the Sure-Jell. Place in sterilized jars. Melt paraffin and spoon a thin layer atop the butter. Once the paraffin has set, screw on the lid atop the jar.

Candy Roaster Pie

2 large eggs, beaten lightly

2 cups candy roaster flesh, cooked and mashed

½ to ¾ cup brown sugar (varies according to how sweet you want your pie)

½ teaspoon salt

1 teaspoon ground cinnamon

½ teaspoon ground ginger

½ teaspoon ground cloves

1 (12-ounce) can evaporated milk

Unbaked pie crusts

Preheat oven to 425°F. Combine and mix ingredients in order listed above. Pour into pie shells and bake 15 minutes. Reduce temperature to 350°F and bake an additional 45 minutes or until a toothpick comes away clean. Cool and serve with whipped cream.

NOTE: For other pie recipes from winter squash, see the chapter on Thanksgiving.

Baked Acorn Squash

Even though the acorn squash belongs to the "keeper" family of squashes, we ate them from the time they first matured in late summer until our supply was exhausted in late winter (usually by February they had all been eaten or else gone bad). The family's favorite way to eat them was baked. Momma would cut the acorn squash in half lengthwise and remove the seeds and pulp. She then placed a big pat of butter, along with some brown sugar or molasses, in the hollow space left from the seeds and pulp being scooped out of each half. The halves were placed in a baking dish or atop a cookie sheet, open end up, and baked at 350°F until the flesh was tender. When served, you could use a fork to mix the melted butter and sweetening with the flesh and then dig right in. The baked squash were sweet enough to have served as dessert, but they always figured as a vegetable in our family menus.

CHAPTER 7

———

BREAD

One of the most familiar of all passages from the Bible, thanks to it being incorporated into the Lord's Prayer, is Matthew 6:11: "Give us this day our daily bread." That humble, heartfelt prayer, addressing the most basic of all longings, the need for sustenance, has always meant a great deal to the deeply religious folks of the Smokies. While I don't recall my Grandfather Joe, something of a religious renegade who read the Bible daily but harbored deep suspicions about organized religion, ever once mentioning bread specifically in the prayer that preceded each meal, he genuinely appreciated food and both savored and did justice to every meal Grandma Minnie put before him. He would return thanks, adjusting his words to the season of the year or perhaps to the foodstuffs gracing the table, but his blessings invariably concluded with a beckoning admonitory sentence: "You'uns see what's before you. Eat hearty." One totally predictable part of what lay before those gathered at his table was bread.

On the mountain menu, bread was a vital part of eating hearty. Whether the bread was made with cornmeal, wheat flour, or rarely, some other grain, it was integral to breakfast, dinner, and supper. With surprising frequency, at least in the households of my parents and grandparents, where I ate almost all my youthful meals outside of school, bread was

Churning butter was a near-constant part of life's routine on many rural homesteads where living from the land, nature, and livestock was standard.
Courtesy of Hunter Library, Western Carolina University.

the meal. Times without number there was cornbread and sweet milk or buttermilk for supper, although you could usually roust up a cold sweet potato or piece of fried streaked meat to go with it. A breakfast of pancakes was considered a feast, and on those special occasions (almost always Saturday nights) when Momma made one waffle after another, with them disappearing just as fast as she could turn them out a pair at a time, I felt like I was sitting at a table in a comfortable spot alongside the gates to culinary heaven.

We pretty much took bread for granted. It was a given, something that could almost have been reckoned as the foundation on which each meal was built. While light bread (the standard term for loaf bread bought at the store) had its place, mainly for sandwiches, in our home, I don't recall Grandma ever putting a piece of toast or a plate holding slices of bread on her table. She had baked bread from her early years onward, and doing so was both a deeply ingrained habit and a part of daily existence. Baking biscuits for breakfast and cornbread for dinner, with the leftovers forming part of supper, was a feature of Smokies living that seemed as natural as the turning of the seasons.

Jim's Pancakes

I don't measure anything when making pancakes, but my approach is pretty straightforward. I use store-bought pancake mix unless I'm fortunate enough to lay my hands on some slow-ground buckwheat meal, something that seldom happens, although you can find it online at somewhat exorbitant prices. I then add a bit of vegetable oil, an egg, and buttermilk (the latter is the key ingredient for light pancakes). Whisk until thoroughly mixed, adding buttermilk as needed to get the right consistency. You want batter that flows fairly easily but that is neither runny nor overly thick. If I'm making pancakes for a larger group or perhaps want some leftovers, I just increase the ingredients, using more flour, two eggs, and extra oil. The batter's consistency lets you know when you have used enough buttermilk. If you are making a lot of pancakes, you may have to add a dollop or two of buttermilk as batter is going on the griddle and pancakes coming off—the batter waiting for the griddle will thicken that fast, and batter that is too thick translates to pancakes that are too heavy.

Heat a griddle until it is quite hot—the batter should begin to show bubbles soon after being placed on the grill—and adjust heat as needed. Pancakes should be turned only once. I like to dress mine up in various ways by adding any of a number of ingredients to the top before turning. Among these are chocolate chips, thin slices of banana, blueberries, raspberries, dried cranberries, blackberries, or chopped nuts. Serve piping hot and slathered with butter and use your favorite syrup, molasses, or my personal preference, honey.

NOTE: If you add any of the toppings mentioned above, they are going to make subsequent batches want to stick on your griddle. Just scrape it a bit with your turner and add a dollop of oil before starting on the next batch of pancakes.

Grandma's Biscuits and Biscuit Bread

In this particular case I'll have to confess that I really have, at best, a minimal idea of how Grandma worked her culinary magic with biscuits. I know that there was buttermilk involved, I know she never measured anything, and I remember watching her with a considerable degree of fascination. I can readily envision the light green handles on her rolling pin, the dusting of dry flour she'd scatter across the dough and a big wooden board where she rolled it out with a flourish, almost as if blessing it, and the biscuit cutter she used to cut the dough. Mostly though, I recall that her biscuits were always perfect—light, fluffy, and big enough to hold a fried egg from Grandpa Joe's chickens without much white sticking out over the edges. In other words, she baked real cathead biscuits. Sometimes, if Grandma was in a hurry or had other chores requiring immediate attention, she wouldn't make individual biscuits. She'd just get the dough ready and put it atop a cookie sheet the same way she did biscuits. She called this biscuit bread. The ingredients were the same, as was, of course, the taste. When it came to biscuits and gravy, a chunk of biscuit bread crumbled on your plate and liberally covered with milk gravy made from streaked meat grease was just the ticket.

While I don't remember Grandma's biscuit recipe, and Momma always left this aspect of food preparation to her when we had family gatherings, a few years back my good friend Tipper Pressley shared and demonstrated her approach to making biscuits at a gathering of outdoor writers. She's also a distant cousin, so for this moment I'm going to use that linkage to claim her as family and thereby keep the general thread of family cooking running through these pages. Tipper's presentation, and the end results, took me straight back to boyhood. It's a can't fail approach that is the essence of simplicity, and while there's none of the buttermilk I'm virtually certain was the secret to Grandma's consistent success, the heavy cream in this recipe doubtless has pretty much the same impact when it comes to end results.

Tipper's Biscuits

Equal amounts of self-rising flour and heavy whipping cream. A cup of flour and one of cream will make six large biscuits.

Mix well and knead once or twice by hand, making sure to coat your hands with flour so the dough doesn't stick to them. If the dough isn't quite "right," add a bit of flour or cream until you have the desired consistency. Cut out biscuits from the resulting dough with a biscuit cutter (or the opening of a canning jar, lightly dusted with flour so the dough comes away easily) and place on an ungreased baking sheet. Bake at 450°F for ten minutes or until light golden brown on top.

About all that then remains is to slather with butter and your favorite sweet biscuit adornment or else cut the cathead open and ladle on some sawmill gravy. Then let out your belt two notches and get busy with your trencherman duties!

Gritted Bread

A sound argument could be made that gritted bread is in reality nothing more than baked corn, but since it is consistently described as bread in the mountain vernacular, who am I to defy linguistic tradition? To make gritted bread, use corn that is past the "milk" or roasting-ear stage. That is to say, the kernels have begun to harden and become starchy. Grate or grit corn from the cobs, making sure to get all of it. A good way of doing this is to use a grater or sharp knife to remove the kernels and then rub the back side of a kitchen knife down the cob, applying pressure, to obtain the last bits of goodness. Pour the gritted corn into a greased baking dish, adding just a touch of milk if the corn mixture seems too thick, and bake at 350°F until done (forty to fifty minutes). The resulting "bread" can readily be sliced, and with a dab of butter it makes a mighty pleasing dish.

NOTE: For cornbread recipes, see chapter 1.

Carl Standing Deer's stepdaughter pounds corn, which was the
way the Cherokees prepared meal for various corn-based dishes.
Courtesy of the National Park Service.

CHAPTER 8

CHEROKEE FOODS

While this work is, for the most part, an intensely personal food memoir embracing things four generations of my family have gathered, grown, cooked, and eaten, it seemed imperative to include a chapter touching on the favorite foods of the Cherokees. Their foodways were, after all, the original ones of the Smokies, and they brought distinctiveness to all aspects of their culinary existence—what they ate, how they farmed, what they grew, their methods of hunting and fishing, approaches to cooking and food preservation, and much more.

My personal exposure to Cherokee foods in terms of dining on dishes traditional to these American Indians and prepared by them is somewhat limited. The annual celebration known as the Cherokee Indian Fair, always held at harvesttime in the fall, was a major event in my boyhood. Every year until I was through high school found me in attendance for at least one day. After all, my Bryson City home was only a few miles from the southwestern boundary of the reservation, I went to school with many tribal members, dated a lovely girl who was part Cherokee for a time, and worked in the town of Cherokee multiple summers. That translated to quite a bit of familiarity with the Cherokees and at least some interest in their foods and closeness to nature.

One of many aspects of the annual fair involved, just like regional and state events of this type across the nation, displays of crops, exhibits of foodstuffs, cooking competitions, and the like. The exhibit area drew my attention in an irresistible fashion and at one time or another I sampled a few traditional dishes such as bean bread and chestnut bread. I never ate yellow jacket soup, but now I wish I had. Bears love the stinging pests and in the fall you frequently find evidence of where they have dug out an underground nest to eat the grubs, clearly oblivious to the pain they have to endure. Yellow jackets are abundant in the Smokies, and they would have offered a ready source of protein. I have no idea of how the nests were raided by people, but it probably involved the use of smoke at nighttime when all the adult yellow jackets were present.

I've also grown some Cherokee foodstuffs, when seeds were shared with me. I particularly love the lore associated with gizzard beans, supposedly rescued from the "grinding gear" of a domestic turkey at some point when the westward march known as the Trail of Tears was getting underway. Similarly, like countless others, I've long recognized the wisdom of the three sisters symbiosis of corn, beans, and winter squash.

I have sampled and savored all the recipes offered here except yellow jacket soup, and Momma frequently fixed a mixed vegetable dish she called succotash. She always used corn, lima beans, and summer squash, with other vegetables often included when available. She did not use pumpkin or other types of winter squash, which is truer to traditional American Indian succotash. The only cookbook focusing specifically on Cherokee foods with which I am familiar is a dandy one dating back to the middle of the last century, *Cherokee Cooklore: To Make My Bread*. Published by two Cherokee icons, Mary and Goingback Chiltoskey, it is short and includes only a few dozen recipes. They are quite general in nature, basically involving description of the food and how it is prepared, with no specifics on ingredient measurements.

Bean Bread

Traditional bean bread was prepared by first using wood ashes to skin corn kernels in much the same fashion associated with making hominy. Once lye had loosened the tough outer covering of the kernels, they would be washed thoroughly (traditional tight-woven baskets were perfect for this effort) and then, while still moist and soft, placed in a section of stump with the top hollowed out to be pounded with a traditional beater (a wooden shaft of four or five feet with additional wood left at the pounding end to add to the impact). The corn pulp would then be mixed with dried beans that had been boiled until they were tender. The resulting corn-and-bean mixture could be wrapped in corn shucks and baked in hot coals for bean bread. An alternative was to drop the corn-and-bean mix into boiling water a spoonful at a time to make dumplings.

Chestnut Bread

Chestnut bread was made following the same basic process as bean bread, with chestnuts being substituted for beans and blended with the pounded corn. The process was a bit more demanding in that the chestnuts first had to be hulled. That involved slitting the individual nut at the top so that it would open up from heat when boiled. The hulls and a leathery layer protecting the nut were then removed and the meat cut into pieces before being mixed with the corn.

Sochan

More commonly known outside the mountains as cutleaf coneflower, sochan has long grown wild throughout the Smokies. It is a perennial that puts on quite a show in late summer and early fall as graceful yellow flowers with their green centers reach skyward atop tall stalks. However, it was the young, tender sprouts, among the first to appear in spring, that gave the plant its greatest appeal to the Cherokees and, later, European settlers. It is so rich in a number of vitamins and minerals that one expert has compared sochan to the "nutritional superstar kale." After long months with minimal intake of vitamin C, and given the plant's hefty content of folic acid, manganese, calcium, and zinc, it was a perfect pick-me-up and welcome dietary change. The young greens were usually parboiled, then cooked in grease from streaked meat, but for a modern and healthier alternative, just steam or sauté them, perhaps using a bit of olive oil and salt to taste.

Hominy and Nuts

Accomplished in using what they grew and what nature offered in tasty, nutritious combinations, the Cherokees had many basic dishes that focused on their most abundant foodstuffs. This dish combines two of the three sisters, corn and beans, with native nuts found in abundance in mountain woodlands. Hickory nuts or chestnuts were most often used, but black walnuts, butternuts, or hazelnuts work just as well.

Hominy (preferably prepared from Indian corn the old-fashioned way, using lye from wood ashes; if you want a far simpler route, substitute the store-bought variety)

October beans, soaked and cooked

Nut meats

Cornmeal

Salt

Mix cooked hominy and cooked beans with just enough water to avoid scorching and bring to a simmer. Add nut meats and cornmeal and stir the mix thoroughly, adding salt to taste. The nuts turn what otherwise might be more of a stomach stuffer than a treat into something special.

Succotash

Although closely identified with American Indians (not just Cherokees but many tribes), succotash is prepared in so many ways, and its ingredients vary so dramatically, that pinning it down as a specific dish is impossible. Cherokee succotash recipes use pumpkin, but that was never part of the dish as I have known it in the Smokies. Instead, the two key ingredients were corn and lima beans, although there might be other ingredients, including what we knew as "shelly beans" (not leather britches but rather green beans that had been allowed to get too big but that could still be shelled out and mixed with immature hulls), okra, crowder peas, or indeed pretty much whatever the garden was yielding in abundance at that point in time.

The ingredients would be mixed in a saucepan with the omnipresent piece of streaked meat and a bit of water added, then cooked until the mixed vegetables were done. The end result was somewhat similar to the soup mix that my family canned, quart after quart, every summer. The biggest difference was that tomatoes were never used in succotash.

Yellow Jacket Soup

As has been previously noted, this is a dish I've never had an opportunity to eat. Accordingly, this recipe is not only an untested one but in fact involves nothing more than a composite based on numerous accounts of the dish.

Locate a yellow jacket nest (they are primarily ground dwellers) and raid it using smoke or perhaps protective clothing. If done at night, all the mature yellow jackets will be with the nest, and you don't have to worry about repelling attackers from outside. Carefully remove the comb or layers (in late summer or early fall an active nest may have four or five sections). Knock all the grubs and immature yellow jackets from the individual cells within the comb into a bowl. Lightly roast the "meat" in an oven or brown it in a greased skillet. Boil the cooked yellow jackets in a soup pot with water and lard (the Cherokees would have used bear grease or fat from a ground hog).

A group "robs" honey. Tracking wild bees to obtain honey,
and often to capture the queen and other bees in the hive and
move them to a domestic setting, was a real art.
Courtesy of Hunter Library, Western Carolina University.

PART II

FOODS FROM NATURE AND SEASONAL FARE

The wild blackberry is a sure sign of Country.

BONNIE LOU COCHRAN, *Ways of Old*

Eatin' a persimmon and wishin' I had not
And ridin' a mule bareback at a fast trot,
Washin' the dishes and disrag fights,
Pickin' blackberries and gettin' chigger bites.

GLADYS TRENTHAM RUSSELL,
It Happened in the Smokies

I n my youth, as had been the case for generations not only in my family but throughout the Smokies, nature's full larder provided a significant, welcome, and tasty portion of our fare. Daddy was an adept fly fisherman, and that translated to trout frequently appearing on the table during the warmer months of the year. By my midteens, thanks to devoting almost every spare moment of the summer, along with weekends during the spring, to wading trout streams, I had actually surpassed his skills with the long rod and whistling line. Momma, for her part, delighted in having a mess of trout at any time and it mattered not who caught them.

Small-game hunting was also a significant part of my boy-hood. We raised beagles, and rabbit hunting on Saturdays from Thanksgiving through the end of the cottontail season the last day in February was a given. There was plenty of squirrel hunting as well, and any chance encounters with quail or grouse where some successful wing shooting came into play meant delicious variety in family foodstuffs.

Important though trout (and other game fish such as bream, bass, and crappie, along with the occasional catch of catfish) and small game might have been, it was the plant side of wild bounty that loomed largest in our diet and those of Smokies folks in general. Vegetables, nuts, berries, and fruits from the fields and woodlands were harvested and used in surprising quantities. Prior to its sad demise due to the ravages of a deadly blight acci-dentally imported from Asia, the American chestnut stood to the forefront in this regard. It offered food, a means of supplement-ing family income, and food for fattening hogs. But a multitude of berries, early greenstuffs that gave a welcome break after winter's rather narrow dietary choices, native nuts, and naturally growing fruits such as persimmons and pawpaws meant food for the taking. All that was required was gumption, and that was a characteristic in abundant supply among hardy, "make do with what you've got" mountain folks. In my case those experiences afield and astream as well as in consuming food from nature have shaped not only my youth but my adult years as well.

For better than two decades, I've earned my livelihood exclu-sively as a writer, and for two decades before that, freelance work as a sporting scribe was a sidelight to my daily duties as a univer-sity history professor. Over all that period, a significant portion of the nonscholarly material I produced dealt with hunting and fish-ing, and I continue to write regularly on the outdoors. My special fields of interest and/or expertise include fly fishing for trout, turkey hunting, the history of outdoor activities in America, the literature of sport, and foods from nature. My literary output involves books in all those fields as well as a regular stream of articles for newspapers and magazines. While their geographical focus ranges widely, and I have even been fortunate enough to hunt and fish in a number of foreign countries and exotic locations, contents of all my nonscholarly works trace in a readily discernible fashion back to a boyhood growing up in the Smokies.

From the time I was old enough to hold enough to tag along, my father allowed me to accompany him on after-work trips to fish for trout, and not many years later that same privilege extended first to squirrel hunts and then to rabbit hunts. Well before I entered high school, I was venturing out on my own, wading nearby trout streams or hunting rabbits, squirrels, and quail in habitat within walking distance of home. One of the most meaningful moments from those halcyon years came when a high school English teacher wrote on an essay where we could pick a topic of our choice and I selected squirrel hunting: "This is the kind of material, in much more sophisticated form, which the outdoor magazines buy." I never forgot those words and they planted a seed that, while it took a long time to do so, eventually sprouted. As a sort of footnote to this early obsession with the outdoors and boyish dreams of writing, I personally consider two books I wrote that are chock full of those glory days of youth as being among the most important I have ever produced. They are *Fly Fishing in the Great Smoky Mountains National Park: An Insider's Guide to a Pursuit of Passion* and *A Smoky Mountain Boyhood: Memories, Musings, and More.*

Any provender produced from my outdoor activities was greeted enthusiastically at home. That was solidly in keeping with traditional Smokies ways, where meat from the wilds involved a welcome break from daily table fare, just as the quest afforded escape from hard work that could all too readily become sheer drudgery. Momma could work wonders with the small game species—rabbits, squirrels, quail, and grouse—which made up virtually all the opportunities the Smokies offered to put meat from the wilds on the table during that era. Deer and wild turkey populations had plummeted to a point where they were virtually nonexistent, and Daddy didn't hunt bears, although it was a sport that had a passionate local following. As for trout, we all loved them, and rest assured Momma wanted no part whatsoever of the angling ethic today popular in many fly-fishing circles (and from a tender age I was exclusively a fly fisherman when it came to trout) known as catch and release. Her views in that regard were quite straightforward. You "released" any trout you caught to hot grease.

Grandpa Joe was just as passionate about sport as Daddy, and he constantly honed my blade of sporting eagerness with tales from his younger years. Those stories included killing a "painter" (the word folks in the Smokies invariably use to describe a cougar); hunting squirrels when, thanks to the presence of the American chestnut, they were incredibly abundant; and catching speckled trout when they were so plentiful as to defy belief. He too loved game and fish on the table, and not surprisingly, Grandma Minnie flat-out knew how to prepare anything nature happened to provide.

My experiences and the manner in which my family enjoyed the "meat on the table" side of the wilds were in no way unusual. From the earliest settlers onward the abundance of game to be found in the woodlands of the high country and of trout filling area creeks, along with other species found in the warmer water of slower-moving rivers, was important to them. Pursuit provided sport and a welcome break from the arduous demands of daily living, and tasty additions to the standard dietary fare were, as Grandpa would have put it, "mighty fine." The only significant difference was that where the big game of the mountains—deer, bear, and wild turkey—had once been of considerable importance, the populations of these animals, especially whitetails and turkeys, had dwindled dramatically.

In time, as I matured and found my niche as a writer, realization dawned that I had a wealth of practical experience in the culinary field. I'd like to think I'm a passing fair hand in the kitchen or over a backcountry campfire, and my wife, strictly through dint of self-instruction, became a worthy successor to the legacy of Momma and Grandma Minnie. As a result, we have cowritten a half dozen or more cookbooks, and the primary focus in all of them is food from nature. Venison probably looms largest, and that was a meat I had no exposure to whatsoever in my youth. However, I did recognize that in earlier generations, before the abrupt decline of deer populations in the Smokies, whitetails, along with coons, bears, groundhogs, and turkeys, were of considerable importance to mountain hunters and in mountain diet. Read accounts of some of the grand old nimrods of the nineteenth and early twentieth centuries—men such as Mark Cathey, Sam Hunnicutt, Wiley Oakley, and Turkey George Palmer—and you soon realize as much. Hunnicutt wrote a book about his experiences, *Twenty Years Hunting and Fishing in the Great Smoky Mountains*. It is the product of someone who was marginally literate, but the vivid descriptions provide an unmatched view of the sporting culture of the Smokies in the early twentieth century.

I was not privileged, as a boy, to hunt big game in the Smokies, mainly because, with the exceptions of bears and wild hogs, it wasn't present in huntable numbers. Today, thankfully, that's a dramatically changed situation. Both deer and wild turkey have made a remarkable comeback from being close to extinction. I never once saw a wild turkey in my youth and had seen precisely ten deer at the point when I headed off to college in 1960. That was despite spending a great deal of time in remote reaches of the Smokies. The animals just weren't there, and most area counties didn't even have an open season for deer and turkeys. We are now in a situation where it is possible to call back yesteryear in a meaningful way. With that in mind, even though it falls a bit outside my personal experiences during a Smokies boyhood, I have included some recipes for venison and wild turkey below. They were, after all, treasured table fare for generations of Smokies residents before my time, and they once more loom large in the diet of many avid outdoorsmen in the region. Grandpa talked about dining on venison and turkey (so Grandma would have cooked the meat), and they predominate among the meats that have graced our family table for the last three decades.

Andy and one of his Wild Turkeys
Hall Cabin

A hunter identified only as "Andy" with a wild turkey hanging from
the wall at the Hall Cabin in the Hazel Creek drainage. Game such
as this, along with fish, formed a welcome part of Smokies diet.
Courtesy of Hunter Library, Western Carolina University.

CHAPTER 9

WILD GAME AND FISH

The importance of small game and fish in my youthful years in the Smokies has already been noted, as has expansion of enjoyment, during adult years, of these aspects of wild bounty thanks to the grand comeback sagas of the white-tailed deer and American wild turkey. Here are some of the recipes, mostly from the past but with a few additions to cover foodstuffs that were important before my boyhood and that thankfully have once more returned to prominence and ready availability.

Pan-Fried Trout

2 to 3 small trout (6 to 8 inches length is ideal—they are tastier than larger ones) per person, dressed

Stone-ground cornmeal

Salt and pepper

Bacon grease or lard

Clean the fish and leave damp so they will hold plenty of cornmeal. Put your cornmeal in a ziplock bag, add the trout, along with salt and pepper, and shake thoroughly. Make sure the inside body cavity gets a coating of cornmeal. Heat grease in a large frying pan (a cast-iron spider works wonders but modern nonstick kitchenware is quite suitable), and when piping hot, place the trout in the pan. Cook, turning only once, until golden brown. You can help the process along by using a spatula or tilting the pan a bit to splash grease into the open body cavities. Place cooked fish atop paper towels, pat gently to remove any excess grease, and dig in. If it is springtime, serve with a backwoods "kilt" salad (see Kilt Ramps Salad recipe in chapter 10), fried potatoes and onions with bacon bits added, and something for the sweet tooth to finish.

Trout Omelet

6 large eggs

½ cup minced onion

½ cup chopped mushrooms

½ cup fresh spinach, chopped

1 cup cottage cheese

2 cups cooked and flaked trout (I like to poach them in butter)

Butter

Sour cream

Salt and black pepper

Paprika (optional)

Parsley, chopped (optional)

Mix eggs and vegetables in a small bowl then combine with cottage cheese and beat until fluffy. Pour into a buttered frying pan and cook slowly on low heat until the eggs start to set. At this point pour previously cooked trout on top, add a dollop of sour cream, and then carefully fold to finish cooking the omelet. Season with salt and pepper and top with paprika or chopped parsley if desired. *Serves 3 or 4*

Fried Quail

Except for hunting preserves and some very special situations involving intensive management, quail in the Smokies and pretty much everywhere else belong to a world we have lost. Yet they were plentiful when I was a boy, and seldom indeed did we go on an all-day rabbit hunt without flushing two or three coveys. We shot at them anytime we had a chance, and the same was true for the occasional grouse we flushed (that happened more frequently when squirrel hunting). This recipe, although I've made some slight modifications, was a favorite way of cooking quail.

1 cup red wine

1 cup olive oil

1 tablespoon minced garlic

16 dressed quail

3 cups self-rising flour

¼ cup seasoned salt

Lard for deep frying

Mix the wine, olive oil, and garlic. Add the quail and marinate, refrigerated, for 4 to 6 hours. Combine the flour and seasoned salt. Remove the quail from the marinade, drain, and then coat the quail in the flour mixture and deep fry in 350°F lard for 15 to 20 minutes. Serve immediately. *Makes 8 servings (quantities in recipe can be reduced)*

Smothered Quail

6 whole dressed quail

¼ pound (1 stick) butter (the real thing)

¼ cup olive oil

2 (10-ounce) cans chicken and rice soup

½ cup cooking sherry

Preheat oven to 350°F. Brown the quail in a mixture of butter and olive oil in a skillet. Arrange the browned birds in a baking dish. Pour the soup and sherry into the pan drippings in the skillet. Bring to a boil and pour over the quail. Cover and bake for an hour. Serve with rice and curried fruit.

Apple Quail

This recipe pairs quail with that old mountain standby, apples, in a tasty union.

¼ cup all-purpose flour

½ teaspoon salt

⅛ teaspoon paprika

6 dressed quail

2 tablespoons butter, plus 1 tablespoon if needed

¼ cup chopped sweet onion

1 tablespoon chopped fresh parsley

¼ teaspoon dried thyme

1 cup apple juice

Mix flour, salt, and paprika and use to lightly flour quail. Melt butter in a large, heavy frying pan, and brown quail. Push quail to one side of the pan. Add onion and sauté until tender (add 1 tablespoon of additional butter if needed). Add parsley, thyme, and apple juice. Stir to mix well and spoon juice over quail while bringing all to a boil, then reduce heat, cover, and simmer until quail are tender (about an hour). Serve quail on a bed of rice or grits with sautéed apples or hot applesauce on the side.

Anna Lou's Squirrel

Anna Lou Moore Casada was my mother. She prepared small game, basically the only type of game available in the Smokies of my boyhood, in a surprisingly wide variety of ways. She could work wonders with rabbit, and I remember a baked young coon that was melt-in-your-mouth fine, but it was when squirrel figured in the equation that she consistently outshone any cook I've ever known. This was my favorite among all her many methods of preparing squirrel.

1 to 2 squirrels, dressed

1 teaspoon baking soda

1 to 2 tablespoons butter

Place squirrels in large saucepan. Cover with cold water, add baking soda, and heat to boiling. Remove from heat and rinse squirrel well under running water, rubbing to remove baking soda. Return squirrel to cleaned pan and cover with fresh water. Bring to a boil; reduce heat and simmer until tender. Place squirrel in a baking dish, dot with butter, and bake at 350°F until browned and crusty.

NOTE: You can prepare rabbit the same way. The broth left when you remove the meat for baking provides the basis for fine milk gravy.

Squirrel Pot Pie

1 onion, chopped coarsely

1 stalk celery, chopped coarsely

1 large garlic clove, minced

4 cups beef broth

Freshly ground black pepper

1 squirrel, dressed

Pastry for a 2-crust pie

1 (12-ounce) can mixed vegetables or a comparable
amount of home-frozen vegetables

1 tablespoon cornstarch

Preheat oven to 350°F. Combine the onion, celery, garlic, beef broth, pepper, and squirrel in a large pot and bring to a boil; simmer until the meat is quite tender and easily removed from the bones. Debone the meat and set aside. Measure out 1 cup of the cooking liquid and reserve.

Fit the bottom crust into a pie pan. Combine the meat, vegetables, reserved broth, and cornstarch in a large bowl and mix well. Spoon the mixture into the pie shell. Top with the second crust, press the edges to seal, and cut several vents in the top for steam to escape. Bake until the crust is brown, about an hour.

NOTE: Rabbit pie can be prepared the same way.

Fried Squirrel

1 cup all-purpose flour

1 teaspoon salt

¼ to ½ teaspoon black pepper

1 to 2 eggs

1 to 2 squirrels, cut up

½ cup canola oil

Mix flour, salt, and pepper, and place in a paper or plastic bag. Beat egg well and place in a shallow dish. Drop squirrel in flour bag, shake to cover well, remove squirrel, and dip in egg mixture. Return squirrel to flour bag and shake to coat well. Repeat with all the squirrel pieces. Heat canola oil in skillet and quickly brown squirrel. Place browned squirrel in roasting pan or baking dish and bake, uncovered, at 250°F for approximately 90 minutes or until squirrel is tender.

Squirrel with Lima Beans

All-purpose flour

Salt and black pepper

2 squirrels, dressed and cut into pieces

¼ pound bacon ends

2 cups dried lima beans, soaked overnight

1 onion, chopped

2 celery ribs, chopped

2 carrots, chopped

1 tablespoon sugar

1 cup sliced okra

3 potatoes, diced

2 cups frozen corn

2 (16-ounce) cans stewed tomatoes or
the home-canned equivalent

1 bay leaf

Dash of thyme and parsley

½ teaspoon crushed red pepper (optional)

Mix flour, salt, and pepper in a bowl and dredge squirrel pieces in it. In a Dutch oven, fry bacon and remove. Brown squirrel in bacon drippings, then add bacon, beans, onions, celery, and carrots to pot, and cover with water. Bring to a boil and then reduce to a slow simmer for 2 hours. Squirrel meat can be removed from bones at this point if you wish. Add remaining ingredients and simmer for an hour longer or until squirrel and vegetables are tender. If desired, thicken with flour-and-water paste and adjust seasonings. *Serves 6 to 8 and is a good way to stretch out a couple of squirrels*

NOTE: This recipe works equally well with rabbits.

Squirrel and Dumplings

Only once during my entire youth did my delight in putting "meat on the table" meet with disappointment. That came when Momma, generous as ever, suggested that I dress a couple of squirrels I had brought home and give them to our next-door neighbors, Marianna and Stanley Black. They were a wonderful old couple, generous with their philanthropic endeavors in the community and pillars of the region in many ways. He was a banker and lawyer while she was a homemaker whose children excelled to the point where one of them, Ellen Black Winston, held a cabinet-level post under first President John Kennedy and later President Lyndon Johnson. Their other children were likewise highly successful in life, and that level of achievement has continued with their grandchildren and beyond.

Momma mainly wanted me to offer a goodwill gesture, but she also figured that the Blacks—who were as frugal in their personal lives as they were generous with the local Presbyterian church, the public library (it bears Marianna's name as its founder), and in quietly lending a helping hand anytime it was deserved and needed—would welcome free meat. Accordingly, I skinned a brace of young, tender squirrels, took extra care to make sure not so much as a single hair clung to the carcasses, and carried them over to their house. When I presented them to Mrs. Black she recoiled in horror. "Oh my," she said, "we don't eat tree rats." Crestfallen, I returned home with my rejected offering, but I feel certain that dining on the squirrel assuaged my disappointment. The dish below may well have been the one Mom fixed.

2 squirrels, dressed

2 bay leaves

1 cup chopped onion

1 cup chopped celery

3 to 4 carrots, chopped

Salt and pepper

2 cups water

Cut squirrels into serving pieces. Place in a Dutch oven and add enough water to cover. Add bay leaves and simmer for 90 minutes or until squirrels are tender. Skim fat or froth from top if necessary. Squirrel may be removed from the bones at this point and returned to stew if you desire (or set aside until the veggies are done before reintroduction). Add onion, celery, carrots, seasonings to taste, and water. Cook for 15 to 20 minutes or until veggies are tender. Increase heat and bring stew to boiling. Prepare dumplings as directed below.

DUMPLINGS

½ cup milk

1 cup all-purpose flour

2 teaspoons baking powder

½ teaspoon salt

Slowly add milk to dry ingredients to form dumpling mix. Drop by teaspoons into boiling broth. Cook for 15 to 20 minutes or until dumplings are done in the center.

Bacon Rabbit

6 slices bacon

2 rabbits, dressed and quartered

½ cup all-purpose flour

½ teaspoon garlic salt

¼ teaspoon freshly ground black pepper

¼ teaspoon paprika

1½ to 2 cups fine dry bread crumbs

Cook bacon until crisp, then strain drippings and set aside bacon. Pat rabbit dry with a paper towel. Roll rabbit (or put in a heavy-duty bag to shake) in flour mixed with garlic salt, pepper, and paprika. Dip in bacon drippings and completely moisten. Dredge in bread crumbs. Place rabbit in baking dish and bake at 375°F for 30 to 45 minutes on one side; turn and bake on other side for 30 to 45 minutes more or until browned and tender. Five minutes before the oven process is complete, crumble bacon and sprinkle atop the rabbit pieces and return briefly to oven.

Country-Style Venison Steak

⅓ cup all-purpose flour

Salt and black pepper

1 pound venison cubed steak

2 tablespoons olive oil

1 medium onion, sliced

1 (4-ounce) jar whole mushrooms, drained

Season flour with salt and pepper to taste. Dredge steak in flour and brown quickly in oil. Place in a 9-by-12-inch casserole dish. Cook onion until tender. Place on top of steak along with mushrooms. Add 2 tablespoons of the remaining flour to pan drippings. Stir until brown, add 1 to 1½ cups water, and cook until thick. Pour over steaks. Bake covered in a 350°F oven for an hour or until tender.

Mustard Fried Venison Steak

1 pound venison cubed steak

½ cup prepared mustard

⅔ cup all-purpose flour

1 teaspoon salt

6 tablespoons canola oil

Brush steaks on both sides with prepared mustard. Mix flour and salt and dredge mustard-painted steaks in the mixture. Heat oil in a skillet and quickly cook floured steaks until golden brown. Do not overcook. One of the cardinal sins in preparing the better cuts of venison is overcooking. Serve immediately.

Venison Meat Loaf

1½ to 2 pounds ground venison

1 onion, finely chopped, or 1 package of dry onion soup mix

1 cup old-fashioned rolled oats, or you can
substitute barley if you prefer

1 egg, slightly beaten

½ cup applesauce

½ cup ketchup, divided

Black pepper

Thoroughly mix all ingredients, except reserve ¼ cup ketchup. Place in a loaf pan and bake at 350°F for 45 to 50 minutes. Remove from oven and top with remaining ¼ cup of ketchup. Return to oven for a further 10 to 15 minutes or until top is browned and the meat loaf is done.

Turkey Pie

6 tablespoons butter

6 tablespoons all-purpose flour

¼ to ½ teaspoon freshly ground black pepper

2 cups homemade turkey broth (or
purchased chicken broth)

⅔ cup half-and-half or cream

2 cups chopped cooked wild turkey

Pastry for a 2-crust pie

In a large skillet, put butter, flour, and pepper, and cook for 1 minute, stirring constantly. Add broth and half-and-half and cook slowly until thickened. Add turkey, mix in, and pour into pastry-lined pan. Top with pastry and pinch edges together. Bake at 400°F for 35 to 45 minutes or until pastry is nicely browned.

NOTE: This is a good recipe for the dark meat of a wild turkey, which is quite tough.

Black Walnut–Crusted Turkey

1 pound wild turkey breast cutlets, pounded
well with a meat mallet

½ cup oil-and-vinegar salad dressing

⅓ cup finely chopped black walnut meats

½ cup fresh bread crumbs

1 tablespoon finely chopped chives

1 tablespoon butter

2 tablespoons olive oil

Place pounded turkey breast cutlets in a quart ziplock bag, pour in the salad dressing, and marinate overnight or for at least 6 hours.

Place black walnuts and bread crumbs in a blender and process until fine. Transfer to a small bowl and add chives.

In a large skillet, melt butter and add olive oil over medium-high heat. Drain cutlets and dip into black walnut mix, pressing to coat if necessary.

Place the coated cutlets in the skillet and reduce heat to medium. Cook for 4 to 6 minutes per side until golden brown and the inside is no longer pink. Serve immediately.

CHAPTER 10

WILD VEGETABLES

As this particular chapter is being written, we've just entered the month of March, and all signs at this juncture point to an exceptionally early spring. The first daffodil blooms showed up well before the month of February concluded. By that point japonica buds were blushing with hints of pink, and yellowbells were starting to sport the color that gives forsythia the name by which it is commonly known in the Smokies. Add fuzzy pussy willows, the telltale white of service tree blooms, and moss greening up in a fashion that to me has always been one of the great attractions of nature's annual renewal.

Vegetables from nature's sprawling, bountiful garden come in many forms and across many months, but none are more welcome than those from greening-up time in spring. The list of edible offerings from early spring used in my youth was a long one, and folks living close to the land in the Smokies knew them with an intimacy born of a combination of necessity and practicality. Among the favorite wild vegetables were dandelions, lamb's quarter, tender young ferns, stinging nettles, saw briar tips, speckled dock, creasy greens (also known as cress though not to be confused with watercress, which many, including some noted writers, have

A fine patch of ramps in the springtime
just inviting a backwoods feast.
Photo by Don Casada.

done), crow's foot, and of course the incomparable poke. A toothsome hallmark of spring that hardy mountain folks have long considered both a feast and a fine spring pick-me-up, the tender sprouts of pokeweed, when cooked, are universally known in the Smokies as "poke sallet."

A bit of explanation is needed at this point. Sallet and salad are two distinctly different edibles. A sallet consists of some type of greens, wild or tame, cooked in water, with a piece of streaked meat usually being added to the pot. Salad, on the other hand, refers to uncooked vegetables such as might engender a comment of this nature: "We caught a mess of trout and that evening enjoyed a fine bait of them with a kilt salad of branch lettuce and ramps." A *mess* probably needs a bit of clarification as well. In terms of amount, a mess is somewhat amorphous, but if asked for synonym or definition, "a precious plenty" comes immediately to mind. In other words, a mess is an ample quantity of some edible.

Poke sprouts show their heads early in the greening-up season, and thanks to dried stalks left behind from the previous year, locating the plant is a cinch. Among sites where you are likely to find poke in abundance are road banks, field edges, recently abandoned agricultural fields or pastures, logging yards where harvested timber was gathered to be loaded on trucks, and indeed almost anywhere that is fairly open without significant overstory. Birds, foxes, and other critters that eat the plant's purple berries in fall guarantee this widespread plant gets seeded in abundant fashion. In fact, foxes enjoy the berries, which are poisonous for humans, so much that their appearance after consuming them engendered a delightfully descriptive if somewhat crude simile I often heard as a boy: "As red as a fox's ass in pokeberry time."

In addition to being free for the gathering, poke is healthy, delicious, and just enough of a purgative to give one's body what Grandma Minnie called "a good spring cleaning." Grandpa had an even more graphic way of describing the side effects of what he invariably styled "a good bait of poke sallet." He would talk about how it had always been a welcome addition to diet at the end of a long winter and how much he enjoyed eating it. However, he would finish with a bit of a cautionary note: "It sure is fine eating, but it also sure will set you free."

Poke grew abundantly in the pasture immediately adjacent to my boyhood home, and once established the plant comes back year after year. The first money I ever earned came from a number eight paper poke crammed with poke. (If that statement seems confusing to some readers, I've just learned something about you—I don't think paper bags are called pokes over most of the country, but I'll guarantee that the word is a part of the vocabulary of anyone for whom Smoky Mountain English is their native tongue.)

My second-grade schoolteacher, Mrs. Emily Davis, absolutely loved poke sallet, and when I presented her with a good mess, she always rewarded me with a quarter. That was big money for a small boy in 1950. For a few weeks it was a cut-and-come-again vegetable, and I knew the location of every poke plant within a half mile of our home.

Poke Sallet with Boiled Eggs

The way both Momma and Grandma Minnie prepared poke was pretty much the standard approach throughout the Smokies. They would rinse freshly gathered sprouts thoroughly in a colander to remove dirt and insects and then bring the shoots to a rolling boil in a sizeable pot of water. Once the water had boiled for several minutes, they would remove the pot from the stove and drain off the water. The process was then repeated, starting with cold water and again draining the greens after they had boiled for 10 to 15 minutes. I have subsequently learned that the plant contains so much vitamin A that this approach is necessary to remove the excess of that vitamin.

The third time around, a couple of slices of streaked meat or maybe bacon drippings would be added to the pot and the greens would be allowed to simmer slowly in their own juice while pork worked its wonders. At the conclusion of this process, we had poke sallet ready for table use. Usually slices of boiled eggs topped the greens, and sometimes bits of bacon or crumbles of streaked meat that had been fried crisp would be added as well.

If you enjoy cooked mustard or turnip greens, or even more so, spinach or Swiss chard, you will find poke sallet a fine offering from nature's rich bounty. Poke's a free annual feast requiring nothing but sufficient gumption to gather it, and as a special spring addition to mountain tables its consumption stretches far back into our high-country roots.

The gastrointestinal impact of poke sallet was one thing, and it has always enjoyed appreciable regional renown. But for a spring vegetable that announced its presence in demonstrative fashion and has become something of a culinary legend in area folklore, nothing can touch the humble yet hallowed ramp. A traditional wild mountain vegetable of early spring that is fairly widely dispersed in the forest understory at higher elevations, today ramps often garner laudatory mention in menus of restaurants famed for haute cuisine. Rest assured any usage involves the vegetable after it has been cooked, for the highbrow epicures who frequent such establishments have no idea of the true nature of the ramp. In its pure, undefiled, raw state, the way hardy mountain folks have enjoyed the vegetable for generations, the ramp is at once a delightful delicacy and the embodiment of gag-inducing noxiousness. Though mild tasting, when eaten uncooked the ramp has a pungent aftereffect that by comparison makes garlic seem a pantywaist pretender in the stink sweepstakes.

My initial experience with ramps came when I was a fifth-grade student at Bryson City Elementary School. A classmate showed up on a Monday after having enjoyed, in his words, "a bait of ramps" on Saturday. Never mind the passage of a day and a half, the lingering and noxious impact of his weekend feast was of a potency defying description with words. He literally emptied the classroom and sent the harried teacher, whose educational training apparently contained no instruction on how to deal with this particular dilemma, scurrying down the hall to the principal's office.

The result was one that would be repeated numerous times over the course of my school days. As was the case when some poor soul showed up with a case of head lice, the odiferous offender was sent home for a three-day vacation. No written rules had been violated and no laws had been broken. It was simply a situation where the welfare of the community—his classmates and indeed anyone who happened to be downwind for an appreciable distance—took precedence over that of the individual.

This sort of situation happened with increasing frequency as I entered high school, with the offending boy (I never once recall a girl having come to school reeking of ramps) always earning a temporary reprieve from the educational process. Most of the enforced absences were intentional although some undoubtedly involved nothing more than a family indulging in a long-established gustatory rite of spring—one that ranked right alongside spring tonics such as drinking sassafras tea or taking a dose of sulfur and molasses.

Eventually I became involved in the consumption side of the ramp equation, albeit my first time was a matter of self-defense. The opening day of trout season in North Carolina was once an occasion for spring celebration as sportsmen shook off the mullygrubs, greeted earth's rebirth, and hopefully caught a mess of trout. The fishing part of the ritual remains strongly in place, so much so that on opening day on some hatchery-supported waters it almost seems you need to carry your own rock if you want a place to stand.

My first experience of this sort came when I joined a group of buddies, all of us avid fly fishermen, to celebrate the annual opener with a weekend camping trip. As we backpacked to our campsite, one member of the party noticed a hillside covered with ramps and stopped to harvest several dozen of them. In camp he cleaned and chopped the ramps, scattered them over a plate of branch lettuce (saxifrage) he had found growing creek side, and dressed the salad with hot grease and bacon bits. He proclaimed this "kilt salad" would be delicious.

This experience involving trout, wild greens, and ramps did indeed produce pure culinary delight. Until you've eaten pan-fried trout dressed up in cornbread dinner jackets and fried to mouth-watering perfection, with side dishes of fried potatoes and a hearty salad of branch lettuce and ramps "kilt" (wilted) by hot bacon grease, yours has been a life of culinary deprivation. Merely thinking of such a feast is enough to cause the accelerator for my salivary glands to stick wide open, and no five-star Parisian restaurant can match such fare.

Truth be told though, it wouldn't have mattered whether the offering from nature's abundant bounty was supremely tasty or odious to God and man alike. All of us were sharing a big tent and had no choice except to follow our companion's dietary example. Once someone has eaten raw ramps, the noxious odor seems to permeate the atmosphere for thirty yards in every direction. The only relief is to join in the feast. As soon as that is done somehow your nasal sensory function alters and the smell magically disappears.

We knew that, and as a result, all of us had a nice ramp and branch lettuce salad to go with our trout and fried taters. It provided the necessary refuge from an aroma that falls somewhere toward the riper end of a nasal spectrum inhabited by unwashed athletic socks, stump water, skunk cabbage, or a midsummer garbage dump. One is almost tempted to wonder if that explains why ramp festivals have long enjoyed such popularity—everyone in attendance consumes the featured vegetable in sheer self-preservation.

For all my numerous personal adventures with ramps, my favorite tale connected with the wild vegetable comes from a stunt perpetrated decades ago by the editor of the Richmond, Virginia, *Times-Dispatch*. He had his printers prepare a special batch of ink that included the juice from raw ramps and use it on a run of newspapers to be mailed through the United States Postal Service. Postal authorities may have persevered with their motto, "Neither snow nor rain nor heat nor gloom of night stays these couriers from the swift completion of their appointed rounds," but they were not at all amused with this situation. Indeed, eau de ramp stopped the distribution of mail in its tracks.

Cooked ramps lose their lingering aftereffects (along with some of the taste), and when scrambled with eggs or included in a batch of hash-browned potatoes they provide first-rate breakfast fare. But for the pure of heart and brave of palate, when it comes to consumption of ramps, the raw route is the only road to travel. Just be advised that if you opt for this exercise in culinary adventure and wish to retain friends or keep your marriage intact, the slender, onionlike bulbs are best consumed with kindred spirits or somewhere back of beyond where you won't return to civilization and the company of others for at least seventy-two hours.

Kilt Ramps Salad

**Freshly gathered ramps, cleaned, with the roots at the
base cut away along with most of the green top**

**Branch lettuce (other spring greens, including dandelions
and watercress, can be included or substituted)**

Hot bacon grease or that from frying streaked meat

Mix coarsely chopped ramps and torn greens and then drizzle hot grease over the top to wilt the vegetables (they are thereby killed, that is, "kilt"). If desired, crumble bits of the bacon or streaked meat atop the dressed salad. Eat immediately.

— MUSHROOM MAGIC —

Many types of edible mushrooms are found in the Smokies, but unless you are an expert mycologist, stick to easily identifiable varieties such as the morels of spring and hen-of-the-woods of fall. For those with sufficient expertise in mushroom identification though, the damp woodlands of the Smokies are a rich larder.

Sautéed Morels

Morels are a great spring delicacy, and they are the most easily identifiable of all the many edible mushrooms. They go by a number of names, including dry-land trout, hickory chicken, and the irresistible merkles (miracles). Morels are indeed something of a gustatory miracle, and there are a number of fail-safe methods of preparing them. In each case, soak the mushrooms in salt water and then clean thoroughly. It is best to slice them in half lengthwise before doing this, because quite frequently insects find the hollow interior of the stem a welcome abode. After cleaning, gently dab dry with a clean cloth or paper towels. Introduce the mushroom pieces to simmering butter in a pan, sautéing until they begin to brown. I find it difficult to resist eating them right from the pan, but you certainly want to serve them immediately while piping hot.

Egg-Battered Morels

Another approach is to beat up a couple of eggs and dredge each mushroom piece in the egg mix before placing in the hot butter to cook.

Breaded Morels

Finally, crumble up saltine crackers or bread, use the same egg dip, but follow with a coating of crushed saltines and then cook. Whatever your choice, it's food for the gods.

Morel Soup

1 pound of fresh morels, cleaned and sliced

1 to 2 tablespoons lemon juice

1 large sweet onion, chopped

3 tablespoons butter (do not substitute margarine)

2 tablespoons all-purpose flour

4 cups whole milk

3 teaspoons chicken bouillon granules

½ teaspoon salt

⅛ teaspoon black pepper

Clean mushrooms and sprinkle with the lemon juice. Sauté in a saucepan with onion and butter until the onion is translucent and tender. Sprinkle with flour and stir thoroughly. Gradually add milk, bouillon, salt, and pepper. Bring to a rolling boil, stirring vigorously as you do so, and continue for 2 minutes. Reduce heat and simmer 10 to 15 minutes. If you like the taste of thyme, add ½ teaspoon to the recipe, but keep in mind that morels have a delicate flavor.

Buttered Spring Greens

4 cups any type of wild spring greens
(lamb's quarters, creasy greens, etc.)

2 tablespoons butter or margarine

Salt and black pepper

Hard-boiled egg, bacon bits, green onions,
and/or vinegar for seasoning

Sauté the greens in melted butter in a skillet until tender. Add salt and pepper to taste, top with egg, bacon, green onions, and/or vinegar, and serve immediately.

Watercress Salad with Parmesan Mustard Dressing

6 to 8 cups fresh watercress

½ cup good quality mayonnaise

¼ cup milk

¼ cup freshly grated Parmesan cheese

2 tablespoons Dijonnaise cream mustard blend

2 tablespoons fresh lemon juice

¼ teaspoon freshly ground pepper

Wash the watercress and trim away largest stems. Whisk together the remaining ingredients in a small bowl. Toss the greens with the resulting dressing. Mountain folks in yesteryear would not have had access to Parmesan cheese and Dijon mustard, but these two ingredients add zest and are a grand complement to the slightly peppery taste of watercress.

CHAPTER 11

———

WILD FRUITS

While wild berries historically loomed far larger in mountain diet than wild fruits, practical, self-sufficient residents of the Smokies were much too sensible to overlook items from nature that were there for the taking. That was especially true when it came to wild bounty in the form of fruit. Persimmons likely merit pride of place, thanks in part to their widespread abundance and also just how sweet they are when fully ripe. The phrase sometimes associated with them, "nature's candy," is an apt and applicable one. Then there are pawpaws, wild plums, and the various types of wild grapes, all of which are not only edible but delicious if properly prepared. Add maypops (passionflower fruit, also sometimes known as wild apricots), crab apples for jelly, ground cherries (not exactly wild but a volunteer fruit that often popped in patches of corn), and mulberries (not a berry despite the name), and you had quite a bit of variety just waiting to be gathered.

Persimmons have long been an integral part of mountain folklore and folkways. Widespread throughout the southern Appalachians and beyond, the persimmon is an interesting, unusual tree. Like the American holly, persimmons have distinctive sexual identities, and only "she"

The James Hannah place on Little Cataloochee Creek with an apple
tree in the foreground and a cornfield beyond. Both apples and
corn were important foodstuffs throughout the Smokies.
Courtesy of the National Park Service.

persimmons bear fruit. Old-timers often checked persimmon seeds, much like they observed the location of hornet nests, thickness of corn shucks, or the coloration and stripes of wooly worms, as a means of predicting winter weather. When a seed is cut open it contains a kernel-like image in its middle. A spoon shape meant lots of wet, heavy snow; a knife shape indicated biting, icy winds and bitter weather; while a fork shape signified sparse snow and a mild winter.

From a more practical standpoint, the heavy, dense wood of the slow-growing persimmon was sometimes used to fashion wedges for splitting firewood, and as late as the 1980s wooden golf clubs featured heads made of persimmon. A craftsman with sufficient patience could carve a well-seasoned chunk of persimmon into a highly effective turkey call in the form of either a box call or suction yelper. Persimmons were also of interest to hunters in another regard, because all sorts of wild animals—deer, bears, coons, foxes, and possums—consumed the fruits once they fell to the ground in late fall.

The fruit likewise figured prominently in mountain diet. To be sure, many a city slicker's first introduction to the persimmon at the hands of country cousins was anything but a treat, for until fully ripe, the lovely orange globes are incredibly astringent. Unknowing folks would be encouraged to take a bite only to then spend the next five minutes trying to rid themselves of the taste. Biting into one produces an immediate, unwelcome understanding of the phrase "pucker power."

Once persimmons ripened though, a magical transformation occurred. The soft fruit provided a sweet, sticky treat with overtones of honey. Delicious eaten raw, persimmons could also be dried and preserved as fruit leather, used to make a meadlike beer, or best of all, to form the key ingredient of breads and puddings. In my mind's eye, I still envision my paternal grandfather pushing back from the table after a hearty dish of Grandma Minnie's persimmon pudding and enthusiastically offering judgment: "My, but that was fine!"

While the vast majority of my initial exposure to various delicacies from the Smokies came thanks to either Momma or Grandma, that was not the case with persimmons. I don't recall Momma ever using the fruit, and while Grandma did so when they ripened in midfall, it wasn't one of the mainstays of her cooking endeavors. In fact, my initial exposure to the pleasures of persimmons, both raw and cooked, came through Daddy. Anytime we were out hunting and came across a tree with the ground underneath littered with fallen, wrinkled, and soft to the point of being mushy fruit, we would eat a few of the burnished globes, spitting out the largish seeds and savoring the succulent pulp. It was also through the auspices of Daddy that I first experienced the wonders cooked persimmons could bring to a dessert.

Over the entire course of that portion of Daddy's working career that my memory embraces, he belonged to one of two local civic organizations—first the Lions Club and later the Rotary Club. I have no idea why he changed groups, or possibly the Lions Club was defunct for a time. Certainly both had a sterling history of service in the local community and I'm not sure which of the two clubs was involved with this particular memory. Each year the club to which Dad belonged when I was a small lad had a sort of special family meeting in December as a part of the general joyfulness and spirit of the season. Spouses and children were invited and enjoyed a meal with the club members. There were also little gift bags for younger children as well as a collection of food and presents to be shared later with those who were impoverished, shut-ins, and the like as a part of the club's community outreach.

My main recollection, however, does not involve the gift bags, carol singing, appearance of Santa Claus, or spirit of togetherness connected with the event. Instead, it is the meal, or more specifically the dessert portion of the feast, that lingers lovingly in the vaults of my memory. The organization met at the Calhoun Hotel, as it was then known (the building still exists and houses the Historic Calhoun House Hotel, a quaint bed-and-breakfast operation), and the establishment employed some local Black cooks who were, any way you look at the matter, flat-out culinary geniuses. I don't remember all their names, but a woman named Stella Jackson was front and center among those wonderful old-time cooks, and she was the progenitor of the persimmon pudding served for dessert.

That evening's menu items included things like fried chicken, biscuits so big and fluffy they could have been gigantic snowflakes colored golden brown, milk gravy, green beans cooked with plenty of streaked meat, and marvelous mashed potatoes. But the meal's true pièce de résistance, the figurative cherry atop the sundae or lace on the bride's pajamas, was persimmon pudding. Richer than the most scrumptious of bread puddings and topped with real whipped cream, it was something to satisfy those with even the most demanding or discriminating sweet tooth.

This particular menu item was strictly a once a year deal, and it garnered sufficient attention for Daddy to have mentioned it in advance. "If we are really lucky," he said, "Stella will have made persimmon pudding for dessert." The background work involved for a gathering of this size—perhaps seventy-five or possibly even a hundred people—had to be demanding and detailed. This was long before the advent of Asian persimmons, which are seedless and can weigh as much as a half pound each. Instead, Stella or someone helping her gathered wild American persimmons, lots of them, and that was only the start. They had to be cleaned, "looked" (checked for bad spots), run through a colander to separate the pulp from an abundance of seeds, and readied for use before the first step of pudding making could commence. The thought of baking enough pudding to serve a gathering of the size involved is mind boggling. Yet Stella somehow managed it, and her only real reward was the deep and delighted appreciation of those who consumed this most delectable of desserts.

I have no real idea of exactly how Stella made her pudding, but I feel pretty confident in suggesting that there wasn't a lot of precise measurement or a printed list of ingredients involved. Like most highly skilled old-time cooks her measurements were in pinches, dollops, dashes, smidgens, "an ample portion," and the like.

About all I can do is offer a modern version of my own creation with specific measurements and a comment to the effect that if you've never tried a persimmon pudding you have a treat in the offing. If you have access to a plentitude of persimmons (and they grow widely in the Smokies), maybe prior to next Thanksgiving or Yuletide you can make plans for a pudding. For my part, every time I work with persimmons in the kitchen, I not only resurrect memories of a grand eating experience from youth. I am also reminded of an aspect of the Smokies scene relatively few were privileged to know in yesteryear: exposure to some skilled African American cooks I knew growing up in Bryson City. The Black presence in the high country has always been a sparse one, but by virtue of living in close proximity to the hundred or so African Americans resident in Swain County in the 1950s, I got to know several outstanding cooks. Stella Jackson was among them; as were Lillie Inabinett, longtime maid of our next-door neighbors; wonderful old Aunt Mag Williams, who lived just down the road; and later in my life, Beulah Sudderth, the doyenne of matchless black walnut cakes.

Here's what I'm confident is a close companion of Stella's pudding. It results in a moment of sweet, succulent magic.

Persimmon Pudding

2 cups persimmon pulp

½ teaspoon baking soda

1 cup sugar

2 eggs, beaten

2 cups all-purpose flour

2 teaspoons baking powder

½ teaspoon ground cinnamon

½ teaspoon vanilla extract

Pinch of salt

2½ cups milk

4 tablespoons (½ stick) butter, melted

Preheat oven to 325°F, and butter a 9-by-13-inch baking pan (or use a nonstick pan). In a mixing bowl, combine the persimmon pulp, baking soda, sugar, and eggs. Mix well. Then add flour, baking powder, cinnamon, vanilla, salt, milk, and melted butter. Mix thoroughly with a whisk. Pour into the baking pan and bake for 50 to 60 minutes. The pudding will fall a bit when it is removed from the oven and allowed to cool.

The pudding should cool for at least a half hour before serving. Small servings are in order because this is an exceptionally rich dessert.

Once my first taste of persimmon pudding had "flung a craving on me," as comedian Jerry Clower used to put it, I turned to Grandma Minnie for repeat performances. I eagerly gathered fruit, rinsed it off, and turned it over to her capable hands. She would mash the persimmons in a colander, using her hands in order to extract every possible bit of pulp, and work on this until she had an ample amount of persimmon flesh for her pudding. Then Grandpa Joe and I, along with anyone else who happened to have the great good fortune to sit down at their table on such occasions, would enjoy the treat that brought forth his previously mentioned words.

Intervening decades have led me to a couple of delightful discoveries that further enhance the culinary appeal of this traditional mountain foodstuff. One is growing Asian persimmons. They taste every bit as good, are far larger than their wild cousins, have no seeds, and sometimes can be found seasonally in grocery stores. They also do quite well in the home orchard and begin bearing after only a few years.

The second breakthrough involves preparation of a dessert I cherish even more than persimmon pudding. This is a rich, sweet persimmon "bread" I first encountered in a recipe developed by famed chef James Beard. My version varies somewhat, but I think anyone who tries it will discover why, as a wizened Swain County octogenarian once said to me, "I'm mighty partial to persimmons." Try this scrumptious offering at Thanksgiving or Christmas. I think you'll see why he was "mighty partial."

Smoky Mountain Persimmon Bread

3½ cups all-purpose flour

1 teaspoon salt

Pinch (maybe ½ teaspoon) of ground nutmeg
or ground allspice

2 teaspoons baking soda

2 cups brown sugar

½ pound (2 sticks) butter, melted and allowed
to cool to room temperature

4 large eggs, lightly whisked

⅔ cup bourbon (a cheap brand is fine)

2 brimming cups persimmon pulp (fruits should be
squishy ripe, and incidentally, pulp freezes well)

1 cup black walnuts (you can substitute 2 cups of lightly
toasted and chopped pecans or English walnuts,
although black walnuts are more flavorful)

2 cups dried fruit, such as apricots, raisins,
yellow raisins, or dates

Preheat oven to 350°F. Butter a pair of loaf pans or use nonstick pans. Sift flour, salt, spice, baking soda, and sugar into a large plastic mixing bowl. Whisk in the butter, eggs, bourbon, and persimmon pulp until thoroughly mixed. Add and whisk in nuts and dried fruit. Place batter in pans and

slide into oven. Check periodically as bread begins to brown by insert-
ing a toothpick. When the toothpick comes out clean the bread is ready.
Cooking time varies depending on configuration of pans you use.

NOTE: Once cooled, wrap to keep moist. The bread will keep several
days (though it is likely be eaten much sooner) and it freezes well. It is rich
and somewhat reminiscent of a dark fruit cake.

— A FONDNESS FOR FOX GRAPES —

One of my many treasured food memories connected with autumn
involves fox grapes. Thanks to family interest in them—both my Grandma
Minnie and Aunt Emma were passing fond of fox grape jelly and made
runs every autumn if they could get the essential ingredient—during the
summer months from early boyhood on I kept a keen eye out for vines. As
anyone familiar with the plant likely realizes, they seem to have a distinct
preference for the banks of branches and streams. That is particularly true
in situations where there isn't dense shade from mature trees.

As a youngster I had two prime sources of fox grapes fairly close to
home—one along a little branch not a mile away that ran through terrain
where I rabbit hunted regularly and a second on the east bank of Deep
Creek. The mother lode of fox grapes, however, was on Burnett family
property near the juncture of Marr Creek and Brush Creek. The vines
there seemed to be heavily laden year after year.

Recently when some twist of my mind brought fox grapes into my
thoughts and in turn evoked a warm flow of memories, I decided to do
a bit of digging into the subject. To my surprise, although I should have
expected it since mountain folks have so many terms and names peculiar to
the region, I discovered that apparently in other regions of the country what
I have always known as possum grapes or frost grapes are called fox grapes.

In my lexicon though, fox grapes are large ones that usually hang alone
or in groups of just two or three instead of being in a tight bunch. By
way of contrast, possum grapes are tiny, come in clusters with dozens or
scores of grapes, and even after several frosts have little if any sweetness.
Fox grapes, on the other hand, can be quite sweet when fully ripened and
are delicious to eat raw. They do have enough acidity, however, to remind
your tongue of that fact should you overindulge. Whether that is pectin
or some other wonder of the wild bounty world, it makes fox grapes ideal
for jelly—you never have to worry about the end product setting well.

I suspect, and again I'm relying on personal experience and the observations of old-timers, as opposed to any pretense of solid scientific knowledge, that what I've always known as fox grapes are simply a mountain variety or offshoot of what folks over much of the Southeast call wild muscadines. Certainly they share the same appearance, taste, preference for stream edges, and time of ripening.

From a practical standpoint, these blurred lines of just what to call the grapes mountain folks designate as fox grapes really don't matter all that much. What is important is the delicious, slightly musky taste they have when made into jelly and the sweet-tart taste treat they provide when dead ripe. Incidentally, fully ripe fox grapes will fall from the vine with a bit of shaking. I remember as a kid gathering all that could be reached from the ground, then giving the vines, which sometimes reached high up into trees, a good, solid tug. We would then scramble around to gather up the grapes that rained down.

A good vine or cluster of vines, and where there's one growing there are usually several, might yield a peck or even a half bushel of grapes. That was enough for a good run of jelly, and the "gatherer" always got a share of the scrumptious end results. Indeed, long after I was grown and gone from home, not to mention far removed from the simple pleasures of gathering nature's wild bounty in forms such as fox grapes, my aunt Emma remembered just how much her greedy-gut nephew enjoyed fox grape jelly.

Invariably when I returned to Bryson City for a visit with my family, it would involve spending some time with my aunt and her family. Sometimes it would be at Thanksgiving or Christmas, and on such occasions, I could count on a jar of Aunt Emma's fox grape jelly being available to adorn hot, buttered biscuits. On other occasions there wouldn't be a holiday involved, but more often than not, as we left her home, she'd say: "Now don't you get away until Frank [her husband] has fetched you a jar of my fox grape jelly from the basement." Those words were music to my ears because I knew that for several breakfasts to come I would feast on something finer than any jar of marmalade or jam carrying a seal saying its producer was purveyor to English royalty.

Fox Grape Jelly

In my family at least, and study of my quite extensive collection of regional cookbooks suggests this is the case generally throughout the South, there was a simple, straightforward method for making fox grape jelly. One of its advantages was that there's enough natural pectin in fox grapes to make the jelly set nicely without using anything beyond fruit and sugar.

Start by squeezing the pulp from the skins and placing in separate bowls. Remove the seeds from the pulp. This is easily done with a plastic sieve with small holes. Discard the seeds. Cook the skins until they are tender and then combine with the pulp/juice mix that you have once the seeds have been removed. For each cup of the recombined mixture add three-quarters cup of sugar or to taste (some folks like fox grape jelly with a bit of tartness or bite to it). Bring the mixture to a slow boil for ten to twenty minutes, stirring frequently, until it becomes noticeably thick. At this point pour into half pint or pint jars and allow to cool. Seal them with melted paraffin or two-piece lids. A cup of fruit with the seeds removed will make about a half pint of jelly.

Scuppernong Pie

3 or 4 cups scuppernongs or muscadines (scuppernongs are green or golden in color while muscadines are dark red or purple, although colloquially the terms are often used interchangeably)

1 cup sugar (or slightly more if needed)

2 tablespoons cornstarch

3 tablespoons butter

Ground cinnamon or apple pie spice

Pastry for a 2-crust pie

Preheat oven to 300°F. Wash grapes. Use two medium-sized enamel saucepans, squeezing pulp into one and placing the hulls in the other. Cover hulls with water, cook until tender, and then drain. Cook pulp until soft enough to run easily through a sieve to remove seeds. Add to hulls. Mix sugar and cornstarch. Add scuppernong mixture and dot with butter. Sprinkle with spice. Pour into pastry-lined pie pan, cover with strips of pastry, and bake until golden brown.

Grape Hull Pie

Gently squeeze pulp from ripe scuppernongs or muscadines and set aside insides to make jelly another time. You will need a pint of hulls. Add three-quarters of a cup of sugar to hulls and stir until well combined. Cook over gentle heat until tenderized, adding a half teaspoon of almond extract and half a stick of butter while cooking. Once tenderized, add cornstarch to thicken, and as mixture begins to cool, pour into a pre-cooked pie crust. Bake at 350°F until crust is golden brown.

— WILD APRICOTS —

My personal experience with wild apricots, which is what both Grandpa Joe and Daddy called the fruit of the maypop, is limited. In late summer and into the fall, anytime I came across the vine, which was common in open areas and readily noticeable when the oval fruits ripened and turned yellow, I would pick a few to eat on the spot. The edible portion was the juicy flesh around the seeds somewhat reminiscent of the pomegranate. It has a tangy, sweet-sour taste that is quite refreshing.

American Indians made a drink from the fruit, and I'm sure that an infusion of juice from the tiny orbs of translucent fluid surrounding each seed, perhaps mixed with lemonade or just water and a bit of sugar or honey, would produce a delightful beverage. It's just something I've never tried, although I've eaten the flesh and seen others do it times without number.

— PAWPAWS —

Pawpaws are quite common in the Smokies, although comparatively few folks know about them (or at least know enough to realize what a delicacy they can be). The father of our country knew though. A pawpaw pudding was one of George Washington's favorite desserts, and presumably the wild fruit grew well around Mount Vernon. In the Smokies you'll most frequently find pawpaws in low, slightly damp areas of fairly rich soil. Once you become familiar with the plants, they absolutely jump out at you in the woods. Pawpaws tend to grow in sizeable patches, and while not exactly what would be styled a tree, can grow as high as thirty or forty feet.

They are readily discernible, depending on the season, because of a number of characteristics. In the spring, the blooms, which are a deep maroon and quite attractive when viewed up close, appear before the leaves have done anything more than begin to swell and show a hint of green. Once spring has fully arrived, the impressive size of the leaves makes the plant distinctive, as does the smooth, almost silvery bark of the shrubs. The fruit, which looks somewhat like a stubby miniature banana in shape, is the largest of any fruit tree indigenous to North America. The fruits, usually in clusters, are green through the summer but turn yellow, with brown spots or almost completely brown, as they ripen in late September and early October. Sometimes they will be heavy enough to bend limbs in a noticeable fashion, and you've got to be on your toes when pawpaws come in season.

That call for alacrity relates to the fact that every critter in the woods seems to like the fruit. It has a flesh with custardlike consistency sprinkled with black seeds. Quite aromatic, the taste is variously described as having hints of pineapple, banana, or papaya. In truth, pawpaws have their own special flavor and texture, and if you want to enjoy them raw, in custard, baked, or in a pudding, vigilance should be your byword. Deer, foxes, coyotes, possums, and coons all eat pawpaws with relish.

Pawpaw Pudding

1 cup pawpaw pulp, seeds removed

1¼ cups sugar

1 teaspoon baking powder

¼ pound (1 stick) butter, melted (the real thing)

1 teaspoon ground ginger (optional)

3 eggs

½ teaspoon salt

1 teaspoon baking soda

2½ teaspoons ground cinnamon

½ teaspoon ground nutmeg

Strain the pawpaw pulp using a plastic sieve. Mix the pulp with all the other ingredients and bake in a well-greased pan for approximately an hour at 350°F (when done it will begin to pull away from the sides of the pan). Cool and cut into squares.

Pawpaw Bread

This sweet dish is suitable either as a breakfast treat, perhaps buttered or served with cream cheese, or by itself.

2½ cups all-purpose flour

1 teaspoon baking powder

2 teaspoons baking soda

¼ teaspoon salt

1¾ cups sugar

½ pound (2 sticks) butter, softened

4 eggs

½ teaspoon vanilla

3 cups pawpaw pulp, seeds removed

Preheat oven to 350°F and grease two loaf pans with a small pat of butter. Whisk together flour, baking powder, baking soda, and salt, then set aside. Cream sugar and butter until light and fluffy. Add eggs one at a time and beat well after each addition. Add the vanilla and pawpaw pulp, then beat until fully combined. Add the flour mixture and blend only until the flour is incorporated. Do not overmix. Pour the batter into the prepared pans and place in oven. Bake for 45 to 60 minutes, or until brown and starting to leave the sides of the pans and checks done when a thick knife blade is inserted. Allow to cool on a rack for 15 minutes before removing from the pans.

Members of the Shelton family of the Tremont
area stand in front of a giant chestnut tree.
Courtesy of the National Park Service.

CHAPTER 12

NUTS

To a considerable degree, early settlers in the Smokies relied on their own gumption to survive. Pieces of paradise such as Cataloochee, Cades Cove, or the low-lying lands along the Tuckaseigee and the Little Tennessee Rivers offered fertile soil with the potential for producing bountiful crops. However, no enterprising, hardworking mountain family was satisfied to rely exclusively on the crops they could grow or the livestock they could raise. Living *off* the land, as American Indians had done for untold generations before them, these hardy individuals became closely attuned *to* the land. To be sure, their linkage with the earth involved subsistence crop farming along with keeping some chickens, hogs, and cows for milk, eggs, and meat.

Yet nature's bounty formed an integral and important part of the process of making a livelihood and a life. Mountain folks hunted, fished, and trapped, but what they could take from the fast-flowing, clear streams and remote woodland fastnesses for meat on the table was supplemented by harvests from the expansive, fertile garden that lay all around them—wild vegetables, berries, fruits, and nuts.

The latter food from nature figured prominently in life during autumn and in diet over much of the year. Fall's gradually shortening days were particularly busy ones. It was harvesttime, with corn to be put in cribs and fodder in shocks, pumpkins to be gathered, apples and pears to be picked and prepared or stored, molasses to be made, hogs to be fattened and then butchered, vegetables to be placed in root cellars, the last green beans to be dried for "leather britches," buckwheat and rye to be cut and winnowed, and field legumes such as October beans to be winnowed and stored. Many farmers, especially the most industrious of them, also tilled the land after harvests had been completed.

On top of all this crammed rush of getting in crops, the hunter's moon of October beckoned sportsmen afield with almost irresistible allure. Cresting the eastern horizon at the time light normally gave way to night, it shone with a brightness sufficient for trees to cast shadows, and the full moon's burnished gold seemed so close you could almost touch it. Along with shadows that lovely orb also cast a spell. In that season no mountain man worth his sporting salt could avoid the temptation of an outing to put squirrel and gravy, a haunch of venison, or maybe a bear roast dripping with fat on the table.

Those game animals knew that lean, mean times of winter were fast approaching, and as a result it was a busy time in the woodlands as well. All too soon bluebird skies and pleasant temperatures of Indian summer would give way to biting winds and bitter frosts. Instinctively animals ate and stored food, and topping the list not only for squirrels and bears but for deer, turkeys, and other game animals were nuts. Humans used them as well and did so with gusto, realizing that in addition to being nutritious they brought welcome taste and variety to their diet.

One of the hallmarks of autumn in the Smokies was what most knew simply as "nutting." An exercise combining genuine pleasure with full use of nature's bounty, expeditions to gather nuts formed a grand example of the important art of making do. While the necessity that once underlay outings to gather nuts increasingly belonged to a vanishing way of life, and that was particularly true once the lordly American chestnut was no more, the practice of nutting nonetheless loomed large in my boyhood a full generation after blight took the chestnuts.

Nutting, especially as an "all hands helping" family outing, had of course originated in times when the American chestnut was incredibly plentiful. Whole families gathered bushels of the predictable, prolific mast. They used the nuts to fatten hogs, earn a bit of welcome cash money through sales (vendors of roasted chestnut were once common on city street corners in the winter), and of course for their own consumption. Before them, American Indians had followed the same practice.

The American chestnut has been gone from the Smokies for a full three generations (the main die-off came around 1930), but fortunately such is not the case with other nuts. Many remain readily available, with the best example being the black walnut, a nut that figured prominently as a food-stuff in my youth. Beginning with the onset of squirrel season in October, Daddy and I would look for trees or for stained white belly fur on bushytails we killed (a telltale sign they were feeding on walnuts). That information was duly filed away with plans for a family outing in the near future.

Widespread in the Smokies and readily identifiable, the black walnut is common along fencerows, at locations where homes once stood, and on the edges of fields in river bottoms. We collected at least a couple bushels of them every year. The task of gathering walnuts then preparing them for cracking, while not physically demanding, consumed considerable time. Hulls had to be removed, but this was not done until several weeks after nuts had been gathered.

Drying hulls for easy removal involved patience more than anything else, but everyone knew that failure to wait meant stained hands and clothing. After all, dyes from walnut hulls and those of the kindred but-ternut were once widely used for coloring homespun clothing. Usually the just-gathered nuts were spread out on floor space in a barn or in some open area where they could dry and cure in the warm sun of fast fleeting fall. Once dry, the hulls could be mashed off by foot one nut at a time or placed in a tow sack hung from a handy tree limb that could be whacked repeatedly using a stout section of hickory as a flail.

Once the hulls had been removed, the time to crack walnuts and pick out meats was at hand. My grandfather used to muse: "The man who fig-ures out a device to crack black walnuts cleanly, leaving big pieces of nut meats, should make a fortune." We still await such an invention, although a good friend up in the mountains who is a machinist with an inventive knack, Ken Roper, has made a quantum leap in the right direction. His cracker uses a flywheel off a car and an attached handle to apply leverage, with the device being fixed to a wooden base for stability. It's an ingenious contraption, but Ken only made a few of them, saying he was having to machine almost all the parts and that few folks wanted to pay the price he had to ask. It doesn't produce perfect halves, but it sure beats the dick-ens out of smashing them to smithereens with a hammer or compressing them to a breaking point in a vise. I'm just happy I got one. Maybe I laid my paws on what will become a genuine collectible.

The method Daddy employed for cracking involved a vise and a hatchet. He placed nuts atop his shop vise, always being sure to turn them at a certain angle, and then cracked them one by one using the back of a hatchet. He would crack a peck or maybe even a half bushel of them at a time. Then came the slow, tedious work of getting the meats out. This effort, known as "nut picking," was almost always a group one. Sometimes it involved relatives but the mainstays were Mom and Dad, my sister, Annette, and me. When it was just immediate family, we often listened to radio programs like *Gunsmoke* or *Amos 'n' Andy*. However, if more relatives were present, laughter, telling of tales, and remembrances of nutting in their childhood punctuated the congenial process.

The considerable effort involved in the end result of obtaining a few quarts of walnut meats was well worth it. Merely thinking about the endeavor conjures up visions of a batch of Momma's oatmeal cookies, still warm from the oven and studded with walnuts and raisins. Similarly, a properly made walnut cake with walnut icing was a delicacy sure to bring tears of pure joy to a country boy's eyes, while on a hot summer's day home-churned walnut ice cream reached the status of near-frozen nectar from the gods.

Grandpa Joe loved everything connected with walnuts, as was, come to think of it, pretty much true of anything edible that grew, swam, ran, or in any way existed in the limited geographical world with which he was intimately familiar. Had he been taken out of the Smokies, he likely would have been a lost and lonesome soul, but on his home heath it was a markedly different story. He seemingly had some kind of thought, folk wisdom, or insight to share with me no matter what the plant or animal.

I loved his description of walnuts. A number of young trees lined the pathway leading from his house to the chicken pen and then on to the hog lot. We walked that path times without number, but seldom did we make the familiar trek without Grandpa pausing before one of the walnut saplings, perhaps six inches in diameter at the time, for a bit of a nature lesson. "Son," he would say, "look at those trees. I'll be gone about the time they start bearing nuts, and it will be at least sixty years before they've grown enough to be cut for timber. This here's good river bottom land, real rich soil, and it will grow stuff about as good as anywhere in these old mountains." Based on the quality and quantity of the produce his garden produced, that was accurate information. "But walnuts demand patience.

They ain't going to be rushed and they ain't going to grow fast. I reckon you could call them a three-generation tree." By that he meant that it took slow-growing black walnuts a full three generations to reach a size where they provided one or possibly two fine saw logs.

He would then woolgather for a moment on the importance of forbearance. I always sensed that underlying the lesson on walnuts was a subliminal message directed at an often impatient and always boisterous boy. "If you wait," Grandpa noted, "walnuts will eventually reward you. They make beautiful wood for furniture, and you know those two guns I've got stored away up at the house, well, their stocks and fore ends are made of fine-grained walnut."

Grandpa knew woods and their uses. If today he could somehow walk that garden path from long ago, he'd light up with that soft grin that was about as close as he ever came to a real smile. The old house has gone through multiple owners, but some of the black walnut trees Grandpa admired (and likely planted, although I don't know that to be a fact) have now reached the three-generation status he so often mentioned. They are tall, straight, handsome trees, precisely the kind that bring significant sums of money from folks anxious to have select wood from mature black walnuts.

As a family we dabbled with other types of nuts as well, and our yard sported a Chinese chestnut tree, which grew so rapidly that it progressed, in the course of only a couple of decades, from a nut-bearing source of considerable pride to a nuisance that eventually had to be cut down. Kudzulike, it was threatening to engulf both the driveway and street serving our house.

Hickory nuts, which come in a number of varieties, some just about as tasty as walnuts, were incredibly abundant. It's no wonder American Indians relied heavily on them, and stands of hickories along with nutting stones are frequently found near Indian mounds. Numerous varieties of hickory are plentiful in the Smokies, and come autumn you can't miss the vivid golden leaves of these sentinels of fall. If anything, however, they are more difficult to crack and pick meats from than black walnuts, and the amount of food you get for your labor will soon have you concluding they are the nutting world's equivalent of truffles.

Hazelnuts, a hillbilly cousin of the filbert, grew widely along creeks, rivers, and branches during my boyhood, and they were among the most predictable of the nut crops in terms of bearing a solid harvest year after year. The bushes—ranging up to fifteen feet or so in height—were simple enough to deal with come harvesttime. The only problem, and it was a significant one, involved squirrels. Once bushytails started cutting on them, they would work nonstop until the entire crop was gone. Our way of besting the treetop tricksters, which normally began cutting on hazelnuts in mid-September, well before the nuts dropped from their husks, was to gather them in the husks and let them dry for a couple of weeks. At that juncture nuts fell easily from the husks and were ready to crack. One distinct advantage of the hazelnut was that its meat came out whole in a single piece.

Three other mountain nuts deserve at least passing mention. Two of them, chinquapins and butternuts, have become increasingly difficult to locate, while a third, beechnuts, can be quite unpredictable when it comes to production. Chinquapins, which were fairly common during my youth, are seldom encountered today. A bushlike relative of the chestnut, they were to some degree affected by the blight that destroyed the American chestnut. Most often they were found on open, south-facing hillsides and particularly in what mountain folks called "fire scalds" (places where a wildfire, sometimes set by arsonists and frequently found in portions of the park, had burned hot enough to kill everything). For some reason chinquapins were a prominent succession plant in such areas, and they were quite plentiful thanks to a few local ne'er-do-wells setting fires out of pure meanness or in hope of being hired by the park or United States Forest Service to help fight the fires.

Those fires occur with less frequency today, but anyone who covers much off-trail ground in the Smokies will still on occasion find bushes bearing the round, deep-brown nuts that look like a miniature chestnut and are enclosed by the same type of protective burr. Growing up I often heard someone say, "she's got chinquapin eyes," and by that they meant luminous, shiny eyes resembling pools of molten dark chocolate. Interestingly, I've never heard the term applied to the eyes of a boy or man.

Butternuts have a mild taste slightly reminiscent of home-churned butter, and perhaps that is where they got their name. Another possibility is that the nut hulls were once used to dye cloth, with the finished product having a buttery hue. The butternut attire associated with soldiers in the Confederate Army gives an indication of how widespread its use for dying purposes was a century and a half ago. An alternative name, one I heard frequently years ago but that seems to have passed out of favor in modern parlance, was white walnuts. They were also sometimes known as long walnuts.

Butternut trees and their foliage indeed look somewhat like a walnut, although the nuts are elongated rather than oval in shape. The wood of the tree was so prized, and such remains the case, that it was unusual to find a grown, heavily bearing specimen. Today the tree is in trouble after a fashion somewhat reminiscent of the chestnut's plight. A disease known as butternut canker showed up half a century or so ago, and by the arrival of the twenty-first century, biologists estimated that it affected as many as three-quarters of all butternut trees. Even those that were not dead were, in most cases, so afflicted they had stopped producing mast.

Then there's the lordly beechnut with its slick, silvery bark so admired by the lovelorn anxious to carve their name, along with that of their sweetheart, into the tree's parchmentlike outer layer of bark. Perhaps the best indication of the appeal of beechnuts from the standpoint of edibility comes from the way they attract wildlife. Squirrels, chipmunks, deer, bears, grouse, wild hogs, and turkeys, all will flock to them, ignoring any and all other types of food, whenever they are available.

The little three-sided nuts develop inside burrs, but for some reason roughly three seasons out of every four the nut hulls are either hollow or else the mast fails entirely. When they do "make" though, and you can readily tell by checking a nut or two in late summer, beechnuts are well worthy of human attention. For my part, I always check a few giants of the species growing along a little branch on some property I own, and on the relatively rare occasions when they carry a fine nut crop, I know two things—I'm going to enjoy some tasty treats and I'll see plenty of deer from a stand strategically placed nearby.

While they can be used in various types of dishes, beechnuts are probably best when eaten on the spot. Just do it in moderation because the fact that they are arguably the sweetest of all nuts notwithstanding, ingestion of too many raw ones can create gastric distress. Grandpa Joe somehow knew this and he'd warn me whenever I seemed hell-bent on overindulgence. A number of massive beeches lined the riverbank near his home, so in a good year the nuts would be available in great abundance. "Son," he would say, "you're about to have another episode like that one with the green apples a few months back." A couple of those green-apple bellyaches were of sufficient severity for painful recollections to linger, or maybe it was just Grandma's castor oil remedy that made it stick in my memory. Anyway, I'd follow his advice. We'd gather a bunch of nuts, parch them atop the stove, and then enjoy a real treat.

Heat destroyed the toxic saponin glycoside in the nuts, and once we had a good quantity of them roasted, Grandpa and I would get down to some serious gustatory business. Beechnut hulls are tender enough to be removed with one's teeth, and while it takes considerable effort to get at the little tidbits, the work was well worth it.

I now realize that memories of nuts and nutting took Grandpa back to a time he held dear. That explains, at least in part, why he spent so much time talking with me about nuts and gathered them at every opportunity. As often as not when we went squirrel hunting, at day's end there was little if any heft in the game bags of our coats. But the side pockets of our jackets and front pockets of our pants were dramatically different. We almost always stuffed them with whatever mast we came across. When Grandpa said, "There ain't no need to be peckish in the fall woods," he was acknowledging the ready availability and importance of nuts in his mountain world.

Today we can still sample and savor such times and the delicious treats they produced. To me, venturing afield for a few pleasant, productive hours of nutting is a fine approach to perpetuating a worthy example of old-time mountain ways. While doing so, mayhap you can wonder as you wander, with lines from Henry Wadsworth Longfellow as a winsome way of wishing. It's almost as if he had an eerie presentiment of the fate awaiting the noble chestnut tree:

> *I see again, as one in vision sees,*
> *The blossoms and the bees*
> *And hear the children's voices shout and call*
> *And the brown chestnuts fall.*

Black Walnut and Banana Bread

½ cup vegetable oil

1 cup sugar

2 eggs

2 cups very ripe bananas, mashed with a fork

2 cups all-purpose flour

1 teaspoon salt

1 teaspoon baking powder

½ cup finely chopped black walnuts

Preheat oven to 350°F. Mix oil, sugar, eggs, and bananas well. Add flour, salt, baking powder, and walnuts, and mix until thoroughly blended. Place in greased loaf pan and bake for an hour, or in 4 small, greased loaf pans for 40 minutes.

TIPS: Ripe bananas can be frozen, and it is also often possible to pick up overripe ones in grocery stores at greatly reduced rates.

Small loaves make a nice addition to a fruit basket or hostess gift.

Black Walnut Cake with Black Walnut Frosting

½ pound (2 sticks) butter, softened (no substitute)

½ cup solid shortening

3 cups sugar

6 eggs

8 ounces of sour cream (optional)

3 cups all-purpose flour, sifted

1 teaspoon baking powder

1 to 1½ cups chopped black walnuts

1 teaspoon vanilla

1 cup milk or half-and-half

Cream butter and shortening thoroughly; beat well. Gradually add sugar and mix until light and fluffy. Add eggs one at a time and beat well after each addition. For a moister cake, stir in sour cream as well at this point. In a separate bowl sift flour and baking powder and add walnuts. In a measuring cup, add vanilla to milk. Add flour mixture alternately with milk mixture to batter. Blend and mix well—beating well is the secret to a successful cake. Pour into a prepared 10-inch tube pan and place in oven. Turn on oven to 325°F (do not preheat) and bake for 1 hour and 15 minutes or until done. When done, cool 10 minutes and remove from pan.

BLACK WALNUT FROSTING

¼ pound (1 stick) butter, melted

1 box confectioner's sugar

Milk

½ cup black walnuts

Blend melted margarine and confectioner's sugar. Add enough milk to reach correct consistency. Stir in walnuts and frost the cooled cake. Once the frosting has been spread over the cake, dot it with additional black walnut meats.

Black Walnut Vinaigrette Dressing

¼ cup coarsely chopped black walnuts

¼ cup coarsely chopped English walnuts

Salt

¼ cup vegetable oil

2 tablespoons wine vinegar

4 teaspoons freshly squeezed lemon juice

Grated peel of 1 lemon

Freshly ground black pepper

Toast nuts, adding a bit of salt, and cool. Add oil, vinegar, lemon juice, lemon peel, and pepper; pulse to blend. Taste to adjust flavors. Wonderful over a mixed greens salad, sliced tomatoes, or an avocado half.

TIP: If you are especially partial to the rich, nutty flavor of black walnuts, double up on them and leave the English walnuts out.

Black Walnut Ice Cream

6 cups whole milk

1½ cups sugar

¼ cup all-purpose flour

1 tablespoon vanilla

½ teaspoon salt

4 eggs, slightly beaten

½ pint whipping cream

1 to 1½ cups black walnuts, chopped fine

Place milk in double boiler and heat. In a medium bowl, mix sugar, flour, vanilla, and salt. Add enough hot milk to sugar mixture to make a paste. Stir the paste into hot milk. Cook until the mixture thickens slightly, and then gradually add the hot milk mixture from the double boiler to the slightly beaten eggs in a separate pan. Cook about 2 minutes longer. Cool in refrigerator (it is best to cool the custard mixture overnight). After cooling, whip cream slightly and add it to the custard along with walnuts. Pour into ice cream churn and run (or crank) the freezer by manufacturer's instructions or until quite firm.

Nut Spread

¼ pound (1 stick) butter, softened

3 ounces cream cheese, softened

1 cup finely chopped nuts (hickory nuts, walnuts,
pecans, and hazelnuts all work well)

1 tablespoon honey

¼ teaspoon salt

Cream butter and cream cheese together. Add nuts, honey, and salt, adding more seasoning to taste. Stir or pulse just enough to blend well. Serve as a spread for bagels, biscuits, or crackers.

Huckleberry Nut Bread

¾ cup sugar

½ teaspoon salt

4 tablespoons (½ stick) butter or margarine, melted

1 egg

2 cups all-purpose flour

2 teaspoons baking powder

½ teaspoon ground cinnamon

½ cup milk

1 cup huckleberries (fresh or frozen—if the
latter, thaw and drain well)

½ cup chopped nuts

Cinnamon sugar

Preheat oven to 375°F. Cream sugar, salt, and butter. Add egg and beat well. In a separate bowl, sift flour, baking powder, and cinnamon. Add flour mixture and milk, alternating, to batter; blend well. Gently fold huckleberries and nuts into batter. Pour into a 9-by-5-by-3-inch prepared loaf pan. Sprinkle a very light coating of cinnamon sugar on top. Bake for 45 minutes or until golden brown and bread tests done in center with a toothpick. Cool in pan for 10 minutes before serving.

Oatmeal Cookies with Black Walnuts

½ cup sugar

¼ cup packed brown sugar

⅗ pound (2½ sticks) butter, softened

1 egg

1 teaspoon vanilla

3 cups oats, quick cooking or regular

1½ cups all-purpose flour

1¼ teaspoons ground cinnamon

1 teaspoon baking soda

½ teaspoon salt

½ cup raisins

2 cups black walnuts

Preheat oven to 350°F. Cream sugars and butter; add egg and vanilla. Place oats, flour, cinnamon, baking soda, and salt in a separate bowl and mix well. Add raisins and walnuts to dry ingredients. Thoroughly combine creamed mixture and dry ingredients. Drop by tablespoons onto cookie sheet. Bake for 8 to 10 minutes or until golden brown (do not overcook if you want soft, chewy cookies). *Yields about 3 dozen cookies*

George Laymon walks among beehives
situated on a raised wooden platform.
Courtesy of the National Park Service.

CHAPTER 13

BERRIES

Some of my fondest, most enduring childhood memories of growing up in the Smokies center on countless spring, summer, and fall days spent plucking the fruits of the good earth and nature's rewarding labor. Foremost among these were berry picking during the late spring and summer months, although there were also the pleasures aplenty that involved gathering walnuts, hazelnuts, fox grapes, and persimmons in the fall of the year. I spent considerable time picking wild strawberries, raspberries, dewberries, and blueberries, but the biggest portion of my youthful efforts focused on the ever abundant blackberry. Some of these pursuits provided welcome pocket money, brought the joy of seeing a big smile on Mom's face, or gave me the "grown up" feel of knowing I had contributed something to the family table. Without exception they offered an unfolding panoply of taste delights. All in all it was glorious fun and even today I derive a great deal of satisfaction from the simple act of picking.

Happily, blackberries ripen at about the same time as another fairly widespread and plentiful fruit, the juicy, yellow-red wild plum. Old-timers, anticipating the ripe plums of months to come, often made a mental note of the whereabouts of plum thickets. The same was true of an overlooked berry, that of the service tree. Service (mountain folks invariably pronounce the word as *sarvis*) trees are one of the earliest of spring bloomers, and you'll see their splashes of white dotting mountainsides when all else is still winter gray. Yet in my experience about the only service trees that consistently bear berries are those growing along creeks, although I must admit that come berry-ripening time, given my love for trout fishing, that's the place I'd be most likely to notice them. I've never eaten them any other form than straight from the tree, but their mild taste, enhanced a bit by the almond flavor of soft seeds, is most pleasant.

Another berry found in great abundance throughout the mountains, and like dewberries they get comparatively little attention, is the elderberry. Yet if you pay attention in mid- to late summer, especially along damp ditches, seep springs, branches, and creeks, you'll see great clusters of ripening elderberries everywhere. They are easy to gather (just take the whole cluster), but processing for jelly, pies, or wine is a tedious, time-consuming process.

Finally, when it comes to berries, there are wild huckleberries, blueberries, buckberries, and gooseberries. All of these ripen in late summer on into autumn, and truth be told, all are the dickens to pick. Yet, as anyone who has ever taken the first bite of a blueberry cobbler fresh from the oven or sat down to a meal of pancakes liberally laced with freshly picked huckleberries knows well, the effort provides wonderful rewards.

— WILD STRAWBERRIES —

Of all the berry world's wild wonders, my personal favorite is the noble strawberry. Adorning late-spring meadows and roadsides, along with abandoned old fields and homeplaces, these little red jewels have merits that could convince even a die-hard Texan that bigger is not necessarily better. In my youth, it was fairly easy to locate decent-sized patches of wild strawberries. They were scattered here and there at many spots in the GSMNP and, to a lesser degree, on old home sites and clearings in the Nantahala National Forest. For example, the Jenkins Fields on Deep Creek were full of them, there were numerous patches around old homesites on Indian Creek, the sprawling fields at Round Bottom on Straight Fork were visited by Aunt Emma and Uncle Frank Burnett on an annual basis to pick them, and the scrumptious tidbits of scarlet sprawled in plentitude in fields along the Oconaluftee River and in the meadows surrounding the park housing complex across that stream from the modern-day visitor center.

At one time or another during my boyhood I picked wild strawberries in all those places, and much closer to home there were two good patches within a few hundred yards of the house in which I grew up. Yet of all the many places where I enjoyed these red jewels straight from nature's berry bucket, none holds quite the same place in my mind of a boyhood midsummer's feast enjoyed along the road leading from Highway 441 out to Clingmans Dome. My stalwart fishing buddy Bill Rolen and I had been on a camping trip using the Fork Ridge Trail as our way into Deep Creek.

We had hiked out at trip's end, and upon reaching the road, were waiting at ease on a sunny afternoon for his father, a park ranger, to show up. Everywhere we looked in the field around us there were ripe strawberries, and it was impossible to walk without crushing the red tidbits of deliciousness winking from beneath their canopy of three-leaved stems. The fragrance of bruised berries filled the summer air and both of us ate to somewhere near the point of being foundered.

Apparently wild strawberries had long been abundant throughout the region. In his *Travels*, noted naturalist William Bartram mentions them growing so densely in ground burned by the Cherokees (which is one explanation advanced for the balds of the Smokies) that they dyed the legs of his horse red and filled the air with their pungency.

The berries my fishing buddy and I consumed featured slender necks and an elongated shape, although, as anyone who has done a fair amount of picking of wild strawberries knows, they come in a variety of shapes and sizes. I don't know the exact reason why, but obviously factors such as soil, genetics, and geography enter into the equation. One thing they do have in common—all are delicious.

Indeed, it is undeniable, as any taste comparison will readily establish, that wild strawberries put their tame cousins to shame when it comes to taste. Domestic berries get much larger and are more durable, easier to pick, and easier to cap. Yet the difference in taste makes all the extra effort associated with wild ones well worthwhile. Without question it was wild strawberries Izaak Walton had in mind when he quoted a fellow named Dr. Boteler in his famed book *The Compleat Angler* on the appeal of strawberries: "Doubtless God could have made a better berry," he wrote, "but doubtless he never did."

Those words of wisdom are well worth keeping in mind during strawberry time, and for proof in the pudding (or certainty in the shortcake, so to speak), here are some recipes using wild strawberries. Of course, lacking the real thing you can use tame substitutes. They are still delicious, but once you've sampled and savored wild strawberries, domestic varieties will never seem quite as good.

Wild Strawberry Trifle

I first ate a trifle (it used raspberries, not strawberries) when in Scotland a full fifty years ago. Talk about an eye-opening dessert! The basics of a trifle are simple—it's a mixture of berries, cake, whipped cream, pudding, and if you wish (and I do!), a bit of rum. Many recipes call for angel food cake, but for my part I think an old-fashioned pound cake made with plenty of eggs is better. Trifles are wonderful any time after they are made, but letting them "set" in the refrigerator for twelve hours or so allows the berry juice to mingle with the other ingredients in wonderful fashion.

> 1 container yellow cake mix, baked according to
> directions, or better still, make a pound cake
>
> 3 large vanilla pudding mixes (enough for 6 cups
> of milk), mixed according to directions
>
> 1 quart wild strawberries, sliced and cooked slightly with
> sugar and a dash or 2 of rum or Grand Marnier if desired
>
> 2 large containers whipped topping (24 ounces total)

Fill a trifle bowl (or any large bowl—it's just that the clear ones made for trifles have a world of visual appeal) with successive layers of crumbled cake, pudding, sliced berries, and whipped cream until you reach the top or run out of ingredients. Anoint with a bit of rum and finish with whipped cream at the top before decorating it with some whole berries.

Wild Strawberry Butter

½ pound (2 sticks) butter, at room temperature
(if you are blessed enough to have home-churned butter,
so much the better)

3 tablespoons powdered sugar

¾ cup wild strawberries, hulled, rinsed, and drained well

Cut butter into pieces and place in a blender. Pulse until fluffy. Add powdered sugar and berries; blend until spread is light and soft. Refrigerate in a covered container. Delicious on toast or biscuits and this is a fine way to make relatively few berries go a long way.

Wild Strawberry Muffins

1 cup self-rising flour

¾ cup sugar

1 egg, beaten

¼ cup milk

¼ cup canola oil

1 cup wild strawberries, capped and cleaned

TOPPING

¼ cup sugar

⅛ to ¼ teaspoon ground cinnamon

Strawberry butter or strawberry cream cheese

Preheat oven to 375°F. Using a spoon, mix all muffin ingredients except strawberries thoroughly. Gently fold in strawberries and fill sprayed muffin tin slots ⅔ full. Combine sugar and cinnamon and sprinkle atop muffins. Bake for 15 to 20 minutes or until lightly browned. Serve warm with strawberry butter or strawberry cream cheese. Again, this is a great way to stretch a small quantity of wild strawberries while enjoying their delectable flavor.

Wild Strawberry Spinach Salad

4 cups washed and torn spinach

1 cup hulled and washed wild strawberries (you can
substitute tame ones)

⅓ cup black walnut meats

DRESSING

2 tablespoons strawberry jam

2 tablespoons apple cider vinegar

⅓ cup oil

Combine spinach, strawberries, and black walnuts, and set aside. Prepare dressing by blending jam and vinegar, then add oil gradually as you continue to process. Use this to dress the salad.

NOTE: If you are fortunate enough to have access to plenty of branch lettuce (saxifrage), it is a grand wild substitute for spinach.

— DEWBERRIES —

The next berry to make its annual ripening appearance is a bit larger than wild strawberries but of distinctly humble origins. Of all the wild berries found in reasonable abundance in the Smokies, dewberries may well be the most overlooked. The child of farmed-out land and exhausted soil, right down to patches of graded red clay, this black beauty is all too often ignored. Yet connoisseurs welcome the berry's seasonal return with a joy born of past experience, for they recognize the dewberry's singular and succulent merits. A cousin of the blackberry, dewberries have a number of distinct characteristics that set them apart from their more common kin. Rather than growing on canes, they send runners along the ground. Where blackberries send up new canes each year after bearing fruit, dewberries spread by sending down roots where runners touch the soil. Of course, they can be spread by birds as well.

To my knowledge no poet has sung the dewberry's praise, and while you'll find its cousin, the blackberry, mentioned frequently in literary passages, this humble berry goes unnoticed. Yet the glories of a dewberry cobbler are such that it may be just as well that relatively few folks have sampled and savored this toothsome dish.

Anyone familiar with the dewberry will be keenly aware of the fact that it comes equipped with thorns on steroids. They are quick to stick, prick, and punish the unwary. Add to that the fact that you've got to do a lot of stooping and bending to pick them (no kneeling, which you can do with wild strawberries, because your knees just won't take the briars), the possibility of encounters with snakes and yellow jackets, along with dealing with a plant that is appreciably less productive than blackberries, and you have some obvious issues. Yet the ultimate reward makes all the agony and hard work worthwhile. I like what Grandpa Joe once said when it comes to the wonders of this wild delicacy. "It's just as well most folks don't know about a dewberry cobbler," he reckoned, "because it's so tasty as to be almost sinful."

Dewberries have afforded intriguing moments in my life well beyond the culinary wonders that can be wrought with their berries. I'd love to have a hundred dollar bill for every rabbit I jumped during my boyhood hunting days in a thicket of dewberry briars. Rabbits find a patch of dewberries the perfect place to spend the day, especially in cold but sunny situations during the late fall and winter.

A dewberry patch and a crippled rabbit also provided a moment of visual high comedy that comes back to me clearly despite the passage of more than a half century. My good friend and boyhood hunting buddy Jackie Corbin (he later became an internationally known research scientist involved in the development of Viagra) got a shot at a rabbit being chased by our pack of beagles. He hit the rabbit with his single-shot shotgun but didn't drop it on the spot. Thinking he could catch the cottontail as it fled through a dewberry patch, he took off after it like a two-legged beagle.

In doing so, he forgot the strength and tenacity of dewberry briars. Grubby (Jackie's nickname) caught one foot on a briar runner and it didn't give even a little bit. Suddenly he was airborne, and at that moment he displayed all the agility and "cattiness" that made him such a great high school athlete. Jackie turned a complete flip, using his gun as a bit of a prop while doing so, and hit the ground running almost as if nothing had happened. Of course, when it was all over (he caught the rabbit), it took Daddy and his best hunting buddy, Claude Gossett, a quarter of an hour to get all the red clay mud out of Grubby's gun barrel.

Dewberries can be used in a wide variety of ways when it comes to table fare—cobblers, pies, muffins, fresh atop cereal or vanilla ice cream, mixed with plain yogurt, or even in cornbread. Although I've never sampled it, I know the plant's leaves can be steeped to make tea. Here are a few ways to use dewberries, and rest assured that anyone who has never sampled them has a rare treat awaiting. I might also note that virtually any recipe calling for blackberries will work equally well with dewberries, though I find the latter to have a richer, more intense taste.

Dewberry Sorbet

2½ cups boiling water

1 regular size tea bag

3 cups fresh dewberries

1¼ cups sugar

¼ cup freshly squeezed lemon juice

Pour boiling water over tea bag and steep for 10 minutes (you can dry and save dewberry leaves for use as a substitute if you wish). Mix dewberries with sugar. Add tea to the berries and crush berries with the back of a spoon to release juice. Cover and cool. Puree berry mixture in a food processor using a metal blade. Strain through a fine sieve. Add lemon juice and mix. Place sorbet mixture in ice cream maker and process according to manufacturer's instructions. Freeze sorbet overnight. *Makes 1 quart*

Dewberry Sauce

2 cups dewberries

½ to ¾ cup sugar

1 tablespoon freshly squeezed lemon juice

Mix ingredients well and refrigerate an hour or more. Allow sauce to come to room temperature before serving. Serve over pancakes, waffles, cheesecake, or ice cream.

NOTE: The same recipe can be used for blackberry, raspberry, or mulberry sauce.

— BLACKBERRIES —

Dewberries are cousins of what is far and away the best known of the wild brambles, the luscious and pretty much ubiquitous blackberry. Old Will Shakespeare, who seemed to know something about everything, once wished, through the voice of King Henry IV, that "reasons were as plentiful as blackberries." Were that the case, ours would be a far more rational world, for most everywhere I've traveled in this country except arid regions, blackberries greet the knowing eye at every turn. Having spent a number of summers in the British Isles back before I became a "recovering professor," I can assure you that blackberries are just as plentiful there as they are in the Smokies. Abundant and delicious, they might be termed everyman's berry.

Botanists tell us that there are hundreds of subspecies of blackberries, and anyone who has picked a pailful has likely noticed subtle variations in the appearance and nature of berries from different vines (it holds true for taste as well). In many cases even vines have a distinct appearance, with some tending to stand tall and erect while others are less canelike and more truly vines when it comes to their looks and growth patterns. In fact, genetic engineering has produced a thornless blackberry, three rows of which (and I admit this a bit shamefacedly) adorned the fruit and berry part of my property for several years. However, no self-respecting blackberry picker feels he has fulfilled all the requirements of his job until his hands are well scratched, briar riddled, and stained an exquisite black-purple hue that Renaissance artist Titian would have loved.

A passion for blackberries runs as a bright thread through the entire fabric of my life. Along with poke salad, they provided the first cash money I earned as a youngster, fetching two bits a gallon in the early 1950s. I worked hard for many a quarter, which would buy one precious trout fly to give me a fix for my insatiable angling addiction. There were episodes where chiggers gave my nether parts a red-specked decoration that looked and itched like chicken pox, briar scratches left me looking like I'd been on the losing end of a tussle with an ornery bobcat, and once I managed to get into a wasp nest. Those stinging brethren of Beelzebub sent me into painful retreat, leaving my bucket behind, and only hours later did I work up the courage to sneak back, survey the situation, and retrieve it. On top of that, there was always, in the back of my mind, concern about an encounter with a rattlesnake or copperhead. Daddy had told me too many tales of snake episodes from his Juney Whank Branch boyhood for it to have been possible to do otherwise.

Such obstacles notwithstanding, I loved to pick blackberries. They were, for the three weeks or so of peak ripeness, a source of significant income for me, and I was by no means the only youngster who picked them. That was the time of year when I earned enough money to keep me in fly-fishing equipment the rest of the summer. Six or eight gallons would enable me to buy sufficient monofilament of various sizes to tie two dozen or more leaders and indulge in other shopping splurges when I had had particularly good picking (this was a product of berry size and finding a place they were plentiful within walking distance of the house). My standard splurge was for two or three trout flies, each of which sold for the same sum I received for a gallon of blackberries, tied by local experts Fred and Allene Hall.

The joy derived from picking blackberries has in no way changed in adulthood. About the only thing that can rival the pleasure to be found in a session of picking is enjoying the fruits of one's labor after the harvest, although I've personally never been able to resist some serious sampling while out picking. Anyone who has dealt with blackberries much knows, by sight and by feel, when a particular berry has reached the peak of perfection in terms of sweet, juicy goodness. Plucking such a berry is, at least for me, simply too much temptation. Dew drenched or sun soaked, it cries out to be eaten on the spot. Only after I've consumed forty or fifty of these morsels of ripened perfection can I resist temptation and put the berries in my bucket, not my mouth. Postharvest there's blackberry cobbler, blackberry jam, blackberry muffins, blackberry sorbet, blackberry wine, and less well known but truly special treats such as blackberry cornbread (if you've never had it, then you have a treat awaiting you, and it involves nothing more than adding a goodly measure, perhaps a cup and a half to two cups, of berries to your standard cornbread batter), and what for me is the ultimate culinary wonder offered by this matchless gift from the wilds, a blackberry stack cake.

We ate blackberries a lot at home. The fresh ones were used for cobblers, but big pickings went straight into runs of jam or quart cans of processed berries. Jam, put up in pint jars, adorned many a biscuit come winter, and in considerable quantities it was a key ingredient in peanut butter and jam sandwiches. My favorite way of eating jam, however, was when Grandma Minnie used it in the preparation of one of her stack cakes. They were the food of the gods. Grandma had several options for the sweet goodness between the thin layers of cake (she always made her stack cakes seven layers high) including applesauce made from dried apples, peach sauce made from peaches that had been similarly prepared, and various jams or jellies. All were delicious, but for me none quite matched blackberry jam.

Mind you, picking blackberries is no picnic. It involves hard work in the summer sun, a full ration of scratches, juice-stained hands (with the juice setting tiny fires anytime it seeps into a deep scratch), and the aforementioned chiggers. They may not bring the instant agony of a bee sting but what they do guarantee is three days of itching misery. About all I can suggest is that you take precautions before setting out and a good shower immediately after a picking session. Otherwise, just recognize that the rewards are well worth the trouble and that "no pain, no gain" is certainly the operative truism.

Finding blackberries is no problem. Throughout these old mountains they adorn fencerows, roadsides, abandoned fields, power line rights of way, and indeed about any open area. They beckon those with willingness to undertake the hard work that picking blackberries undeniably presents with the promise of rewards beyond measure.

Even today, the better part of six decades removed from my first picking days, I don't consider a summer complete until I've picked a few buckets of blackberries and enjoyed the treats they offer. Mom's invariable words of praise (she was masterful in recognizing what worked best when it came to motivating a youngster) are no more, but the berries remain there for the picking. I just have to wonder how many folks in today's world take advantage of their abundance, because sometimes, as is the province of older folks, I'm prone to think the stock of mountain gumption has begun to run out.

Blackberry Dumplings

1 quart blackberries

1 cup sugar

DUMPLINGS

1 cup all-purpose flour

2 teaspoons baking powder

¼ teaspoon salt

1 tablespoon sugar

1 cup milk

Place blackberries, sugar, and enough water to make berries thin enough to cook dumplings in a saucepan, and bring to a boil. Meanwhile, mix dumpling ingredients thoroughly and drop by tablespoons into boiling berries. Cook for 15 minutes or until dumplings are cooked through the center. Serve hot with cream.

— WILD RASPBERRIES —

Wild strawberries are the season's first offering of what might be termed nature's "dessert" bounty, but once the harvest of these spectacularly tasty morsels has come and gone, along with dewberries the promise of wild ripening raspberries lies in the near future. They ripen close on the heels of dewberries and more or less simultaneously with blackberries.

There are actually two types of raspberries in the Smokies. At lower elevations, found mainly around field edges and along roadsides, grow what are sometimes called "black cap" raspberries. At higher elevations, especially from four thousand feet up, you will find red raspberries. Often these do not ripen until late summer. They are common in areas known as balds, fire scalds, and other relatively open high-altitude places. Black cap raspberries are found on long, somewhat spindly canes, while red ones grow on shorter, stubbier canes. The last time I walked the path from the parking area up to Clingmans Dome, there were ripe red raspberries all along the trail. Apparently not one in a hundred passersby knew what they were, because with minimal effort I picked a hearty treat for my granddaughter and me while barely leaving the path.

In the late 1950s the family of my boyhood fishing buddy Bill Rolen had just moved into park housing at Luftee following the promotion of his father (also named Bill) to district ranger. That general area had a fine growth of black cap raspberries, and one day, taking a break from the serious matter of dealing with trout on nearby streams, our favorite summertime pursuit, we set out picking. Bill's mother, Lola, had indicated she would make us a cobbler if we would show enough initiative to provide her with a big mess of raspberries. The task was accomplished in good order, with our picking efforts producing the better part of a gallon in no time at all—there were canes hanging heavy with berries everywhere.

Lola Rolen was as good as her word. I don't recall any other item on the supper menu, although this staunch daughter of the Smokies was a gifted cook, but thoughts of a big bowl of that raspberry cobbler, fresh from the oven and adorned with a scoop of vanilla ice cream, linger ever so strong. It was truly a memorable food moment.

Of course, the park's confines are not the only place to find raspberries. They are fairly plentiful in many places, and in the case of black cap ones, the telltale purple tint of their canes, readily visible in winter, give you a "heads up" on locales for some fine picking come early summer. There are lots of ways to enjoy raspberries, but for pure sweet tooth satisfaction combined with simplicity, it's difficult to beat a recipe Mom used countless times over my boyhood and beyond. It is as near to a "can't miss" baking approach as you'll ever slip into an oven, and it works well not only with raspberries but with most any kind of berry found in the Smokies, and it is perfectly suited for apples and peaches as well. If wild strawberries offer culinary nirvana when it comes to a hearty helping of shortcake, arguably nothing produces a finer cobbler than raspberries (see Peach Cobbler on page 68—just substitute raspberries for peaches).

— ELDERBERRIES —

Most mountain folks with a passing acquaintance with the natural world are familiar with elderberries. They notice their striking white bloom clusters in late spring and then the profusion of reddish-purple berries in late summer. Yet few indeed are those who have enjoyed the delights of this plant, which loves damp feet and is commonly found in open or semiopen areas along ditch lines, tiny branches meandering through pastures, roadsides, and the like.

Such may be the case on the local level, but elsewhere, especially in Europe, elderberries are cherished and put to a variety of culinary uses with delicious results. The same can be done in the high country, where the elderberry is found in great abundance. There are actually two types in the Smokies, but only the common elderberry, with berries that are deep purple when ripe, is edible. The red elderberry, a high-elevation plant, should be avoided, and because of the presence of glycosides, the common elderberry should be cooked before any type of human consumption. Before turning to matters connected with the kitchen and good eating though, at least passing mention should be made of aspects of the humble plant's other uses.

When I was a youngster, and I hope some of the same sort of simple pleasures still exist today, large elderberry bushes were avidly sought for two reasons that had nothing whatsoever to do with table fare. A short, straight section of an elderberry stalk with the pith removed from the middle made a most satisfactory pop gun, while a longer section could become a blowgun. Similarly, tuneful flutes could be fashioned from a hollowed section with three or four air holes bored in with the tip of a pocketknife. I have also seen pieces of elderberry used as a conduit for drinking water from a seep spring.

Perhaps the most interesting application in my experience came from one of the grand old Tar Heel turkey hunters of yesteryear, the legendary Simon Everitt. In his delightful and rare little book *Tales of Wild Turkey Hunting*, Everitt gives a detailed description of how to craft a suction yelper. One of the yelper's key components is made from an elderberry stalk.

Still, the elderberry shines forth in its brightest light when the tiny berries (drupes is actually the more accurate description) are turned to food and drink. In the latter context, one of many memorable experiences from my boyhood was stopping by an impressive country home in neighboring Jackson County for Daddy and his good friend Claude Gossett to seek permission to hunt. The owners, in a stellar example of mountain hospitality, insisted that we stop by for some refreshment after our day afield. Among the offerings were hefty slices of stack cake, fried apple pies, and for the adults, little glasses of elderberry wine. Of course, I was too young to partake of the wine (I did ample justice to the foodstuffs and a big glass of milk from the owner's cow), but the moment has always stuck in my mind.

Many years later I had my first sip of elderberry wine—in Austria of all places—and I've enjoyed the bounty of this plentiful plant in other forms including jelly, jam, pies, and fritters. Check out the recipes below, and maybe you'll try one or two of them and add some joyful variety to your table fare. It probably should also be noted that various concoctions featuring elderberry juice have long enjoyed popularity for medicinal reasons among mountain herabalists and granny women.

Elderberry Fritters

Long before the berries ripen or even form, the flower clusters of the elderberry can be used in a fashion similar to many other edible blooms, such as squash flowers, violets, nasturtiums, and pansies.

1¾ cups all-purpose flour

2 eggs

½ cup milk

Pinch of salt

16 elderberry blossom clusters with stems

Powdered sugar for dusting

Lard or shortening for frying

Mix flour, eggs, salt, and milk into a batter with the consistency of that for pancakes. Rinse the elderberry blossom clusters thoroughly, then pat dry. Dip the blossom clusters in the dough, and deep-fry until golden brown. Drain, dust with powdered sugar, and serve.

Elderberry Mush

1 pound elderberries with stems removed

Sprinkling of sugar

½ cup milk

1 tablespoon all-purpose flour

Pinch of salt

1 tablespoon honey

3½ tablespoons butter, melted

Briefly cook the elderberries, which should be sprinkled in sugar, in a skillet with a tiny bit of water added. Then, in a separate pan, make a roux using milk and flour. Add the roux, salt, and honey to the cooked elderberries and bring to a rolling boil, stirring constantly. Pour melted butter on top. You can eat the mush as it is, pour over ice cream, or better still, add to toasted cubes of pound cake for a dessert that is as colorful as it is tasty.

Elderberry Soup

Fruit soups are more common in other countries than here, and this one is a favorite in the central European countries of Germany, Austria, and Switzerland. I've never encountered it in the Smokies, but I'd like to think that scattered hardy settlers of the area with central European roots prepared this unusual soup.

2½ pounds elderberries with stems removed, washed

9 cups water

Zest of 1 lemon

4 tablespoons cornstarch

6 tablespoons cold water

2 tablespoons lemon juice

¾ cup sugar

Place berries in a soup kettle or deep pot. Add water and lemon zest. Cook until the berries soften. Strain through cloth into a bowl, pushing through as much of the pulp as possible. Return the liquid to the kettle, bring to a boil, and then remove the kettle from the stove.

In a small bowl, combine the cornstarch, cold water, and lemon juice, pressing out all the lumps. Add to the soup, together with the sugar, and stir thoroughly. Place over medium-low heat and cook, stirring constantly, until thick. Adjust the sugar and lemon to suit your taste (honey can be substituted for sugar if you wish). Can be served hot or cold.

Easy-Peasy Elderberry Jam

2 quarts crushed elderberries

¼ cup vinegar

6 cups sugar

Combine berries, vinegar, and sugar, and bring to a slow boil, stirring to make sure the sugar dissolves completely. Then cook rapidly until thick. As the mixture thickens, be sure to stir vigorously to prevent sticking. Pour boiling hot mixture into sterilized jars. Adjust lids, and process in boiling water for 5 minutes. Remove and cool. *Makes 6 half-pint jars*

— BLUEBERRIES AND — HUCKLEBERRIES

Plentiful in the Smokies and in far-flung reaches around the world (I've nibbled on them in Alaska, Austria, and far northern Quebec), blueberries and their low-growing cousins, huckleberries, are a pure delight when it comes to fine eating. There can't be many breakfast foods that outshine a stack of blueberry pancakes cooked in a backwoods setting with the berries having been picked the evening before. I can almost taste a breakfast from a decade or more ago, well up the Hazel Creek drainage in the GSMNP, which featured pancakes liberally laced with blueberries that my brother had picked during a lengthy hike the previous day. Given the fact that the breakfast was the next meal we consumed after a hearty feast of trout the night before, I reckon we were living like backwoods kings.

In yesteryear, American Indians and the famed mountain men of the West relied heavily on pemmican, and one of the key ingredients of that protein- and fat-rich foodstuff was dried blueberries.

I have no awareness of such trail rations ever being prepared in the Smokies, but it wouldn't have been because of the lack of key ingredients. In this part of the world both blueberries and huckleberries are plentiful. They seem to like higher elevations and are commonly found on balds or as new growth in fire scalds. One of the attractive aspects of those growing at elevations up to and even above six thousand feet is that they ripen in late summer, long after most other berries have come and gone.

Picking either of these dark, delightful little packages of intense taste is, any way you want to put it, a chore. It takes a lot of picking to make a gallon, and when I read of whole families going on pickings back in the days when reliance on nature's bounty was an integral and important part of mountain life, the thought that one such venture might produce the many gallons of berries sometimes mentioned astounds me. Yet I have no doubt such was the case. My father often talked about family outings of this sort, with buckets made from lard pails forming receptacles for berries. Incidentally, those same lard pails also served as lunch boxes for schoolchildren, with the contents normally being a chunk of cornbread and some molasses or maybe a cathead biscuit and a cold sweet potato.

Both blueberries and huckleberries dry nicely, can be canned or frozen, and are at their finest when eaten fresh. Used in cakes, pies, to top ice cream or cereal, make syrup, or in other ways, they provide a rare treat. I must confess that these days most of my sampling and savoring of blueberries takes the form of eating tame ones (I have a big patch that has been thriving for better than four decades). However, anytime I come across ripe berries while hiking or fishing the backcountry, it is immediately time for a break and a delicious snack.

Here is a passel of tips before turning to a couple of recipes:

- Blueberries and huckleberries are a great health food, thanks in large measure to being loaded with antioxidants.

- Add blueberries or huckleberries to your favorite muffin, cake, or pancake or waffle batter.

- Serve kids a purple cow by whirling milk, berries, and sugar together in a blender (I guess in today's lingo it would be a smoothie).

- Stir blueberries or huckleberries into plain or vanilla ice cream. Better still, make a run of homemade berry ice cream.

- Add berries to a melon medley of watermelon, honeydew, and cantaloupe.

- Make a blueberry trifle using an old-fashioned pound cake.

- Partially fill an ice cream cone with blueberries then top off with a scoop of vanilla ice cream. Tell children (or the young at heart, no matter their age) they are eating an ice cream surprise and let them discover the surprise in the form of berries as they get into the cone.

- Make a pan of snow cream (see page 194) and sprinkle it liberally with frozen blueberries.

Blueberry Backstrap

Should you be so blessed as to have the backstraps or tenderloins from a deer, those tastiest of venison cuts go wonderfully well with blueberries. This recipe offers a fine example.

6 tablespoons butter, divided

4 venison loin steaks, cut a half inch thick (half of one backstrap or a pair of tenderloins will be enough meat)

Juice and peel of 1 fresh lemon (about 2 tablespoons)

1 cup chicken broth

1 cup fresh blueberries

Ground cinnamon

Ground ginger

Salt and freshly ground black pepper

Melt 2 tablespoons of the butter in a large skillet and cook venison loin steaks until medium-rare and browned on both sides. Place on platter and keep warm. Deglaze skillet with lemon juice, lemon peel, and chicken broth. Cook over high heat to reduce liquid to about ½ cup. Lower heat to medium and whisk in, 1 tablespoon at a time, the remaining 4 tablespoons of butter. Add blueberries, several generous dashes of cinnamon, several dashes of ginger, and salt and pepper to taste. Pour blueberry sauce over steaks and serve immediately. *Serves 4*

Berry Larrup

As a boy I would occasionally hear some dish, usually a dessert, described as "larruping good." That was high praise and perhaps explains the derivation of berry dishes known simply as larrup. Almost any wild berry—such as blackberries, dewberries, raspberries, elderberries, blueberries, or mulberries—could be used to make larrup. This basic recipe will work for any of them.

4 cups (or more) berries

1 cup sugar for every 4 cups of berries

⅓ cup all-purpose flour for every 4 cups of berries (a bit less cornstarch can be substituted for the flour if desired)

In a large saucepan holding a half cup of water bring the berries to a full boil and then add the sugar and flour. Stir steadily at a slow boil for 5 to 7 minutes. Serve hot as a topping for buttered biscuits, on pancakes, or with homemade ice cream.

CHAPTER 14

SWEETENINGS—
MOLASSES, HONEY, MAPLE SYRUP, AND MORE

As was true for anything that had to be bought from the store, refined sugar was considered a luxury in my grandparents' heyday. Daddy often talked about "sweetenings" from his youth, and it was obvious that sugar was precious and little used. It could be purchased along with some of the basic cooking necessities that were otherwise unavailable—salt, black pepper, and the like—but whenever possible substitutes that could be grown or obtained through barter were used to satisfy the sweet tooth. There were plenty of options available from nature. Most required hard work and considerable expenditure of time, but those were two ingredients of life in the Smokies that folks living there possessed in ample quantity.

The most common sweetening was molasses (if you want to get technical, it was sorghum syrup, but in my linguistic experience the usage is completely interchangeable). Families typically set aside a plot of good ground for their patch of cane, saved seed to plant the crop year after year, and made a special event out of cutting the stalks come harvesttime. When it was gathered in the fall they turned to someone who had the equipment to press the juice from the stalks and boil it down until the syrup reached a satisfactory color and consistency. Almost every community had a resident living not too far away with the necessary skills

Men boil sorghum syrup while a pair of youthful onlookers enjoy sucking
the sweet juice out of mature sections of cane and watch the process.
Courtesy of Hunter Library, Western Carolina University.

and machinery (press, large vatlike containers, skimmer, horse or mule to work the press, wooden paddles, and other essentials). Much like a miller, that person usually received a portion of the syrup as payment for use of the equipment. Often "molasses makings" were a community event with families hauling in their crop of cane and helping out in feeding the press, seeing that the animal that provided the power to do the pressing kept moving, regulating the fire beneath the vat of juice at the right temperature, skimming the foam off the top with a special device made for that process, and all the while being part of a holidaylike atmosphere. There would likely be a picnic as part of the festivities, sometimes imbibing of moonshine or the "skimmings," which quickly developed significant alcohol content, music, and dancing.

The end product, stored in cans or lard buckets, would keep indefinitely and could be used in a variety of ways. Daddy enjoyed talking about his school lunch often being a big chunk of cornbread or a couple of biscuits with molasses to sop them in, and any true-to-its-roots recipe for stack cake will call for molasses instead of sugar. Dried beans were sometimes cooked with molasses and known as baked beans. The sweetening had a distinctive flavor, and folks developed specific preferences for variations ranging from light-colored syrup to blackstrap molasses with its hearty hint of an iron aftertaste. In that context, one of the notable features of molasses, unlike refined sugar, which has no nutritional value, is that it contains a number of vitamins and minerals. Ironically, in a sharp reversal from the past, today molasses, while still available, is far more costly than sugar.

Along with a patch of cane, many well-rounded farms sported a stand of bee gums somewhere on the property. They were usually at the edge of a sunny, open area that gave the bees easy flying routes to and from their hives. Some folks took great pride in their ability as bee trackers, using a salt or sugar water lure to draw bees to a spot where the bees would be coated in flour or something readily visible, and then following their flight path until the wild hive was located. Sometimes it would require several attractant stations and "coursings" of the bees before the hive was located. Once the "bee lining" resulted in the bee tree being found, it would be chopped down to obtain the honey, and unless someone was being a shameful wastrel, to capture the queen and reposition her in a gum at the homeplace.

The gums earned that name in the same way rabbit gums did—they were fashioned from hollow sections of black gum trees. It took some ingenuity to get them shaped right, protected from the elements, provided with a suitable entrance for the worker bees, and fashioned with an internal support framework that aided the bees in their amazingly complex construction of combs. Spring brought swarming time, when a hive that had become too populous would see a queen and a cohort of worker bees leave. It was at that point a good beekeeper needed to be ready to capture the swarm and provide them with a gum of their own.

That happened once on our property when I was a youngster. Coming home from school one day I noticed a huge mass hanging from one of the apple trees. As I drew closer, awareness dawned that it was a gigantic swarm of bees—they would have easily filled a peck basket—weighing down a limb. As soon as Daddy got home from work, I rushed out to tell him about the swarm and show it to him. He called a beekeeper friend who showed up in short order, captured the queen, and gave the swarm a new home.

Two of the most prized flowers for honey, sourwood and locust, grow in abundance in the Smokies. While it is all but impossible to get honey that is exclusively constituted from nectar of these or any other blossoms from a hive, bees will select them by preference when they flower in abundance. Sourwood, with its large bloom clusters featuring scores of individual flowers on each of them, has the welcome characteristic of staying in bloom for an extended period. It makes a fragrant, light honey many Smokies natives prize above all others.

Sugar maples were widespread throughout the Smokies, and residents prized them for the wood, which had many uses, and the resplendent beauty they brought to the landscape each fall with their shawl of scarlet. Although maple syrup is generally associated with New England and Canada, it figured prominently in Smokies diet for generations. There was none of the sophisticated network of tubes and collecting stations associated with today's production, but "syruping" was an integral part of the bustling times of early spring in the Smokies. One region, the lovely valley and sloping hillsides of the drainage of the West Prong of the Little Pigeon River above Gatlinburg, had so many of the trees that it was known as the Sugarlands (an alternative explanation for the name, likely originating as a "windy" from some mountain storyteller, suggested it derived from the immense amount of sugar hauled into the area for production of moonshine). An oft-quoted couplet describing the Sugarlands before it became part of the park reflects both the serene beauty of the area and the hardscrabble nature of the existence eked out by residents of the rocky bottomlands and hardwood coves:

> *The Sugarlands so clear and clean*
> *Although our meals were mighty lean.*

Production of maple syrup was never a community enterprise to the same degree as molasses making, but families would take time to tap trees and perhaps boil down a few quarts of the tasty sweet treat. They also enjoyed maple tea, which blended sap with a tablespoon or two of honey for a pick-me-up that offered a most welcome break along with hydration in the midst of arduous agricultural labors associated with mountain springtime.

Birch Syrup

Although it never figured in Smokies diet to the degree of molasses or honey, some enterprising folks took advantage of the abundance of birch trees to make syrup from them when sap was rising in the spring. The process was similar to that for production of maple syrup, although birch trees do not have anywhere near the run of sap of that associated with sugar maples. More common than the actual production of birch syrup was stripping a section of bark from a tree and then using a knife to scrape off the sap that accumulated and boiling the cambium (inner) layer in water to make "sweetwater," or birch tea, which was drunk as a refreshing beverage. Sidney Saylor Farr, in *My Appalachia*, describes having done this as a child.

Popcorn Balls

Frequently, mountain gardens during my youth included a couple of rows of popping corn, with its tight little cobs of strawberry-colored kernels that puffed up with a glorious symphony of noise when coated with a bit of grease and shaken in a popper over an open flame or atop a wood-burning or electric stove. If you lack the real deal, and that's likely the case, store-bought popcorn will work just fine for this recipe. Pop the corn as you normally would (but without adding any salt or butter). To make the syrup for the popcorn balls warm a cup or so of molasses, a hefty chunk of butter, and a pinch or two of salt. Heat, stirring constantly, to boiling. At that point add a spoonful of vanilla and "just a tetch" of baking soda and blend them in by more stirring before allowing the syrup to cool. Once the syrup mixture cools, pour over a big mound of popcorn placed on wax paper atop a flat surface.

You are now ready to form the popcorn balls. In my experience this has always been done with greased number-eight pokes (for the uninitiated, that's mountain talk for paper bags) over your hands, although presumably latex gloves would work as long as they haven't been powdered or scented. Once gently rolled and shaped into spheres roughly the size of baseballs and placed on cookie tins, some of the popcorn balls demand immediate consumption while others will keep for a day or two as monuments to savory stickiness so sweet as to be irresistible. The whole process is a glorious mess and will eventually require liberal application of soap and warm water once production is completed. Incidentally, young kids love making popcorn balls. Just be prepared for some serious cleanup efforts in the aftermath.

Smoky Mountain Snow Cream

Snow days, times when it snowed enough for the winding country roads that comprised most of the bus routes in Swain County to become treacherous or impassable, formed special moments in my boyhood. Depending on the nature of the snow, which could range from an icy skiff to what the old folks called a "cross-legged snow," when wind blew hard and flakes seemed to fly in all directions, closure of school could mean a rabbit hunt, sled riding, snowball fights, or just enjoying being free from classroom drudgery. If the snow was a heavy, soft one, with big flakes that accumulated rapidly, Momma would often say, "Let's make some snow cream."

I think she enjoyed the festive mood about as much as her offspring, although she did have some specific instructions when it came to gathering the snow. We used an aluminum dishpan and had strict instructions not to dig too deep in order to avoid leaves or trash. Momma preferred to wait until there were several inches on the ground. Once we carried the essential ingredient back into the house, fine eating was only moments away. Here's how it came about.

1 cup whole milk (or for added richness, use half-and-half)

½ cup sugar

½ teaspoon vanilla

Sizable bowl of snow (3 quarts or more)

Blend all ingredients gently but quickly—you don't want the snow to melt or the mixture to turn to slush—and eat immediately. There are many variations to this recipe. If you want chocolate snow cream, add powdered cocoa mix to the above ingredients. For a richer, and to my way of thinking, tastier snow cream, add a beaten egg before you stir the snow cream. Other possibilities are using a couple of mashed, overripe bananas for banana snow cream or stirring in some cinnamon sugar for an eggnoglike taste. You can even soak some raisins in water in advance, drain them, and add them and a bit of rum flavoring to the snow cream as it is being mixed.

Whatever approach you use, avoid the first and lowest couple of inches of snowfall. It carries a lot of pollutants from the air to earth, as well as holding the trash Momma worried about.

Birch Candy

Although I never had the privilege of eating candy made from boiling down birch syrup, I do recall either Grandma or, more likely, Grandpa talking about it. Certainly, there were birch trees aplenty in the Smokies and you could strip some bark off one and lick the sap in a fashion somewhat similar to pinching the bottom off a honeysuckle bloom and "sucking" that sweetness. Sidney Saylor Farr covers birch candy in her delightful *More than Moonshine*, and you can find other descriptions of the process with a bit of digging. Although the setting for Farr's experiences is eastern Kentucky rather than the Smokies, careful reading of her prose works and cookbook leaves no doubt in my mind that she knew her traditions and reflected them accurately. In this case her experience would have been similar to that in the Smokies with one significant difference. The birch tree does best at higher elevations in Appalachia, and the Smokies had far more suitable topography to offer than Farr's home stomping grounds. The main problem with this recipe is that it required a precious commodity—sugar—and would accordingly have been a real luxury.

1 cup birch sap

2 cups sugar

Combine the birch sap and sugar in a kettle and bring to a boil. When a tiny amount from the kettle is dropped into cold water and immediately hardens, the candy is "made." Pour the liquid from the kettle atop a lightly greased cookie sheet or other flat, rimmed surface, and as it cools, use a knife tip to score it. When it is fully set, the glazelike candy can be broken along the scoring marks.

Molasses Candy

Sometimes called taffy, because pulling is part of the process, this sweet is distinctively different and a real treat for anyone who likes molasses and enjoys sucking on a piece of hard candy.

3 tablespoons butter, divided

1 cup brown sugar

**¾ cup Dixie Dew (or other light corn or cane syrup—
Momma was partial to Dixie Dew and I've always loved
its label proclaiming the syrup "gives a biscuit a college
education")**

2 teaspoons vinegar

¾ cup molasses

Pinch of baking soda

Grease a baking pan with 1 tablespoon of butter and set aside. Combine sugar, syrup, and vinegar in a saucepan and cook slowly on low heat, stirring regularly, until the sugar dissolves. Increase heat to medium, stirring as needed, until a candy thermometer reads 250°F (Grandma would have pooh-poohed the very concept of a candy thermometer) or until the mixture is fairly firm.

Add molasses and the remaining 2 tablespoons of butter, and continue to cook, stirring as needed, until the candy mixture reaches its previous consistency. Remove from heat, add baking soda, and beat well with a whisk.

Pour in the prepared pan and let cool until you can handle it with buttered fingers. Pull and work the mix as you would taffy, making it into ropes. Cut in 1-inch pieces and wrap in waxed paper.

Old-Timey Honey Cookies

¼ pound (1 stick) butter, softened
(do not substitute margarine)

½ cup sugar

1 large egg, beaten

½ cup honey

2 cups all-purpose flour

2 teaspoons salt

1 cup finely chopped black walnuts

Cream the butter and add the sugar gradually until fully integrated. Mix the beaten egg and honey with the dry ingredients and stir into the butter mix. Chill the resulting dough, create a roll, and wrap it in wax paper. Place in the refrigerator for 15 to 20 minutes or until firm. Remove and cut into thin slices. Place these atop a cookie sheet and bake in a preheated oven at 350°F for 12 to 15 minutes or until they just begin to brown on top. Allow to cool and store in a cookie tin or other container.

Metheglin

A traditional mountain beverage, often enjoyed in the Christmas season, metheglin is in essence a type of mead. It was a favorite among Smokies old-timers and was considered much more acceptable among "church-ified" folks than moonshine.

2 quarts honey (sourwood was preferred, but then that was true for anything using honey)

4 quarts pure water (Smokies folks swore by spring water, and with good reason—I've never tasted anything finer anywhere)

½ cup sugar

2 egg whites, well-beaten

Zest and juice of 1 lemon

1 ounce baking yeast

Mix honey, water, and sugar, and simmer slowly while adding eggs, lemon, and yeast. A scum will form. When the scum disappears, allow the liquid to cool until it is lukewarm. Place in a stone crock covered with cheese-cloth until the liquid stops working (that is, ceases to bubble or effer-vesce). At that point the drink can be stored in bottles with cork stoppers.

Syllabub

I always considered syllabub a drink with mountain origins until under-taking considerable work on the writings and career of Archibald Rut-ledge, perhaps the most prolific outdoor writer of the twentieth century. A resident of Hampton Plantation in South Carolina's Low Country, he often mentioned the drink in connection with Christmas and New Year's celebrations at his ancestral homeplace. His directions for preparation of syllabub are somewhat similar to those used in the Smokies.

1 quart cream

**Half pint of sweet wine and half pint of Madeira
(in the Smokies, homemade wines such as elderberry
or blackberry would have been used, perhaps in
conjunction with a measure of brandy)**

Juice of 2 lemons

Pinch of ground allspice

Sugar, to taste

Briskly whisk all the ingredients until a froth rises. Skim away the froth and set aside. Partly fill glasses with a portion of the liquid and top with froth. Repeat the process to obtain more froth for topping the drink.

Molasses Pie

When I finished undergraduate school and ventured out into the real world beyond the blessed bosom of the Great Smokies, my first position found me teaching and coaching in a military academy in Chatham, Virginia. The school furnished lodging (of sorts), but there was no kitchen or cooking facilities. Accordingly, I was reliant on the food eaten by the cadet corps, which was adequate but nothing more, or eating in one of the few local dining sites. In one of them I noticed they had brown sugar pie on the menu. Curious and possessing a sweet tooth always in need of some satisfaction, I ordered a slice. It was enjoyable but after the first bite I thought to myself: "I'm eating molasses pie made from brown sugar." It lacked the extra taste touch molasses offers, or maybe I was merely a gustatory prisoner of my raising. Whatever the case, a molasses pie made with syrup from homegrown cane, along with free-range eggs and home-made crust, is a genuine mountain sweet treat.

2 cups molasses

4 large, free-range eggs (regular cackleberries will
work, but they aren't as good)

2 tablespoons cornstarch

Pie pastry shell

Preheat oven to 325°F. Pour the molasses into a small pot and heat it until it shows the first signs of bubbling, then turn down the heat, keeping the syrup warm. Break the eggs into a bowl and beat them well with a whisk. Slowly add the eggs to the molasses, stirring constantly as you do so. In a small bowl, mix the cornstarch with a bit of the syrup-and-egg mixture to make a paste, and then place it back in the pot and mix in well. Turn the heat back up and allow the mixture to come to a slow boil, stirring consistently as you do so. Once the mixture thickens and stiffens enough to make stirring a bit difficult, pour into the pastry shell and bake until the pie sets, usually in about a half hour but you can check with a toothpick.

A woman stands on her porch, where jars of canned goods indicate she has been busy preparing for coming winter. The canned goods would have been moved into the cabin or a cannery before the onset of cold weather.

Courtesy of the National Park Service.

PART III

PREPARING AND PRESERVING

Diggin' the potatoes and pickin' wild greens,
Makin' sauer kraut and picklin' beans,
Out puttin' the hay crop into the barn
And getting' up before daylight to hoe corn.

GLADYS TRENTHAM RUSSELL,
It Happened in the Smokies

The ability to preserve food so that it would last for many months was a defining part of life in the Smokies until well into the twentieth century. You didn't make a weekly trip to the grocery store to purchase fresh vegetables, butchered meat, canned goods, loaf bread, packaged dry goods, or other essentials of daily existence. Trips to the store, especially for those living in more rural areas, were an occasion, and sometimes a rare one at that. They might involve some barter, sale of items such as ginseng or yellow root, which fetched cash money, and actual purchase of the relatively few essentials that could not be cultivated, raised, or obtained from nature. Among these were salt, certain types of spices such as black pepper, refined sugar, and a few other items. For the most part though, self-sufficiency, invariably embraced with a "make do with what you've got" perspective, was a cardinal rule of life.

Making do meant not only the ability to produce or procure virtually everything a family ate; it required a mixture of knowledge passed down through the generations with an ability to work hard. If you didn't pick blackberries and can them when they ripened in the height of summer, there wouldn't be cobblers in the winter. If you failed to raise and fatten your hogs properly, or if you did an inadequate job of curing hams and let skippers get at the meat, times could get lean in a hurry.

Accordingly, "putting up" food in various ways was a required skill for daily life. It took many forms. Dairy products such as milk and butter could be kept cool and enjoy a decent shelf life through placement in the family's springhouse. Carefully monitored souring of sweet milk to produce buttermilk or clabber was another approach to handling the result of daily milking of the family cow or cows. My father loved to relate the tale of how, as a boy, he would slip off to the springhouse during the heat of summer for a cool, refreshing drink of buttermilk. Can you imagine a youngster in today's world thinking a few surreptitious sips of buttermilk were a special bit of sneakiness? Some vegetable crops, notably corn, could be allowed to cure in the field and stored in dry places, with protection from rodents and other critters, until needed for use. Numerous other crops could be dried as well, although they required considerably more human effort.

Many of the fruits and vegetables harvested in the fall—apples and pears on the fruit side and winter squash, dry beans, turnips, potatoes, cabbage, carrots, parsnips, and more in the vegetable line—could be stored in the ground; in specially designed housing such as an apple house, root cellar, or cannery; beneath corn shocks; or in other protected places. There they awaited usage as needed, although vigilance was required to avoid spoilage. There was truth aplenty in the suggestion that one rotten apple can spoil the whole bunch.

Meat required extra effort, with salting and canning being pretty much the only preservation options available. That was one reason pork enjoyed such prominence in mountain diet. It was easier to handle than beef, not only in terms of butchering but also when it came to salting, smoking, and curing. Pigs were also, to a considerable degree, self-sufficient. They could be turned loose to feast on mast in the fall, and even when they were penned up, the omnivorous habits of swine contrasted sharply with the comparative pickiness of cattle. Barnyard fowl were almost never preserved. They were cooked and eaten immediately after being killed, and chicken was pretty much reserved for special occasions. The regular production of eggs far exceeded one-time gratification from a meal of yard bird in terms of culinary importance.

Pickling was a part of the picture, and it ranged across a spectrum embracing near necessities such as kraut to luxuries such as pickles and relishes both sweet and sour. Apple vinegar was a readily available commodity, and while many types of pickling required days or even weeks for completion, it was perhaps not as demanding an overall process as many other types of preservation. While it remained important, pickling went into something of a decline, at least when it came to amounts, once canning arrived. Of course, canning did allow pickled items to be put up in jars, as opposed to the storage crocks that had previously been the standard containers.

As for canning, someone of my generation finds it difficult to imagine what life's culinary aspects of life must have been like in the Smokies prior to the popularization of that method of food preservation around the dawn of the twentieth century. During the winter months diet would have taken on a dreary (and unhealthy) sameness focused on cured pork, various corn dishes (no wonder mountain folks were so ingenious in figuring out diverse ways to prepare corn), and dried legumes. Only dried fruit and fruit leather broke the dietary monotony.

The advent of canning and the dramatic expansion it brought to Smokies diet must have seemed almost miraculous. All I can say with certainty is that my mother, grandmother, and virtually everyone I knew embraced canning with something not too far

removed from religious fervor. Neither Momma nor Grandma
Minnie really felt comfortable with the existing state of affairs at
summer's end until row after row of quart jars lined shelves, and
as winter strengthened, they carefully watched empty glass jars
replace filled ones. That was in part a way of gauging how much
they would need to can of a given fruit or vegetable when the
growing season once more arrived, but it was also comforting or
concerning, depending on the shelf stock, to know where matters stood with the family supply of comestibles.

In my personal experience, canning loomed larger in terms
of overall family food preparation than anything else. Canning
jars were zealously procured and protected. The pressure canner
holding six quart jars was considered a must-have kitchen item.
From the first bounty of the spring garden through laying by
time and on into the autumn season of harvest, there was always
something to justify a run of canning. It might be whatever berry
was in season; the pressures of ripe peach time when preserves,
dried peaches, peach leather, and pickled peaches all cried out
for attention; or the necessity of getting garden truck canned
when half a dozen or more vegetables reached their peak of
productivity more or less simultaneously.

"A woman's work was never done" held true in no small
degree at all seasons, but the adage took on added meaning
when the demands posed by canning peaked. In truth though, it
wasn't just woman's work. Canning demanded that everyone be
involved. Even a small boy was perfectly capable of pulling and
shucking roasting ears or gathering tomatoes, while girls could
be busy stringing and breaking beans or silking corn and cutting
it from the cob. When really large runs of canning were in the
offing, such as bushels of apples to be peeled, pecks of green
beans to be strung and put on thread to dry as leather britches,
or especially when hog-killing time rolled around in November,
all who were capable worked and worked hard.

Yet those times of communal effort, when entire extended
families or maybe even significant segments of the local

community turned out, were not viewed with dismay. Quite the opposite was true. It meant togetherness, good times, fine food, maybe some frivolity, and certainly the deep-rooted sense of satisfaction derived from seeing gleaming jars of canned sausage or cracklings in lard as hallmarks of the group's labors. When Momma looked at the shelves in our basement after she had reached her annual quota of two hundred quarts of apples, one hundred quarts of green beans, along with jars of at least a score more fixings in the form of everything from soup mix to canned tomatoes, Concord grape juice to blackberries, it was always with a pleased gleam in her eye and the hint of a smile playing across her lips. She had done her labors and done them well, and her tiny tribe was assured of fine vittles for another winter.

The advent of freezers and frozen food changed things, although in my experience at least, it was gradual. Grandma Minnie never froze anything, although she would occasionally put leftovers from a family gathering or something like a whopping pot of soup into containers she placed in the small freezer at the top of her refrigerator. Of course, the refrigerator had come into her life when she was well beyond middle age, and it's remarkable to realize that in the course of her eighty-odd earthly years she went from indentured servitude as a girl, where there was no canning; through married life, which saw canning, then an ice box, and eventually a refrigerator; from open hearth cooking to a wood-burning stove to an electric one. Maybe, with that degree of transition, it is understandable why she resisted when freezers became all the rage. Either flat worn out from a life with more than its share of hardship, or maybe because she had seen enough change, she never wanted or owned a freezer. Momma, on the other hand, thought the first one she owned, a chest type that was the very dickens to defrost, was the cat's meow.

More or less simultaneously with the arrival of home refrigeration came other massive changes on the food front. Somewhere around midcentury, life in the Smokies left linkage to the land as the primary way of existence and gave way to nonagricultural jobs. If those jobs weren't available locally, many traveled the so-called hillbilly highway to the automobile factories of the upper Midwest. Grocery store shelves stocked with goods that had once been primarily the preserve of those living in towns or folks who earned their livelihood in some way other than farming increasingly drew a more diverse clientele. A barter system gave way to cash or credit. It was progress, but at a price.

Lost were treasured times of togetherness. Slipping away, bit by bit, were the skills and knowledge of those who knew self-sufficiency as their way of life. Community and family closeness suffered. The automobile and avenues of asphalt meant far greater mobility, but they also often meant far less day-to-day interaction with others in a close-knit church group, extended family, or rural community. We can't call back yesteryear, but we can reflect on the means by which those who were our Smokies forebears made and preserved their daily bread. To do so, at least for those who realize the past holds deeply meaningful messages for the present and future, is to wander through a lost world that had great allure.

CHAPTER 15

DRYING AND DRIED FOODS

By the time of the central years of my adolescence in the 1950s, preserving foodstuffs through drying was in steady decline. Virtually all homes had electricity, and as soon as folks could afford one, a chest freezer, usually stationed on the back porch, became a must-have appliance. Freezing food required less work than canning, and some fruits and vegetables were tastier when frozen. Even before the widespread advent of freezers, canning had already sent drying into retreat. Nonetheless, despite the availability and usage of both methods of putting up food, drying continued to have its place.

If the kitchen and cannery areas of my grandparents' home can be taken as a typical example, and given the fact they had lived close to the land ever since moving to Swain County in the second decade of the twentieth century with a passel of kids, I think that is a reasonable assumption, then drying still had an important role in mountain life. From early autumn well into the following summer there would be a number of hot pepper plants, laden with pods, hanging upside down from rafters in the cannery. Grandpa loved the flavor of hot pepper on soup beans, in soup, in pot likker, and even in a beverage he called pepper tea. He

Sarah Parton alongside leather britches (dried green beans), which were a staple of mountain food.

Courtesy of the National Park Service.

made it by parching drying pods of hot pepper, so filled with capsaicin that just touching one to my lips set them on fire, then crushing the pods before pouring hot water over the flakes. The resultant brew seemed to me something likely to make raw horseradish bland by comparison, but he would drink it (piping hot in temperature as well) and smack his lips with his ultimate compliment to food or drink: "My, that's fine."

Nearby would be long strings of leather britches—dried green beans that had been strung but not broken then pierced with strong sewing thread. After being thoroughly dried in the summer sun—they needed to be so dry they would crumble if you mashed a pod—they were stored where there was plenty of air flow and minimal humidity. The taste and even appearance of leather britches when cooked was dramatically different from green beans, so both made welcome appearances on the family menu without anyone thinking along the lines of "Oh no! Green beans again."

The primary focal points of dried food in my family, however, if you left out corn, were fruit and various types of shelling beans. Corn was a sort of special deal. It dried on its own on the stalk without much need for human intercession. All the work required, once it had dried, was to pull ears and put them in the crib for storage. It was easy enough to see whether the corn was suitably dry. Smokies folks didn't have any of the fancy devices to measure moisture content found on massive midwestern acreages of corn, but they knew that once the formerly upright ears turned toward the ground while still on the stalk, they were ready to be pulled. Sometimes, particularly if the husks were especially thick and tight that year (something deemed a harbinger of a hard winter), they were just left on the stalks in the field until needed. However, Grandpa considered that practice shoddy land management, and besides, he gathered a lot of the stalks for shocks, which provided a protective storage area for things like pumpkins, cabbage, and turnips. He would wait until afternoon on a bright, sunny day in the latter part of Indian summer, when the corn husks had had several hours to dry out, and then do the pulling. The corn, with the husks still intact, was stored in a well-ventilated crib protected from rain or snow.

In our family I only recall a lot of special attention, when it came to drying, being given to two types of fruit. Those were apples and peaches. Other families, however, dried plums to make leather and sometimes dried pears. Drying apples and peaches was a standard part of summer and fall harvesting work. As the ingredients for fried pies or the sauce between layers of that most representative of all Smokies desserts, stack cake, they were prized items.

Drying fruit was accomplished in one of two ways, at least within the bounds of my experience. Apples were peeled, cored, and sliced thin while peaches were peeled, pitted, and sliced. Sometimes, though infrequently, the still-moist fruit would then be sulfured (bleached and dried by burning a bit of powdered sulfur to smoke them in some type of enclosed container such as a barrel). Prepared this way, fruit could be stored for long periods without any real concern about it going bad. The sulfur dioxide fumes, in combination with removal of most of the moisture, took care of any bacteria that could have caused spoilage. The process turned the fruit quite white, and it would have to be thoroughly rinsed before use. I always thought a bit of sulfur flavor lingered as well and much preferred fruit dried in the standard fashion.

Straightforward drying, in our family at least, was far more common. The prepared fruit slices would be spread out atop a clean, worn-out bed sheet, cheesecloth, or similar material. Alternatively, they might be placed atop old window screens that had been carefully scrubbed. The screens had the advantage of allowing more air circulation. Then the fruit was placed where it got plenty of sun, or better still, in a sunny spot with reflected heat as well. A tin roof was ideal, but most folks preferred doing the drying beneath a roof. It wasn't quite as quick as when the fruit was atop a tin roof right out in the sun, but with that approach you had to wait until the sun was out, keep close watch for threatening rain, and get the drying fruit in daily before the first hint of evening dew.

Once the fruit was deemed sufficiently dry, which basically meant reaching a tough, leathery texture not too far removed from being brittle, it would be stored in a homemade muslin pouch, section of cheesecloth tied into a bag, or something similar. Grandma liked to keep her dried apples in the kitchen, ready at hand and close to the stove. That kept any threat of damaging moisture at bay, and I suspect her practice dated back to days when she cooked over an open fire or on a wood-burning stove. The heat from either approach would have been ideal for keeping the dried fruit well protected.

When it came to beans and peas, seemingly endless varieties were grown by mountain folks, but in the final analysis, those that made it to the drying stage all received pretty much same treatment. There were October beans, perhaps the best known of them all; black-eyed peas; crowder peas; lima beans; butterbeans; speckled butterbeans; navy beans; gizzard beans; Indian beans; and goodness knows how many more types of legumes. With rare exceptions, beans and peas cultivated for use when dry were climbers. That was because those that climbed enjoyed obvious advantages over bunch beans or even half-runners. Once established with the accompanying planting of corn, they required no further attention until harvesttime. They climbed the stalks of Hickory King or a similar field corn as it reached heavenward (ten to fourteen feet in fertile ground during a good growing season), and come harvesttime, afforded the additional benefit of requiring no stooping to pick the beans. Also, growing well off the ground meant less exposure to moisture in periods of rainy weather. Bunch beans or butterbeans, which were close to the ground, could rot during a summer wet spell. That didn't happen with climbers.

As the dried beans or peas were picked, the hulls went into a basket or possibly a sack, but whatever the exact nature of the picking container, the beans normally would be hulled not by hand but by being flailed. A tow sack was ideal for this. It could be tied to a limb of the proper height, a barn rafter, or some similar means of suspension. Then someone (in my case it always seemed to be a preteenage boy with lots of energy) could pound the sack with a stout hickory stick, a scrap piece of lumber, sawmill slab, or my favorite, a baseball bat. Once plenty of whacks had separated the beans from their hulls, they would be spread atop a sheet or other sizeable piece of cloth and winnowed using an autumn breeze. This took at least two people, and if it was a really large section of cloth or a lot of beans, four were better. The idea was to toss them into the air, time after time. Each toss or flip of the cloth saw more chaff and pieces of hull blown away until eventually you had mostly beans.

At that point it was time for the penultimate step in preparing the beans for storage until time to cook a batch. They would be placed in a large colander and shaken repeatedly to remove as much remaining foreign matter as possible. Imperfect beans spotted by watchful eyes would also be removed. The final step before beans went into a pot, and this might be weeks or months down the road when the dinner menu called for a big pot of soup beans cooked with a ham hock and partnered by a pone of cornbread, was to work through them by hand, known as "looking your beans," to remove any remaining bits of inedible material.

Meanwhile, the beans were stored in a dry place, usually but not always in the kitchen, in cheesecloth, maybe half-gallon jars with cloth tied across the top, or whatever receptacle happened to be available. The main thing was to keep mice and insects out of the beans. Sometimes a bit of a particularly pungent herb, tied in a sachet, would be placed with them to keep insects away. I don't ever recall any problems with moisture. It was just crucial that the beans be completely dry when stored.

October Beans

The October beans mentioned above are quite large and speckled with splotches of brown or red claylike color. They were the most popular of all the soup or dried beans grown in the Smokies. Used as a key ingredient in vegetable soup or by themselves, they are as tasty as they are hearty. Both Momma and Grandma Minnie prepared them in a simple way and often used them as a main course for winter meals. They would wash and drain the beans two or three times, then "look" them, before placing the beans in a large pot half full of water to soak overnight. When this was done, most any unwanted material that remained would float to the top, as would bad or worm-eaten beans. That detritus was easily removed with a handheld strainer. The following day would see the addition of water and generous chunks of streaked meat or a ham hock before putting the pot on the stove. The cooking process began by bringing the pot to a rolling boil before cutting the heat back to a slow simmer. The beans would cook this way for several hours, perhaps with the addition of a cup of water once or twice during the process.

The aroma from cooking beans would fill every room of the house with an almost irresistible odor. Often the beans, accompanied by a crusty pone of cornbread, possibly a few slices of fried streaked meat, and perhaps a bowl of turnip greens, would be our main meal for the day. Sometimes they would be prepared, after cooking, with molasses and bacon. Slow cooked in an oven until no longer soupy, this produced the mountain equivalent of baked beans.

Leather Britches

For those who don't recognize the term *leather britches*, first let me extend my sympathy regarding your lifelong trek down a trail of culinary impoverishment. Then, that gap in your gustatory pleasures being duly recognized, the good news is that the situation can be easily rectified.

In the mountains of yesteryear, especially in prefreezer days, about as much food was dried as was canned. In the vegetable realm, among items that had to be artificially dried (unlike corn and certain types of beans and peas) green beans stood out. There were many types or varieties of green beans, seeds of which were carefully saved year after year. They included runner beans, half-runners, cutshorts, bush beans, creasy beans, and more. All were dried, along with being eaten fresh and canned. Properly done and then suitably stored, the result, leather britches, would last right through the winter. The process of drying was the essence of simplicity. In our family we just strung the beans (not taking the time to break them) and then threaded the result, one pod after another, on strong pieces of string or sewing thread. This was done with the aid of a heavy-duty sewing needle. You just ran the needle through the middle of a bean the way you would start out to sew a stitch, pushed the bean down the thread out of the way, and moved on to the next pod. Once you had a long stringer of beans, perhaps a couple hundred pods to a string, they were ready for drying in the fashion described above.

Once fully dried, leather britches were a cinch to store. You just hung them in some out of the way place, such as high up near the ceiling in the kitchen, to await use. When it came to cooking them, preparing a mess of leather britches was the essence of simplicity. They were placed in a big pot with plenty of water and a chunk or two of streaked meat for seasoning and set to simmering. Slow cooked in this fashion for a few hours they would reconstitute as they absorbed moisture while becoming tender and tasty in the process. All that was required was the occasional check to be sure there was plenty of water in the pot (they soaked up an amazing amount of it) and seasoning to taste at the end. Salt and a bit of black or red pepper did the trick, and alongside a fine pone of cornbread they were a dish to stick to the ribs. I can't describe the taste other than to say it is distinctively different from fresh green beans. Try it and you'll find this old-time mountain dish a pure delight, and I for one like harkening back to the food customs of my forebears.

Bean, Ham, and Vegetable Soup

½ pound dried beans

1 cup chopped, cooked ham, or a ham bone
with considerable meat on it

1 cup frozen green peas

2 carrots, chopped

2 potatoes, peeled and chopped

1 small onion, chopped

Salt and black pepper

Soak dried beans in a large kettle for several hours or overnight and then cook until they are almost at the point of being tender enough to eat. Add ham, peas, carrots, potatoes, onion, and seasonings to taste to the beans, retaining the water in which they were soaked. Bring to a boil. Reduce heat and simmer covered for 1 hour or until beans and vegetables are tender. Add water if needed. With a potato masher, mash the vegetables right in the kettle, and then simmer uncovered about 15 minutes for a thick, hearty soup.

Soup Beans and Ham Hock

"Soup beans" always meant either pinto or navy beans in my family, but this simple recipe will work with any kind of dried beans. In fact, my personal favorite is October beans. No matter what kind of dried bean you start with, whether store-bought or homegrown, it is highly advisable to rinse them thoroughly in a colander as your first step. Any grit or dirt left from the harvesting process should be washed away, and rest assured that even packages of beans from a store will contain foreign matter. Then "look" your beans one final time and remove any that appear suspect. The next step is to put the beans in a large stew pot or soup pot and cover with water.

Soaking can go in one of two directions. I usually cover the beans with a couple or three inches of water above the beans and let them soak overnight. They will soak up most if not all the water and you'll likely need to add more when you are ready to cook. Alternatively, you can bring the dry beans to a rolling boil and then back off, letting the beans set for twenty to thirty minutes.

Either way, once you are ready to cook, add a ham hock (or a soup bone if you are lucky enough to have one left from a ham), and bring the pot to a boil before turning the heat back to a slow simmer. I like to add black pepper and a bit of red pepper at this point, although I hold off on any salt until the beans are tender and ready to serve. That's because the ham or ham hock will have considerable salt, and there's nothing more distressing than getting a big pot of soup beans too salty. Cook until thoroughly done and tender, adding water if needed, but avoid overcooking and having the beans turn to mush. Serve with a big pone of cornbread and a fruit salad and you are every bit as well off as folks eating fancy fixings in restaurants where maître d's flutter around like butterflies hovering over a bed of zinnias.

Crowder Pea, Spinach, and Ham Soup

I've always been a great one for experimenting in the kitchen, and many of my experiments involve situations where I've got a surplus of some garden truck or need to clean out the freezer a bit. I don't know that this is a recipe with deep-running roots, but I'm perfectly confident it follows the kind of pattern that shrewd "use what you've got" cooks would have used in the Smokies of long ago.

Cook a big pot of dried crowder peas, with a ham hock or a chunk of streaked meat, until they are tender. You can cook them in water, but I find using chicken broth or putting a tablespoon of chicken base in the water preferable. When the peas are just done (cooked through but still quite firm), add water as needed and dump a bunch of fresh spinach (kale, chard, or turnip greens will work just as well) in the pot and simmer until done and the flavors blend nicely. Add some red pepper flakes if you like a bit of heat in such dishes, and serve with a big chunk of cornbread. You can turn this from a soup to a stew by using less water, but the broth from the cooking peas will give it plenty of richness even if you add a considerable amount of water.

Black-Eyed Pea Soup

While most of the recipes found in these pages come from the paternal side of my family, this one's origin is a bit uncertain. I found it while
combing through thousands of recipes my wife accumulated over her
many years of devotion to the culinary arts. Usually she gave an attribu-
tion of origin, and scores if not hundreds of the three-by-five cards filling
her boxes mention my family. That is not the case here. It is possible,
of course, given Ann's ever strong eagerness to experiment and special
love for soup, that it is original with her. At any rate, the soup's central
ingredient is a familiar dried legume, one that could easily be replaced by
crowder peas or October beans.

2 strips bacon, or a chunk of streaked meat

1 small onion, chopped fine

1 garlic clove, minced

1 cup cooked black-eyed peas

1 cup canned (or frozen) tomatoes

½ cup water

¼ teaspoon cumin

¼ teaspoon mustard

1 pod hot pepper, crumbled fine

⅛ teaspoon curry powder

⅛ teaspoon black pepper

Pinch of sugar

Fry bacon or streaked meat until crisp and drain on paper towels. Using
1 tablespoon of the drippings, sauté the onion and garlic until tender.
Add black-eyed peas, tomatoes, water, and seasonings. Bring to a full boil,
reduce heat, and simmer for 15 to 20 minutes. Sprinkle crumbled bacon
or streaked meat atop individual servings, and if desired, top with shreds
of sharp Cheddar cheese.

Dried Sweet Potatoes

Sweet potatoes can be a promising crop when dug at the proper time and dried. Unfortunately, autumn rains can ruin them, either because the ground is wet at the appropriate time to dig or as a result of the rains coming during the several days of the immediate postdigging period when sunshine is needed for curing). But there is an alternative. Dig the sweet potatoes in early fall and wash them thoroughly. Then cook in a large pot or outdoors in a big cast-iron kettle of the type used for tasks varying from making hominy to rendering lard, adding a bit of salt to the water. Bring the water to a boil and cook at a simmer for twenty to twenty-five minutes or until the skins slip easily (you can test with fork tines—the peeling will slide right off if the sweet potatoes are sufficiently done). Cool and then peel. Once cooled, slice lengthwise in fairly thick slices (about a quarter inch) and then dry in the sun (you can also use a dehydrator). Drying in trays, atop cheesecloth, or on clean screen wire atop a tin roof is ideal. They should dry until they are hard enough that a slice will break under pressure. The waxy type of sweet potato that has pale flesh rather than red—we always knew them as white sweet potatoes—do particularly well when prepared this way.

The dried slices can be reconstituted in water for sweet potato pies or a dish that was a regular menu item at King College (Bristol, Tennessee), where I attended undergraduate school. Overall the college fare was nothing to get excited about, and that's being charitable. But the woman who carried the title of dietitian (I doubt seriously if she had any formal training) could work wonders with sweet potatoes. I don't know exactly what she did, but her offering was the consistency of mashed Irish potatoes, sweetened with a bit of brown sugar, spiced with either cinnamon or allspice, and had some butter in the blend. Had there been a sufficient quantity—we ate family style, and with hearty adolescent appetites there were never leftovers unless it was some singularly unpalatable offering—I would have foundered myself.

Persimmon Leather

To my way of thinking, fruit leathers rank well toward the top of over-looked but worthy mountain food items. They can be eaten as a snack, reconstituted for use in sauces or desserts, and are easily prepared. For the hunter heading out for a long day, a ziplock bag filled with persimmon leather is at least as tasty as and far healthier than jerky. You really need a dehydrator for this, but once you own one, you'll soon wonder, "Why didn't I get this years ago?" My mother would have considered one a mir-acle right up there alongside a chest freezer.

Puree persimmon pulp in a blender (for taste variety you can mix two parts persimmon to one part pineapple). Spread thinly atop plastic wrap or waxed paper and oven dry at 135°F until leathery. Normal drying time is four to six hours. When the leather is ready, it will be shiny, nonsticky to the touch, and flexible. Allow it to cool, and then roll into cylinders and wrap with plastic wrap. When fully dry (don't overdo it and let the leather become brittle), persimmon leather will store in a dry place, preferably in a plastic container such as those designed to hold cereal or pasta, and keep for months.

Peach or Plum Leather

Follow the same basic process used to make persimmon leather. Clean and pit the fruit and mash in a colander or sieve to separate the pulp from the peelings. Once this is completed, dry the pureed fruit until it is leathery but not so dry it will break when you fold a piece. Store either in a dry place in containers or, if you have sufficient room, in a freezer. Leathers can be dried in the sun, but that's an iffy proposition what with insects (the fruit will draw yellow jackets like sourwood blossoms attract honeybees, not to mention being the ideal locale for a fruit fly farm), the need to watch the weather, and the slow nature of the overall process.

CHAPTER 16

SALTING AND CURING

The word curing (or *cure out,* as I have heard it used throughout my Smokies years) can be somewhat nebulous, although most often it applies to some approach to preserving pork. At one time it was also commonly applied to the drying process associated with burley tobacco, but with the ongoing disappearance of that crop, formerly an important source of cash money to many in the Smokies who had allotments, that usage is almost anachronistic.

In my family the curing of hams was a highly competitive, somewhat secretive, and immensely important process. Daddy, Uncle Hall, Uncle Frank, and Grandpa Joe all had their own approach to curing hams. I strongly suspect they differed very little, but you would have thought the quantity of the key ingredients (salt, brown or white sugar, black pepper, red pepper, and possibly saltpeter) was a matter of vital importance deserving of at least the same degree of protective secrecy surrounding the gold at Fort Knox or matters of national security.

Whatever the exact makeup of the cure, it could be used for hams, shoulders, or side meat. Given how salty the end product would be, and that is particularly the case with streaked meat but also held true for hams

Butchering a hog. Virtually every family in the Smokies raised hogs, fattened them in the early fall, and then had the annual "hog killing" once suitably chilly weather arrived. Pork was the staple meat in mountain diet.

Courtesy of the National Park Service.

and shoulders, it was surprising how little cure was needed. The basic process varied some, but not a great deal. It began by mixing the cure together prior to application to the meat. (If sugar was one of the ingredients, it was styled a sugar cure.) Then the meat would be covered with the dry cure, rubbing it in vigorously while being sure to cover the entire exposed surface. Daddy had a wooden tray he had made specifically for this purpose, and other than when in use, it was stored away from one fall until the next.

After the meat had been treated with the cure, it was loosely wrapped in brown paper and then in a bag made of muslin, heavy-duty cheesecloth, or a similar fabric. At that point the meat was hung, shank-end down in the case of hams and shoulders, in a cool, protected place for about a month and a half. Periodic checks were necessary to make sure flies did not gain access in an unseasonable spell of warm weather and "blow" the meat. Similarly, the storage place had to be sufficiently protected from the elements so there was no chance of rain intruding or temperatures dropping below freezing. If there was a floor beneath the hanging meat (as opposed to dirt), there needed to be some type of container to catch the moisture that dripped out during the curing process. Students of the Civil War's impact on the Southern home front may remember accounts of digging up dirt and mixing it with water to strain out salt. That would have come from places where pork had once been cured.

The curing of the meat was considered complete once all dripping stopped and the outer edge (or rind) of the meat had fully hardened. It was then hung, often in the same place where the curing had occurred, until ready for consumption. The cloth bag made a handy container, and a ham could be removed for the cutting off of a few slices, and then the rest of the meat could be placed back in its holder.

A standard sugar cure for a single ham would have include a pint of salt, four tablespoons of brown sugar, two tablespoons of black pepper, and one hot red pepper crumbled into fine bits. Sometimes a tiny amount of saltpeter was added, but given widespread though fallacious belief that the ingredient dramatically reduced libido, that was not usually the case.

One significant difference from home-cured meat, no matter what portion of the pig was involved, and the bacon, cooked butts, hams, and shoulders you buy in today's grocery stores was water. Store-bought meat is liberally infused with moisture, and if you have any doubt and the luxury of makings to use for comparison, just compare the shrinkage from slices of home-cured bacon with that from the grocery. Or look at the difference in the grease that cooks out. Brine water introduced with the use of needles is standard with commercial pork. An old-timer in the Smokies who took justifiable pride in his curing would have had a red-eyed hissy over such practices.

In our family the curing process ended and the meat considered ready when the meat ceased to drip, but that was by no means universal. A further step, incorporating hickory wood, a smokehouse, and the tedious work involved in a smoke cure marks the boundary line between cured ham and smoked ham. Smoked hams go through the salt or sugar cure and then continue with smoking. John Parris describes the process in a delightful little essay, "The Art of Smoking Hams," found in *Mountain Cooking*. It continues for months, in the heart of winter and on into early spring, but in his view, "There's nothing like a good hickory-smoked ham cured the mountain way."

CHAPTER 17

CANNING

During my boyhood, canning was our family's primary approach to preserving food. Our house included a basement, where Daddy had constructed rough shelves to hold canned goods, while the home of my paternal grandparents featured a separate cannery, where jar upon jar lined three walls. All sorts of vegetables, along with apples, were processed in quart jars, while pint ones contained jams, jellies, preserves, pickles, and butters. Some meat, primarily pork, was canned as well. I particularly recall cracklings and cooked sausage, both with rendered lard poured over them to fill the spaces around the meat, being put up ("putting up" was the standard terminology used to describe canning).

Momma had specific goals connected with her summertime canning, and looking back on those goals leaves a strong impression of just how much we relied on our garden and little apple orchard for sustenance. In terms of quantity and perhaps overall importance to diet, cooked apples led the way. As has already been noted, Momma's annual target was a whopping two hundred quarts of what we variously described as cooked apples, applesauce, or just fruit. Another target involved one hundred quarts of green beans. Although she probably had other specific

Missie Oakley making a batch of apple butter.
Courtesy of the National Park Service.

quantities in mind, those are the two goals I remember being mentioned on a regular basis. There would be lesser amounts of soup mix, tomatoes, crowder peas, pickles, relish, corn, chowchow, peaches, grape juice from our Concord vines, blackberries, cherries, and a variety of jams, jellies, and other sweets to decorate biscuits or go on sandwiches.

The latter, incidentally, were pretty much in their first generation in my family. I don't recall Grandma ever making sandwiches or indeed even having store-bought loaf bread in the house, although it may well have been present. If so, it took a distinct and distant back seat to biscuits and cornbread. Our sandwiches tended to be pretty basic—peanut butter and jelly, butter and brown sugar, or for something in the exotic range, banana and mayonnaise. Sandwiches were for the most part just fill-ins when Momma really had a lot of work needing her immediate attention or perhaps when our preserved food, whether canned or dried, was running low.

Those times when the stock in the rows of canned goods had been pretty well depleted (late winter and early spring) were when we were most likely to have beef. Momma would buy a rather small amount of hamburger, maybe three-quarters of a pound, and make hamburger gravy from it. With a lot of milk and flour, some grease, and relatively little meat, it could be stretched a long way when served atop cornbread or biscuits. It would be a meal's main dish for a family of five, and if one of the children had a friend over or someone spending the night, that simply translated to more flour and milk to stretch the gravy.

When we had surplus vegetables or fruit, no matter what they might be, the foodstuffs were put up in some fashion. Nothing went to waste. Momma derived a great deal of satisfaction from looking at bulging basement shelves in the fall. Once the last run of apples had been canned, followed by hog-killing time and jars filled with lard, cracklings, cooked sausage covered with rendered fat, and maybe a few quarts of backbones and ribs, you had a colorful tableau of months of work in raising, harvesting, and preserving food. The scene before her eyes, and it was one she viewed with justifiable pride, sent a silent but significant message: "We are ready for winter."

Things were quite similar at Grandma Minnie's, and in retrospect, I'm surprised at how much canning she did despite only she and Grandpa being there for three meals on a daily basis. Part of it no doubt involved habit. She had worked arduously all her life, and putting up food during the spring, summer, and fall had been an integral part of her lot through the decades. Also, even in her later years there would be grandchildren around with great frequency, and if others had capacities similar to mine, she needed to put up plenty of foodstuffs.

Not only did she work hard, hers was a hard existence and always had been. She could have sung words from the old spiritual "Nobody Knows the Trouble I've Seen" and been amply justified in doing so. Yet other than occasionally grousing along the lines of "a woman's work is never done" or strongly suggesting that it would be a good idea for Grandpa Joe and me to get out of the house and out of her way, she simply persevered in the only fashion she had ever known—work from first light until near bedtime.

Her life's tale of unremitting labor, poverty, and general hardship began with a childhood in which she was what amounted to an indentured servant. The census records for her early years simply describe her as "indentured." I suspect most folks living today, and it was certainly true in my case until I did some study in census records, have no idea that such a status, a rather short step removed from slavery, existed long after the Emancipation Proclamation. Yet it was a harsh reality in Grandma Minnie's early years.

A member of her extended family, Charles Price (she was born Minnie Price), has written quasi-fictional accounts of the childhoods of Grandma and her brother, who was likewise indentured. They grew up next to each other but not in the same household. The books describing their respective youths are *Hiwassee* and *Freedom's Altar*.

For Grandma, escape from indentured status, in the form of marriage, came at a fairly early age. Yet before the passage of too many years, she found herself, in at least one sense, again a victim of harsh circumstances and to a degree imprisoned by the straitjacket of life's sometimes cruel dictates. That came when a virulent attack of scarlet fever affected some aspects of the mental abilities of her husband (Grandpa Joe) when he was a young man still in his twenties. She endured a move by wagon over extremely rough and dangerous terrain (from Clay County to Swain County) in the midst of bitter winter weather, lost two of her nine children not long after the move, and found herself scraping along from year to year and from one house to the next while never really knowing what lay in store just months down the road.

Hers was, in short, always a life with more than a fair share of difficulty and opportunity aplenty for an attitude of despair. She was in no way unique in that regard. Grandma Minnie's lot may have been somewhat harder than most, but women of the Smokies in her generation, like their men, well understood the oft-used phrase "root hog, or die." To Grandma's credit, she accepted her fate in life, and other than certain aspects of her temperament, never showed much sign of depression or lack of willingness to deal with her circumstances. She made do with what she had, worked with a will, and that was that.

A significant part of making do involved canning, and for most of Grandma's adult life it was the primary means of preserving many kinds of food. As has been noted, she never owned a freezer, other than the tiny upper portion of her household refrigerator, and the heart of her years embraced the period, from around the turn of the century until the 1960s and 1970s, when canning in glass jars and using a pressure canner was at its peak not only in the Smokies but nationally.

Much the same was true of Momma, although she did eventually take considerable pride in owning freezers—first one of the chest types and in her later years a much handier upright appliance. Canning was a tedious, hot, arduous process, yet each year witnessed an ongoing ebb and flow of scores of pint and quart jars being added to or taken from shelves. By the welcome arrival of spring each year, their once bulging ranks would have been thinned, and most space in the cannery or basement would be occupied by empty jars. A few months later in October, at the point where the filled jars were at their most numerous, it would be obvious we were once again ready for the lean times of coming winter. It was a cycle, not only in our family but throughout the Smokies, which was as predictable and constant as the changing of the seasons. It was a way of life, a means of existence, and a necessity.

Canning was a key part of mountain life. Our rough basement
had shelves built against dirt walls, while Grandma Minnie had
a real cannery quite similar in nature to what is shown here.
Courtesy of Hunter Library, Western Carolina University.

CHAPTER 18

———

PICKLING

Pickling was important to Smokies settlers because it provided a means of preserving foodstuffs that did not necessarily lend themselves to other means of keeping, and the practice continued long after other means of preservation had become commonplace. Of course, the mere thought of drying cucumbers or cabbage is laughable, and even in the case of foodstuffs that could be put up in other ways, pickling meant a different taste. Moreover, a key ingredient of the pickling process, vinegar, was readily available. A portion of a fine crop of apples could be made into cider vinegar with minimal trouble. All else needed for most pickling recipes was salt or sugar and maybe some spices. Some indication of the prevalence of pickling and just how variegated it could be is given by Cleo Hicks Williams in her interesting book *Gratitude for Shoes: Growing Up Poor in the Smokies*: "I reckin you can pickle just about anything. We had pickled corn, beans, beets, okry, green tomaters, and cucumbers. They even pickled the cabbage stalks. Sometimes they used salt brine, and sometimes a vinegar and sugar mixture. They made kraut and chow-chow in churn jars. . . . The big barrels and churn jars full of pickles was kept out in the spring house."

Pickled Peaches

During the summer months, Grandma Minnie always had a jar of pickled peaches in her refrigerator. I loved to come into the house after Grandpa and I had been involved in some sort of "doings"—and they might range from hard, honest work such as hoeing out the corn to something like knocking down a wasp nest so we could get some prime fishing bait—and eat one of those peaches. They had been peeled whole and then put up in a pickling mixture that ranged distinctly in the direction of sweetness. There were always a few cloves hanging around the bottom of the jar, and the tangy sweet taste, with more than a hint of vinegar in the background, seemed to me especially refreshing. Some family members didn't care for the pickled peaches, but Grandpa, who had an appetite for pretty much everything, loved them as much as I did.

4 cups sugar

1 cup white apple vinegar

1 cup water

2 tablespoons whole cloves

4 to 5 pounds Indian peaches (what mountain folks called clingstones), blanched and peeled

Several cinnamon sticks

Combine the sugar, vinegar, and water in a sizeable pot and bring to a full boil for 5 minutes. Press a clove into each peach and place in syrup. Boil for an additional 20 minutes. Spoon cooked peaches into sterile jars and top with liquid to within ½ inch of the rim. Place a cinnamon stick and a couple of loose whole cloves in each jar. Use a towel or kitchen paper towel to wipe the jar rims clean and close with lids and rings. Process in a hot water bath to seal.

Watermelon Rind Pickles

Another snack treat regularly present at Grandma's was watermelon rind pickles. While most recipes call for cutting away the outer peeling and removing any red flesh next to the rind, Grandma Minnie left the rind intact as well as a bit of the melon next to the rind. It made for a more colorful end result.

BRINE

4 tablespoons salt

1 quart water

Watermelon rinds

PICKLE SYRUP

8 cups sugar

4 cups vinegar

8 teaspoons whole cloves

12 cinnamon sticks

Pinch of mustard seed (optional)

Dissolve salt in water. Cut the watermelon rinds into 1-inch cubes and allow to soak in the brine overnight. The next morning drain off the liquid, add fresh water, and cook the rinds until tender.

Then prepare the pickle syrup. Combine all syrup ingredients and boil the mixture before allowing to sit for 15 minutes. Add drained watermelon rind and cook until the cubes become somewhat transparent. Process in sterilized jars. Properly done, this sweet pickle will be crunchy, tasty, and appealing to the eye.

Chowchow

A relish that belongs to a bowl of October beans the way redeye gravy partners cured ham, chowchow sometimes goes by the name of picca-lilli (although I've seldom heard that usage in mountain talk). It offered mountain folks a way of preserving a wide variety of vegetables through what was, in essence, a pickling process. Other than common denominators of cabbage and vinegar, the variations on chowchow contents are almost endless. Here's a recipe as true to Grandma Minnie's method as my memory allows.

> **2 heads cabbage, diced fairly fine**
>
> **6 large green tomatoes, diced**
>
> **4 tablespoons pickling salt**
>
> **4 pods dried red pepper, crushed**
>
> **1 cup water**

Place the vegetables in a large stoneware crock and then add the other ingredients. Mix thoroughly and pack tightly, being sure the liquid (brine) rises over the top. Cover with cheesecloth and let set in a warm room until the chowchow "works." "Working" is basically a process of fermentation, and bubbles atop the mixture will tell when it has reached that stage. Store in pint or quart jars.

Kraut

Cabbage forms a central ingredient in all chowchow recipes, but it is *the* key one in another Smokies standby, kraut. As the name readily suggests to those familiar with the language, sauerkraut is German in origin. That sets it apart from the vast majority of regional dishes, which almost always came from the Scots-Irish or American Indians, but it is also a reminder that folks of German descent were an important part of the process of migration that saw movement southwestward down the spine of the Appalachians into the Smokies. Of course, it is, nomenclature aside, nothing more or less than pickled cabbage.

The standard approach to making kraut involved plenty of cabbage, a vegetable that does especially well in the Smokies; apple vinegar; and large stoneware crocks or churns. Other ingredients would include pickling salt and possibly a pick-me-up in the form of hot pepper. Grandma made kraut, but as was true of most of her cooking and preserving, measurements had no part in her approach. She simply used whatever amount of cabbage she wanted or had available, along with a few dried pods of cayenne pepper, and went from there.

She began by chopping the cabbage quite fine, and all of the head, including the interior part of the stalk (the core), was used. She then added salt and a bit (not a lot) of apple vinegar and stirred this into the cabbage. Next came the "canning" process, although all she did was put the cabbage-salt-vinegar mix in quart jars. She packed the cabbage into the jars very tightly, using a homemade wooden device Grandpa had probably whittled out at some point to press it in (she called the tool a "pusher," which ordinarily saw duty as she ran various things through a colander). She finished by using a heated rubber sealing ring and a screw-on zinc lid. The lids would not be fully tightened. The jars, which were filled to within about an inch of the top, would then be stored in the cool, dark recesses of what she called the cannery. This was a building built of cement blocks and nested in the shade of overhanging trees and situated a few steps from the back porch. There she would let the kraut "work" (ferment) for a couple of weeks and then wipe the jars clean, tighten the lids as much as she possibly could, and store the quarts alongside other foodstuffs decorating her shelves.

Before she turned to this process, which produced smaller quantities better suited to her needs, she had made huge runs, which were stored in earthenware crocks in the springhouse or a cool place. The process of preparing the cabbage was the same, but the manner of closing the containers differed quite a bit. Once the cabbage mixture had been packed and tamped into a crock, a few large leaves from the outside of a cabbage head would be used to cover it. That would be topped by cheesecloth, a piece of wood cut to size, and the whole thing weighted down with a rock, old flat iron, or something similar. When a mess of kraut was needed for the supper table, the covering was removed, the necessary amount taken out, and then the protection put back in place.

Pickled Okra

Most of the okra we grew either found its way to the family table in expeditious fashion as fried okra or else went into soup mix. I don't ever recall Momma using it for a dish I later came to love, Stewed Tomatoes and Okra (see page 85), nor did she prepare pickled okra. On the other hand, Grandma, who did a great deal more pickling in general, annually made at least a couple of runs of okra pickles. There would always be pickled pods on a relish tray alongside pickled cucumbers and beets at large gatherings of the extended family, and Grandpa, who in truth found pretty much everything toothsome, was powerful partial to pickled okra that had appreciable bite thanks to the use of several hot red peppers in its preparation.

4 pounds okra pods

4 to 8 pods hot red pepper (8 pods means a fiery pickle)

Garlic cloves, 1 for each jar

½ cup pickling salt

**1 cup apple cider or white vinegar
(for color emphasis white is best)**

1 cup water

Thoroughly wash the okra pods and cut the stem away quite close at the base. Pack the whole pods, stem end down, into hot, sterilized pint jars. Add pepper and garlic cloves to each jar. Dissolve salt in vinegar and water and bring to a boil. Pour brine in each jar until full and seal at once. *Makes at least 6 pint jars of pickles*

Pickled Beans

When it came to pickling, cucumbers, beets, okra, and corn received more attention in most households than green beans. Most of the time beans to be pickled would be strung and broken just as if they were to be cooked fresh from the garden with a slab of streaked meat, but whole beans stacked vertically in a jar when pickled made an eye-catcher on the shelf, at a community gathering or church picnic, or perhaps for an entry at a county fair or the Cherokee Indian Fair.

Peck or half bushel fresh-picked green beans

¾ cup salt per gallon of green beans

Corn shucks, outer leaves from cabbage, or grape leaves

Clean, string, and break beans (or leave whole if you want to take that route). In a large stew pot, cook beans with water until the beans are beginning to soften. Drain and rinse in cold water, draining three or four times until the beans are cool. Add salt, being sure to mix it thoroughly with the beans, and place in a large stoneware crock. Cover with leaves or shucks that have been carefully washed. Top with a plate and weigh it down with a brick, old hand iron, or a rock. Cover the top of the crock with cheesecloth and tie the cloth down tight. Allow the beans and brine to work for a week, and then remove beans from the crock, reserving brine. Rinse beans once, quickly, in cold water, and then bring the beans to a boil in a large pot. Place them in sterilized quart jars straight from a hot water bath, and then cover with enough of the reserved brine to reach the top of the beans before sealing. *A peck should produce 6 quarts and a half bushel 12.*

Bread-and-Butter Pickles

Bread-and-butter pickles were probably the most popular of the many types of pickled items put up during my childhood. They were relatively easy to prepare, had multiple uses as a condiment, in egg and other salads, or as a stand-alone item. They offered the versatility their name suggests.

8 cups slices of small- to medium-sized cucumbers, unpeeled

4 cups sliced onion

¼ cup salt (regular or pickling)

2 cups sugar

2 cups apple cider vinegar

2 tablespoons pickling spices

2 teaspoons turmeric

½ teaspoon celery seed

Place the sliced cucumbers and onions in a large container (do not use aluminum) and sprinkle the salt atop them. Stir and allow to stand for 10 to 12 hours (or overnight), stirring a few times. Drain cucumbers and onions, pour the sugar and vinegar, along with the remaining ingredients, over them, and allow to stand a few hours. Place in a heavy kettle or stew pot (again, avoid aluminum) and bring to a full boil. Reduce heat to a slow simmer and cook for 20 to 25 minutes. Pack in hot, sterilized jars and seal. *Makes 6 quart jars of pickles*
    NOTE: Quantities may be doubled.

Fourteen-Day Pickles

Grandma Minnie made fourteen-day pickles, but perhaps because of the time span involved, or more likely as a result of a woefully inadequate attention span, I never absorbed the details of how she went about the process. Fortunately, my good friend Tipper Pressley has a recipe she's graciously allowed me to share. It has a rich history, like so many recipes from the region, in that it was given to her by her mother-in-law, who in turn noted it traced back to her grandmother. In other words, we are talking about a recipe passed through at least four generations before it found its way to these pages. Tipper's thoughts on fourteen-day pickles go pretty well to the heart of matters: "Let's just say, in my opinion, they put the smack down on bread-and-butter pickles." Here's her recipe, step by step, and as I've previously noted, I can't resist adding she's a distant cousin. So this isn't going totally outside the family bounds that form the parameters of virtually the entirety of this book.

DAYS 1 TO 7—Wash 3 dozen cucumbers (do not peel). Place in a stoneware crock and cover with brine made with 1 pint of pickling salt and 1 gallon of cold water. Let stand for a week with a weighted plate or other device to keep the cucumbers submerged.

DAY 8—Pour off the brine, cover with boiling water, and let stand overnight.

DAY 9—Drain and cut the cucumbers into thin slices. Cover the sliced cucumbers with boiling water containing 2 tablespoons of alum and 2 tablespoons of prepared horseradish. Let stand overnight.

DAY 10—Drain, add boiling water to cover, and let stand overnight.

DAY 11—Drain well and prepare a syrup made of 3 pints of apple cider vinegar, 5 quarts of sugar, 6 cinnamon sticks tied in cheese-cloth or just added loose, 2 tablespoons of whole cloves, and 2 tablespoons of celery seed. Bring the syrup to a boil and pour over the pickles. Let stand overnight.

DAY 12—Drain syrup from pickles, bring it to a boil, and pour back over pickles. Let stand overnight.

Day 13—Repeat the process of day 12.

Day 14—Bring pickle mixture to a boil, then remove cinnamon sticks. Pack in sterilized hot pint jars and seal.

A group portrait just before a corn shucking. Such events were part work, part celebration, but many hands of extended family or a group of neighbors made for fast and enjoyable work.

Courtesy of Hunter Library, Western Carolina University.

PART IV

HOLIDAYS AND SPECIAL EVENTS

Who can assess all the merits of progress?
Have all changes been for the better?
I wonder about all this now
As I walk through the vast stillness
Of the woodland of my old homeplace,
Remembering the simple life there
And grateful that I'm still a mountaineer.

GLADYS TRENTHAM RUSSELL,
It Happened in the Smokies

Historically, Smokies folks treasured their solitude, and the old chestnut about neighbors being too close if you could see smoke from their chimney had some validity. Yet it would be a mistake to think the mountains held nothing but misanthropes or that people avoided each other to an inordinate degree. My father loved to talk about how he communicated with boys headed down Toms Branch on the way to the Deep Creek School while he and his brother were making their way down the steep lower portion of the Juney Whank Branch drainage on the opposite side of the main creek where their home was located. They would whoop or yodel, joying in the sounds ringing down the hollows and along the ridges while knowing that soon they would meet at the point where a bridge today crosses the main creek. Underlying that cherished memory from his Smokies childhood was a clear message—interaction with others was valued.

Indeed, far from idolizing isolation, almost all sorts of opportunities for a "gathering" or "frolic" were welcome. The one exception would have been a death and the ensuing funeral service and burial. Even then those who gathered for the somber event, while saddened, were pleased to see family and friends. No one in the Smokies had to be a rank stranger unless they specifically wanted to avoid the company of others.

The most common types of gatherings were Sunday church services, Wednesday night prayer meetings in more populous areas, and revivals. Either religious or family connections also provided the setting for homecomings, which like revivals, generally took place during the summer. More often than not, food was an integral part of these times when neighbors came together for worship. Even if there wasn't a communal meal or at least cookies and coffee, religious observances meant special culinary endeavor. In my own family Sunday dinner was, without exception, the fanciest meal of the week. It was chicken time, along with all the fixings.

Most events with indeterminate dates took place in the summer. Mild weather was conducive to holding them outdoors, something that could be of considerable importance with a sizeable number of people involved and indoor space often at a premium. The largest building in many rural communities would be the church or one-room school (often a single structure served both religious and educational purposes), and it was by no means ideal for a picnic. On the other hand, simple homemade tables or just some boards placed atop sawhorses and covered with cloths could be set up on the grounds with relative ease.

Another reason for holding observances during the summer linked to a crucial part of the festivities—the abundance of food. Late June, July, and the first part of August found mountain gardens at peak productivity. There was no finer time of year to celebrate the tried-and-true Smokies wisdom that "you ate what you grew and you grew what you ate." Seasonal plenty meant variety along with ample quantities. Cooks who, at certain seasons of the year, had to make do with a rather sparse range of options, could select from lots of fresh vegetables, along with melons and fruits, to prepare favorite dishes.

There might well be unusual or fancy foodstuffs, the sort of offerings prepared only a few times a year, at events such as homecomings, family reunions, and Decoration Day, but the basis of any such gathering was traditional staples—green beans, roasting ears or creamed corn, fried squash, sliced tomatoes, boiled potatoes and potato salad, deviled eggs, ham biscuits, fried chicken, an array of relishes and pickles, and a wide selection of desserts so toothsome as to make a grown man turn visibly emotional.

Then there were the myriad of work-related gatherings where many hands were not only needed but lightened the effort through camaraderie. Among these were barn raisings, corn shuckings (also known as shucking bees), corn pullings, corn shellings, hog killing, Decoration Day, molasses making, quilting bees, gatherings to help a family whose home had burned, and indeed any project requiring a considerable number of laborers.

Purely social occasions had their place as well. They included weddings and housewarmings, dances, turkey and beef shoots, pie suppers, bake sales, candy pulls, music making, and the like. Music almost always had its place in community gatherings and those who played stringed instruments such as mandolins, fiddles, banjos, and guitars would bring them along almost as a matter of course. There would likely be someone who could play spoons and quite possibly a mouth harp (harmonica) as well. Food and musical frivolity went together like cornbread and pot likker.

Along with religious observances, work, and social gatherings, major holidays had a place of prominence. Some of these, such as Easter and Christmas, were religious in nature, while others, notably New Year's Day, Independence Day, and Thanksgiving, were secular. Again, as was true whenever there was a gathering of friends and family, or neighbors and church members, food came to the forefront. These occasions provided unrivalled opportunity for Smokies cooks to strut their stuff. While on the surface womenfolk may have seemed modest about their culinary skills, rest assured that they kept an eagle eye on how their dishes did at picnics or church suppers. Many of them became so well known for a particular item (especially desserts), that there would be quiet comments along the line of "I sure hope Aunt Emma brings her orange slice cake" or "Do you reckon old Granny Smith will have made a big batch of her chicken and dumplings?"

Expressions of appreciation such as "that stack cake was larruping fine" could buoy a mountain woman's spirits in rare fashion. Similarly, a picnic basket or box supper prepared by a single girl of courting age for some type of fundraiser was a source of keen interest and highly competitive bidding. The fierce jockeying could be the product of would-be suitors drawn by beauty rather than bounty, but foodstuffs from a renowned kitchen hand had at least as much appeal. Smokies cooks, no matter what their age, found stellar performances over a wood-burning stove or before an open hearth sources of quiet satisfaction and a reason for pride.

Special occasions sometimes provided fare seldom consumed at other times of the year. Fermented skimmings from molasses, for example, would be available only at syrup-making time in the fall, and there were always some fringe elements of a mountain community anxious to obtain this potent seasonal intoxicant. Beef, a scarce item on most mountain menus, would be sampled and savored with great gusto if someone slaughtered a steer. Even the milling for some flours, such as buckwheat and rye, might bring bread treats, which were especially welcome because they were seldom offered. In my own life I remember, with great fondness, the occasions when we had buckwheat pancakes.

If you want to plumb the most meaningful depths of the folkways associated with Smokies food, holidays and special events are the place to turn. For quantity and quality, they formed the culinary lodestone of life in the region. Small wonder that old-timers looking back on memorable moments of their early years so often reminisce about Christmas meals or the free-flowing joy associated with sumptuous repasts, when what could have been back-breaking work magically transitioned to pure celebration. Food not only sustained life, it provided sustenance for the soul.

CHAPTER 19

NEW YEAR'S FARE

Momma always was a great one, on the food front, for starting New Year's off right. We normally ate our main meal of the day at noon, but every January 1 that routine changed. We had our big meal at supper. The male members of the family always spent the heart of New Year's Day, from dawn until somewhere well into the afternoon, rabbit hunting with some friends and our pack of beagles. That gave Mom all day to prepare a traditional feast, and the menu was as consistent as it was tasty.

Her thoughts on a fitting meal to start the New Year were simple, straightforward, and unvarying. The menu had to include greens to promote economic success during the coming year, with the idea being that the cool-weather vegetables represented the color of money. Normally her pot of greens included a mixture of mustard and turnips, often with diced bits of turnip root included.

Of course, Momma's method of preparing greens, and for that matter about any other vegetable that readily comes to mind, would have left today's health food enthusiasts apoplectic. She invariably used chunks of streaked meat as seasoning. Sometimes it was fried first and then the grease and crisp meat added to the pot; on other occasions she just added

A young man with a pair of calves. Beef was not a significant item in Smokies diet, but milk and milk products were of vital importance.
Courtesy of Hunter Library, Western Carolina University.

a few slices of cured meat to the pot and set things asimmering. This process conducted a marvelous marriage ceremony between the greens (or whatever vegetable was in the pot) and streaked meat. The end result was delicious flavor, just the right degree of saltiness, and pure, lip-smacking pleasure.

Accompanied by a sizeable chunk of cornbread, at most times a big bowl of greens and perhaps a few slices of streaked meat fried to a crisp crunchiness more than sufficed for supper. At New Year's though, Momma never stopped with just greens and cornbread. She would also have a big bowl of either black-eyed peas or crowder peas. Like the greens, they were seasoned with streaked meat. Momma said the peas represented pennies and were a symbol of good fortune for the coming year.

The final dish in Mom's quartet of must-have edibles, joining the greens, cornbread, and black-eyed peas, was backbones and ribs we had put up at hog-killing time back before Thanksgiving. While most associate hog jowl with New Year's dining, she went "higher on the hog." Incidentally, don't go to the nearest grocery store asking for backbones and ribs. On two different occasions recently, at different establishments, I've inquired about the availability of this delicacy. In each instance I got a thousand-yard stare and a sense that the butchers thought I had lost my mind. They had no idea what I was talking about, but Momma fully understood the old adage "the closer to the bone the sweeter the meat," while Daddy, for his part, loved marrow sucked from the soft bones where ribs connected to the spine.

Quite possibly there would be other dishes for New Year's as well. More meals than not, from late fall until spring, we had cooked apples on the table. There would also likely be leftover desserts from Christmas feasting, and a personal favorite of mine was to take a hefty slice of her applesauce cake and lather it with a goodly helping of canned apples. That alleviated any possibility of the cake being a bit dry and made for a wonderful flavor combination.

While we ate, Momma and Daddy might reminisce a bit about New Year's traditions from the past, but mainly they expressed hope that coming months would bring good cheer, good fortune, good health, and a bright outlook for our clan. It formed a sensible approach to new beginnings, and as a youngster I could always count on one great blessing—awareness that the year ahead would unfold in the embrace of my beloved Smokies.

Mustard Greens and Turnips

Wash a big bait of greens fresh from the garden, being sure to give them multiple rinses to remove all dirt and grit. If they are overly large, it is best to remove the stems. Chop up two or three turnips in small pieces (diced is best). Place both in a large pot with plenty of water. Throw in a couple of slices of streaked meat and bring to a boil. Reduce to a simmer and allow to cook until greens and turnips are done. This will depend to some degree on how tender the uncooked greens are, and for newcomers to the dish, don't be alarmed when the foliage darkens appreciably while cooking. That's normal and actually an indication that things are reaching a point where the greens will be ready. It doesn't hurt to simmer quite a while for tougher greens, and they reheat wonderfully well. Add salt to taste. Serve piping hot. Be sure to save the cooking liquid. It makes for mighty fine eating when you dip a chunk of cornbread in it, or as Grandpa Joe used to do, pour it in a bowl and crumble cornbread over the rich, vitamin-filled juice. Both turnip and mustard greens can be cooked this way, but my personal preference is for the latter. Collards are the green of choice in South Carolina, where I now live, but you can have my part of them. No one I knew in the Smokies grew collards.

Backbones and Ribs

I have no idea what happens to the backbones of today's hogs when they go to the abattoir, but they don't show up in meat market displays. Ribs do, but only in forms such as baby back racks of ribs with no sign of the backbone they once adjoined. But there's a lot of meat tucked away in those crevices where ribs join the spine, not to mention between the ribs, and it is also worth noting that the stock from a pot of backbones and ribs comes in mighty handy when making dressing or for sopping with cornbread. In my family, there was only one way to prepare this particular cut of pork.

When cooked slowly and for a long time, not only did meat fall from the ribs but the bones became a delicacy in their own right. Marrow sucked or chewed from pork ribs is incredibly rich, full of minerals, and best of all, extraordinarily tasty. The joint where the ribs join the backbone becomes so tender after a spell of simmering that you can easily chew it, and from that point forward this simple son of the Smokies literally sucked the bones. Many years removed from my boyhood, while holding a postdoctoral fellowship in England, I discovered there was actually a dining utensil known as a marrow spoon. We didn't have such specifically dedicated, fancy-dancy tableware in the Smokies, but that certainly didn't mean that marrow went to waste.

In today's world, good luck on obtaining this particular cut, unless you butcher your own hogs or know someone who does. Cheaper cuts of bone-in pork, while not quite the same, have to suffice as a substitute. Cut away larger pieces of fat (there'll still be plenty when you start cooking) and place in a crock pot or slow cooker on medium heat. Add salt and allow to cook, covered, for hours. Other than maybe turning the pieces of meat once or twice and checking the level of the liquid, you don't need to do anything else. If you cook long enough, meat will fall off the bone and the actual bones will soften to the point you can gnaw them for marrow. Then you are in hillbilly heaven.

Crowder Peas

I've never known for sure the "proper" name for these members of the legume family. In my family we interchangeably dubbed them field peas, crowder peas, or clay peas. I've also heard them called zip peas, purple hulls, and shelly peas. They come in dozens of varieties but all share a couple of things in common—they produce prolifically and are delicious to eat. Today's annual freezer allotment is normally thirty quarts or so, with the standard approach being to blanch the shelled peas, put them in freezer bags, and finish the cooking when they are ready to be eaten. I've always been partial to cooking them with streaked meat, but if I wasn't vigilant, my health-conscious wife sometimes yielded to the dictates of weight and cholesterol and used bouillon. It's good but it ain't the same. If you happen to be a fan of chowchow as I am, top the cooked peas with it. Otherwise, just enjoy them with cornbread and the rest of your New Year's victuals.

The lower reaches of a 250- to 300-year-old sassafras
tree, said locally to probably be, at more than one
hundred feet tall, the world's largest tree of that species
in the Ohio River city of Owensboro, Kentucky.
Courtesy of the Library of Congress.

CHAPTER 20

───────────

SPRING TONICS

Other than a note on calendars indicating the date is the first day of spring, there's no national holiday or special observance connected with the arrival of greening-up time. But rest assured the coming of spring was both welcome and anxiously awaited in the Smokies. Finally another period of cabin fever had come and gone. Longer days and earth's reawakening put pep in an old man's step and lifted the spirits of the young. Mullygrubs and miseries magically vanished. Yet this welcome time of transition was never complete until everyone had been "dosed" or "doctored" with one or more spring tonics.

When it comes to that traditional mountain rite of spring from days gone by, it's tempting to claim, decades after the fact, that I was the victim of child abuse. If so though, child abuse was once near universal in my highland homeland. This particular spring tradition involved an annual "tonic," with the underlying premise being that after a long, hard winter everyone's plumbing needed a thorough cleansing—a sort of internal pick-me-up. The restorative came in numerous forms including sassafras tea, various types of wild greens, and the remedy that reigned supreme in my family, sulfur and molasses.

Every year during the early part of my boyhood, as frogs began to peep on warm afternoons; buds on maples swelled and showed red; and bluets, bloodroot, dogwood, and other early spring wildflowers burst into bloom, the subject of spring tonics entered adult conversation. Although my mother was a firm believer in cleansing the inner body, not to mention every crevice, cranny, and corner of the house, at that season, the leading voice in the call to action when it came to the administration of spring tonics was that of Grandma Minnie. As moderating weather brought the first hints of escaping winter's doldrums and the dreaded mullygrubs associated with cabin fever, she would become increasingly fixated on the subject. To a boy who found the whole process completely repugnant, it seemed like her pronouncement, "It's about time for everyone to take a spring tonic," entered the conversation every time I saw her.

At some juncture, Grandpa Joe would add his pithy commentary to the spring tonic groundswell, although as a rule he sagely did so out of earshot of Grandma Minnie. I didn't really mind his opining on the subject, since he staunchly maintained the finest of spring tonics came in either the form of sassafras tea or perhaps better still various wild vegetables—poke salad, dandelion and creasy greens, watercress, ramps, greenbriar tips, dock, lamb's quarters, fiddlehead ferns, and the like. "Eat a big bait of any of them spring greens," he reckoned, "and they will loosen you up and set you free." Many years later, long after he was gone, I became aware of the fact that most of the wild vegetables he mentioned are not only filled with vitamins but function as a mild purgative. Only then did I fully understand the situation and the full meaning of "set you free." I'm not sure Grandpa ever stopped to analyze the matter in detail. He just knew, thanks to traditions passed down to him, that the edible wild plants of the Smokies had salutary effects.

They also tasted good. Since I was quite fond of the various wild greens popular in the Smokies and regularly consumed by mountain folks and remain so until this day, I was all for spring tonics as Grandpa defined them, never mind aftershocks as predictable as preparation for a colonoscopy. Then too, although my preferences leaned toward vegetative tonics, plenty of honey and a bit of lemon juice made "sass" tea palatable.

Another reason for my partiality to Grandpa's thoughts on tonics was that the process of gathering the raw materials, whether it involved wandering around hedgerows and along field edges while grubbing sassafras sprouts or gathering poke and other green delicacies from nature's rich larder, suited me to a T. As I've already noted, gathering poke sallet brought me the first earned cash money of my boyhood, and a ritual of spring I cherished throughout my youth involved celebrating the opening of trout season with a backcountry feast of fried fish accompanied by a salad of branch lettuce and raw ramps. Activities of this sort gave me a feeling of importance and satisfied an inner drive connected with wild foods that has continued to motivate me in a powerful fashion throughout my adult years.

On the other hand, the female side of the family spring tonic equation troubled me to no end. It involved noxious nostrums sternly administered and carefully observed for proper aftereffects, and discussions leading up to the actual event were at least as troubling as the terrible taste. It was sort of like anticipating a visit to the dentist, knowing you had to see the school nurse for a vaccination, or being told by Momma, after some particularly egregious act of misbehavior, "I'm going to let you wait until your father gets home so he can give you a real whipping." Indeed, to my way of thinking everything Grandma and Momma had in mind when it came to spring tonics wasn't merely unpleasant, it was diabolical. While undeniably effective, the tonics smelled bad, tasted worse, and were administered under considerable mental duress.

I would have already had more than a fill of cod liver oil during winter, because throughout my early childhood you took a government-supplied capsule of it daily at school during the cold weather months whether you wanted to or not. Yet the foul taste of the fishy oil, never fully disguised by the gelatinous capsule containing it, was a mere child's play in comparison to the foulness of the key ingredient in Grandma's favorite spring tonic—powdered sulfur. Since I loved blackstrap molasses, a nectarlike gift from the culinary gods, the first time I was on the receiving end of a hefty two-tablespoon treatment of sulfur and molasses, I thought I was in for a treat. Talk about disillusionment. You simply can't employ enough sweetening to hide the noxious taste of a big dose of sulfur.

Once the first mixture of sulfur and molasses was in my mouth, realization immediately dawned I'd been hoodwinked, hornswoggled, bamboozled, and in general led down a fool's path by two determined females. From that point forward until I "outgrew" the dictates of wily female family members (for some reason administration of spring tonics ceased about the time I reached adolescence), I dreaded the annual administration of spring tonic worse than a shot, and as a kid I had a mortal fear of inoculations whether administered in the arm or posterior.

Although such was decidedly not the case in my family, there were always some who thought the ideal way to render spring tonics innocuous or even downright pleasant was to accompany them with a good slug of peartning juice. Not too long prior to his final arrest and subsequent suicide, I had the opportunity to discuss such matters with the late Popcorn Sutton. Popcorn was a genuine mountain character and lifelong producer, purveyor, and partaker of corn squeezings. His studied opinion was that "a body needs some properly made likker, along with a mess of trout and bait of ramps and branch lettuce, to get into spring in fitting fashion." I'm not about to defend his musings on medicinal approaches connected with changing seasons, but there's no denying his prescription is one that has long enjoyed a considerable following.

Bitter draughts and bootleg liquor aside, the story underlying spring tonics is one typifying the practicality of hardy mountain folks and the manner in which a close connection with the good earth formed an integral part of their lifestyle. In old days, especially before the advent of freezers or even widespread reliance on canning, mountain diet during winter months was long on starches (cornbread, biscuits, and potatoes), salted meat, and dried foods such as fruit and leather britches. Even the winter squashes and root crops lacked essential vitamins, especially vitamins C and K, along with fiber, calcium, and iron found in green-leafed vegetables. It was a time when a balanced diet was pretty much an impossibility.

Mountain folks didn't talk about eating a balanced diet, but they did discuss blood thinners, purging the body after winter, and come spring had an understandable craving for fresh victuals. That's why the first greens of spring were so prized, and they were indeed a tonic to the body as well as a dietary approach that uplifted the spirits. After all, how can anyone resist the beauty of a warm spring day, the loveliness of a world gradually turning green once more, and the appeal of mountains aglow with flowers as the good earth reawakens? To me, that's the ultimate spring tonic. To use the words former politician Zell Miller chose for the title of a fine book, these practices associated with ever-returning spring are *Purt Nigh Gone*. Yet to recall them is to relish, even revere, such traditions.

Sassafras Tea

1 cup small sassafras roots, thoroughly washed and
pounded with a meat hammer or similar tool until well
broken up and yielding their spicy scent

½ cinnamon stick

6 cups cold water

3 tablespoons honey

Put the crushed roots and cinnamon in a saucepan with the water and bring to a rolling boil. Decrease the heat and simmer for 15 minutes. Pour the tea through a fine strainer (cheesecloth topped by a coffee filter works just dandy), and then add the honey and stir it in. The beverage can be drunk hot or poured over crushed ice.

Sulfur and Molasses

I wouldn't prescribe a dose of sublimed sulfur and blackstrap molasses for my worst enemy, but for sake of completeness I'll share the method Grandma Minnie used to prepare the pernicious "remedy." She mixed a tablespoon of flowers of sulfur with two tablespoons of blackstrap molasses, thereby deterring the latter from its ordained mission as adornment for a cathead biscuit. Nothing would do until the entire tonic had gone "down the red lane."

Hazel Chosewood and a young boy with a hen and a pair of chicks. Most homesteads had a flock of chickens for eggs and the occasional special meal of yard bird.

Courtesy of Hunter Library, Western Carolina University.

CHAPTER 21

EASTER EATS

What I remember most about Easter, at least when it came to food, was the importance of eggs. For one thing, eggs were particularly plentiful at that time of year, especially if Grandpa Joe or some of his offspring who lived locally had bought a bunch of baby chicks from the local Farmers Federation rather than relying on setting hens for a new crop of peeps. The domestic layers that had made it through the winter without ending up in the oven, pushed by the powerful urges of procreation, had a distinct instinct for nesting somewhere other than in the perfectly comfortable, boxed nesting areas provided for them. It almost seemed as if they wanted an extra bit of privacy when it came setting time. Laying their daily egg and proudly cackling about that accomplishment was one thing; keeping a clutch of eggs warm while resting atop them for hours on end, day after day, was quite another proposition. Any self-respecting hen wanted some privacy for her spell of setting.

It took considerable vigilance to keep up with wandering springtime hens hell-bent on raising a brood of peeps, but for me, and I rather suspect the same was true for Grandpa Joe, the battle of wits between human and barnyard fowl was plain out fun. I loved wandering about his place looking for a nest, watching wary old hens trying to sneak off to some secret place, and I took real pride in finding a remote nest. Grandpa liked having plenty of eggs for eating available, and buying peepers meant that no hen had to be given a leave of absence from regular duties to raise a brood.

An abundance of eggs also kept Grandma in good spirits, something not always easily accomplished; it meant eggs to share with her children and grandchildren; and maybe allowed for a few extra to sell. An infusion of cash money, maybe a quarter or thirty cents for a dozen eggs, was always welcome. Having plenty of eggs available at Easter loomed particularly important, because our baskets didn't contain any of the pull-apart plastic eggs or foil-wrapped pieces of candy shaped like eggs that are commonplace today. We boiled eggs—lots of them—and dyed them in a wide variety of colors. In my mind's eye I still see the packets of Rit dye, together with an ingenious little wire device shaped to hold an egg while it was dipped in the coloring liquid. Momma, with youthful "help," which was in truth likely a considerable hindrance, might dye as many as three or four dozen eggs each Easter.

After all, there were multiple Easter egg hunts—school, church, and ones with friends—along with plenty of egg fighting to be done. Those joys lasted from Good Friday on into Saturday, but usually come the evening of the latter day it was time for our treasured eggs to make the transition from frivolity to functionality. In other words, they were destined to become egg salad or deviled eggs. The former might well be featured on supper sandwiches the day before Easter, and you could count on deviled eggs being offered on Sunday whether we ate as an immediate family unit or the more extended family got together.

Depending on when Easter fell in a given year, we might also have new peas on the menu, although usually in the mountains they didn't make until several weeks later. Ham was a given, maybe the last glorious hurrah of those smoked or cured back in November, and with it would go the obligatory redeye gravy and biscuits.

Egg Salad

Peel and chop a number of hard-boiled eggs finely (two per serving if you are planning on sandwiches or offering them as a main course for a light meal). Dice sweet or bread-and-butter pickles and add to the eggs. Add enough mayonnaise to allow the mix to blend nicely with a spoon or whisk (a teaspoon per egg is a rough approximation the amount needed), along with a bit of mustard if desired, and add salt and black pepper to taste, along with a sprinkling of paprika.

Deviled Eggs

Peel and cut hard-boiled eggs in half lengthwise and empty the yolk portion into a bowl, setting the white portion aside. Add mayonnaise, Dijon mustard, apple cider vinegar, and salt and pepper to the egg yolks and mix until creamy. Use a spoon to put the yolk mixture back into the egg halves and sprinkle paprika atop the result.

NOTE: Often eggs that were boiled a day or two earlier will have a dark tint to the outer edge of the yolk. This in no way affects the taste and will for the most part disappear when you mix the yolk and other ingredients together.

Redeye Gravy

You can start a heated debate on the proper way to prepare redeye gravy, probably the most renowned of all mountain gravies, although a solid case can be made for sawmill gravy, merely by mentioning the subject in a group of country ham aficionados. Some hold tenaciously to the view that without coffee as an ingredient it isn't true redeye gravy, while others are equally adamant that the intrusion of coffee is a taste-destroying abomination. My personal preferences lean distinctly toward the noncoffee persuasion, but I've never been known to turn down a biscuit anointed with coffee-based redeye gravy.

Fry slices of country ham in a large skillet, browning on both sides and being sure the fat around the edges cooks away sufficiently to produce plenty of hot grease drippings (placing another pan atop the ham as it fries will prevent curling). Remove the ham and set aside. Add water to drippings (a half cup for each two slices of ham), and bring to a sizzle. If you absolutely have to add coffee, do so at this point. Some spoon gravy over grits, others atop a slice of ham, and still others follow my preference and put a bit atop a halved biscuit. It's a thin gravy, but a biscuit soaked through with it makes breakfast something truly special.

NOTE: There are even arguments about the origin of *redeye*, although the most logical one is that a bowl with the gravy in it has an uncanny resemblance to the eyes of someone who consumed too much tanglefoot the night before.

CHAPTER 22

HOMECOMING,
FAMILY REUNIONS, DECORATION
DAY, AND OTHER GATHERINGS

In some cases homecomings and family reunions were synonymous, and that was especially true for those folks who had moved away from the Smokies. They left the bosom of the mountains for many reasons, with economic improvement topping the list. No matter where their search for a better life took them, the automobile factories of Detroit at the northern terminus of the "Hillbilly Highway," the mill towns of the lower piedmont regions of the Carolinas, or possibly military service, the mountains retained a firm hold on their souls. The mental impulse to "go back home" ran as a constant refrain in their minds, and a key aspect of that magnetic draw involved food. Comments such as "there's nothing like the way Momma used to cook," "what I'd give to sit down to the kind of dinner we used to have every day," or "I miss fried pies like you wouldn't believe" were commonplace. Folks cherished the foods they became accustomed to as youngsters, and when they visited home, being able to enjoy such fare figured prominently in what was always an emotional time.

In my experience and the region's lexicon, homecoming has most frequently been associated with churches. Homecomings offered opportunities to celebrate one's raising, a testament to enduring godliness,

The James Caldwell place in Cataloochee Valley. This panoramic view offers
an example of a prosperous mountain farm embracing good land.
Courtesy of the National Park Service.

recognition of the closely intertwined nature of faith and family, and maybe a chance to spruce up the graveyard on the hill beside or behind the little country place of worship. They were, as a rule, held in the summer. That was traditional vacation time. The weather lent itself to eating outdoors, side visits with family and old friends could be part of the occasion, and not infrequently there would be a weeklong tent revival associated with homecoming.

Such events seem most often connected with small rural churches. Today, much as it was a century ago, traversing country roads anywhere in the Smokies will find you passing numerous small churches. Usually there will be an adjacent cemetery as well, with maybe a half dozen to a dozen family names dominating the tombstones. Alongside the little church, perhaps in the form of a long, narrow, one-room building or possibly a "Sunday school wing" added to the original structure in an L shape, chances are you'll find a pavilion covered by a tin roof. Underneath will be permanent picnic tables or a place where sturdy wooden tables can be placed. Such are the backdrops for traditional mountain homecomings.

My firsthand experiences with that type of homecomings are limited to a special anniversary celebration at the Presbyterian church in Bryson City (this was a one-time event and to my knowledge that congregation has never had annual gatherings), along with gatherings dating from early childhood. For the first few years of my functional memory, every summer found my family traveling to nearby Clay County for a homecoming connected with Momma's family. I have three distinct memories of those events. The first involved what seemed to a small boy an interminably long church service, where the primary sources of interest for me were dirt daubers and wasps flying about in the rafters and the syncopated fluttering of fans wielded by elderly ladies seated in nearby pews. Still, those innocent distractions evidently kept my squirming to a manageable level, because I never underwent the humiliation of being carried unceremoniously from the church. Usually when other antsy youngsters were led out, sounds of the particular offender would soon be heard through open windows as parental retribution in the form of a solid spanking was meted out. Those distant lamentations had a noteworthy side benefit. They worked wonders in behavioral improvement on the part of other youngsters who had been twisting and squirming.

My second recollection is far more pleasant. It involves long rows of cloth-covered tables. They were loaded with an orderly assembly of food to feed the gathered multitudes. Separate tables would be devoted, in strict order, to pickles, relishes, and what highfalutin society might style hors d'oeuvres (probably not one in twenty of those in attendance would have recognized that verbiage, and if they did, it would be dismissed as "Frenchified"); fresh fruits and vegetables such as sliced cucumbers and tomatoes, the colorful appeal of slices of watermelon and cantaloupe, and possibly even an offering or two of store-bought stuff not found in the gardens of those in attendance; a panoply of cooked vegetables, with dishes using potatoes, squash, or green beans being predominant; the meat section with fried chicken taking pride of place but also offering country ham, beef stew, and chicken and dumplings; an impressive array of bread with cathead biscuits in the ascendant; and finally, a selection of enough cakes, cookies, cobblers, and pies to sate even the most insatiable sweet tooth.

If the previous paragraph hasn't made it abundantly obvious that culinary aspects of homecoming loom large in my mind, then I haven't gotten my point across. These were occasions where that wonderful word from mountain talk, *founder*, came into play in significant fashion. Although this greedy-gut youngster always seemed capable of stuffing himself to the gills, amazingly there were never any repercussions beyond possible hints of a tummy ache on the way home. Momma rightly had little sympathy with such maladies, and she also had a ready restorative. She'd remind me of previous warnings not to overeat (incidents involving green apples always came readily to mind) then offer rumblings to the effect that a good "dose of soda" or a big spoon of milk of magnesia might be just the ticket. Such verbiage had remarkable curative effects.

My final memory of those early gatherings involves a temporarily lost pair of shoes. After the preacher's long-winded reminder to everyone to get right with the Lord, and after I had partaken of the finest renditions of a regiment of superb mountain cooks, my sister and I adjourned to a little branch running nearby for a spot of play. I could no more resist the allure of flowing water than I could turn down a slice of Grandma Minnie's stack cake, and in no time at all shoes and socks had been shed, Sunday-go-to-meeting britches had been rolled up, and awading I went. Apparently when Momma discovered me splashing happily about, she was so irritated with the fact that I had managed to do a splendid job of dirtying my best clothes and so busy hunting a suitable switch (the instrument of corporal punishment that day was a long limb from a yellowbell growing alongside the little church), she didn't notice my lack of footwear. We were actually in the car and on the road home before that particular matter came to light. The repercussions for my nether regions (a repeat dose, no less) and my psyche were obviously severe enough to remain with me from that day forward. Fortunately, after a reversal of our route, with Daddy mad as a wet hornet, I found the shoes right where I had left them.

Ann Fox Casada serving fried turkey tenders.
Courtesy of the Casada family.

CHAPTER 23

THANKSGIVING

During my boyhood days, the Thanksgiving holiday was special in many ways. It was marked by family togetherness, concerted efforts to help those who were less fortunate, the opening week of rabbit and quail season, and something that was always of note for a schoolchild, a few days of freedom from the classroom. In my family a love of Thanksgiving and what it symbolizes still remains strong, and an integral part of the celebration involves looking back on traditional holiday dishes and high-country food folkways.

Come the season I always think of the glorious hallelujah chorus of a pack of beagles hot on the trail of a cottontail, and if you think a bunch of fine dogs that have spent plenty of time together don't give voice in harmonious fashion then I would simply offer the mountain metaphor: "You ain't been there." Another thread of my memory for this particular holiday wanders back to a quail hunt with my new father-in-law and the manner in which a fine pointer, bevies of birds, and at day's end a sumptuous meal of quail with all the fixings brought us much closer than we had been to that point.

Then there are recollections, haunting yet hallowed, of the manner in which Mom and Dad always saw to it that folks poorer than us had a feast. Mind you, it wasn't until I was grown and off at college that reality dawned regarding the fact that our own family circumstances were decidedly modest. Maybe that was because almost everyone we knew shared a similar lot. But a charitable conscience, of a genuine and personal sort completely unassociated with government intervention, was an integral and important part of the way Smokies residents lived in the 1940s and 1950s. Folks might disdain a government handout, but they understood and appreciated the concept of both giving and getting a hand up.

These and other Thanksgiving-related memories remain strong, but there's no question that pride of place belongs to warm reflections and recollections connected with food. Most high-country families, and certainly those with roots running deep in the Smokies soil, have substantial food traditions associated with the holiday. It was a day not only for giving thanks but for pausing to ponder while indulging in warm remembrance.

For me, it likewise remains a day when nostalgia reigns supreme. I can now look back to youth and early days of manhood and realize that my younger years were truly blessed ones. Some of my most cherished Thanksgiving memories focus on our celebratory family feast. They encompass not only actual menu items but the means by which they were procured, methods of preparation, and the manner in which they were identified with the holiday.

We normally ate just two meals on Thanksgiving—breakfast and the family feast in midafternoon. That was because it was the opening day of rabbit season and in our family chasing cottontails was a passion, an obsession, a fixation, and an addiction all rolled up together. No matter what the weather might offer, we were going to spend a good many hours afield listening to the incomparable music ringing and resonating down hollows and bouncing off ridges, of a pack of beagles hot on the cottontail trail. Such outings meant we needed an especially hearty breakfast to get us going.

If hog-killing time was in the recent past (it normally occurred a week to ten days before Thanksgiving), there might be fried fresh tenderloin for breakfast. If not, there would be bacon or sausage. Some type of pork, served along with cathead biscuits, sawmill or redeye gravy, eggs, and an impressive selection of sweeteners, including sourwood honey, molasses, jelly, jam, and Dixie Dew, offered fodder aplenty to start the day. If that spread of Lucullan-like dimensions somehow didn't suffice, you could always count on there being a big bunch of fried apple pies available. Taken as a whole, it made for a lavish and scrumptious breakfast.

Although store-bought turkey replaced chicken once my paternal grandparents had become too old and feeble to raise their own yard birds, for many years the centerpiece on the festive family holiday table was baked chicken. One chicken wouldn't suffice, thanks to an extended family of grandparents, aunts, uncles, and cousins assembling for a time of togetherness. Instead, there would be several chickens, guaranteeing not only plenty for everyone at Thanksgiving but the makings of soup, sandwiches, salad, or chicken and dumplings in the days to come.

Whether the hens came from Grandpa's chicken lot, live from the local Farmers Federation, or in later years, from the grocery store, once they were dressed and ready for kitchen use it was a matter of turning them over to Grandma and getting out of the way. The kitchen was her undisputed kingdom and she ruled with a sure hand that tolerated neither foolishness nor interference. Year after year she worked her kitchen wizardry with dressed birds, and the mere thought of getting into the middle of one of those baked hens, where miniature yolks of eggs in the making provided a special treat on Thanksgiving Day, still sets my gustatory juices aflowing.

Along with Thanksgiving's baked hens, there would be splendid arrays of vegetable side dishes, pickles, relishes, and other provender. Standard fare included Aunt Emma's ambrosia; brimming bowls of leather britches and October beans cooked with streaked meat; stewed greens with small bits of turnips blended in; creamed corn; casseroles featuring sweet potatoes, green beans, lima beans, and squash; mashed or scalloped potatoes; cranberry relish; a variety of pickles made from cucumbers, beets, watermelon rind, okra, and peaches; chowchow (for the leather britches and October beans); hominy; and more. Other than the baked chicken though, two dishes stand out in my mind as truly emblematic of a mountain Thanksgiving.

One was the dressing that served as the standard accompaniment for the chicken and giblet gravy. It was prepared with cornbread made from stone-ground meal, but the key to its distinctiveness involved incorporation of plenty of chopped chestnut meats. Alas, these weren't the American chestnuts my father and grandfather had known but instead mast from a Chinese chestnut that grew on our place. To me the sweet, starchy nuts tasted delicious, but Grandpa would often say, with about as much emotion as this hickory-tough old man ever displayed, "They are good but they just ain't the same."

A half century and more has come and gone since those halcyon days of youthful Thanksgivings, but I still gather Chinese chestnuts from my own trees and save them for dressing. For most it might seem a minor or even meaningless gesture, but to me it represents continuation of a deeply meaningful family tradition. Dressing featuring chestnut meats is a memory to cling to all my days.

The other item that had special appeal, then and now, was stack cake. It offered one example among many in which Grandma Minnie's kitchen skills came to the forefront. She always made her stack cakes using seven thin layers of cake interspersed with applesauce prepared from fruit she had dried in late summer or early fall or blackberry jam she had canned. The cake would be prepared three or four days in advance, left to cool in an unheated downstairs room, and by the time Thanksgiving rolled around, sauce between the layers had soaked into the cake to produce a marriage of indescribably delicious taste. No matter how much I ate before the family moved from the main meal to dessert, there was always room left for a hefty slice of stack cake. Partly for diplomatic reasons but mostly because in those days my innards seemed capable of expansion in a fashion reminiscent of a timber rattler consuming what seemed impossibly large prey, for good measure a smaller slice of Mom's pumpkin chiffon pie would rest alongside my stack cake.

All of the above-named dishes, amplified by orderly ranks of biscuits, hot cornbread, rolls, and maybe some type of sliced tea cake ready at hand on a sideboard, would be on glorious display come Thanksgiving Day. Year after year the womenfolk worked their collective wonders and brought everything together to a fragrant, delectable finish. The bounty atop the big old dining room table and laden sideboards at my paternal grandparents' home was a joy to behold. When the time was at hand and all was in readiness, the entire family would gather around the food, linking hands in a sense of thankfulness and togetherness.

Then in a voice so soft you had to strain to hear him, Grandpa Joe would bless the feast. He would allude to the harvest, express appreciation for health and another good crop year, and as has been previously noted, always conclude with encouraging words: "You'uns see what's before you. Eat hearty." On Thanksgiving, what was before us was a panoply of mountain culinary wonders.

Rest assured I adhered to Grandpa's closing suggestion with a degree of gustatory delight that must have been a source of amazement to my elders. Looking back though, it is not only the wonderful food memories of those simpler days and simpler ways of long-ago Novembers that warm my heart and fill me with thanksgiving. Joining the feasting was a time of togetherness and family closeness, along with appreciation for another year of sowing and reaping, that endures and still endears. I now know that this was but one aspect of a youth filled with treasure beyond measure.

Chestnut Dressing

Both my father and grandfather frequently spoke of the "good old days" when the American chestnut was the dominant tree in the Appalachians as well as a dominant force in their livelihood. Grandpa Joe cut chestnut timber for "acid wood," fence rails, shingles, and rough lumber for building barns and outhouses. Each autumn when the nuts were ripe and falling, the entire family would set out on all-day nutting expeditions. They collected bushels of them. Some were for family use—eaten raw, boiled, roasted at the open fireplace that served as the source of heat in their home high up in the hollow of Juney Whank Branch, and consumed in other ways. Much of the harvest, however, was sold for what Grandpa always called "cash money." They were destined for the stands of street vendors in big cities who sold piping hot chestnuts at intersections and other busy locations.

The meaty, nutritious nuts were also important for fattening hogs, and traditional killing and butchering time came shortly after what might have been called chestnut season. That found free-ranging pigs in prime condition from consumption of chestnuts, and often as a youngster I heard old-timers say: "You've never tasted fine pork until you've eaten meat from a chestnut-fattened hog."

By the time I was born, the dominant tree of the eastern forests was already long gone. Most of the trees in the Smokies of my boyhood died in the late 1920s and early 1930s, but the family kept up a long-established tradition by substituting Chinese chestnuts for the real thing in dressing. Here's the recipe used by Grandma Minnie and Mom and subsequently by my wife. Incidentally, if you don't have access to chestnuts just substitute pecans.

6 to 8 cups cornbread crumbs (Homemade cornbread is
infinitely preferable to using purchased crumbs, and that
is doubly so if you make it with stone-ground meal.
Using buttermilk to make the cornbread
makes it much lighter.)

¼ pound (1 stick) butter

1 cup cooked, chopped chestnuts

1 cup finely diced celery

1 cup finely chopped onion

2 eggs, well beaten

2 cups turkey or chicken broth or stock

Salt and black pepper

Sage (optional)

Montreal Chicken Seasoning

Preheat oven to 350°F. Pour cornbread crumbs into a large bowl and set aside. Place the butter in a skillet and add chestnuts, celery, and onion. Cook slowly over low heat for 10 minutes. Stir frequently, as it can easily burn. Add this to cornbread crumbs and mix well. Add eggs and turkey broth. Add more liquid if necessary, as the mixture must be very moist. Season to taste with salt, black pepper, sage (if you like it—I don't, and it is a dominant and dominating taste), Montreal Chicken Seasoning, or whatever you prefer. Bake for 40 to 45 minutes.

Giblet Gravy

While I thoroughly enjoy dressing with a slice of turkey or by itself, it really cries out for a lavish ladle of giblet gravy poured over it. I'll leave the gravy-making details to your individual tastes, but I do have a suggestion (at least for turkey hunters) that will make it meatier. The next time you kill a wild turkey, save not only the giblets (heart, liver, and gizzard) but all of the dark meat (legs, thighs, wings, and medallions on the back). Place the dark meat in a large stock pot and keep it simmering for at least a couple of hours. The meat will never get really tender, but it will reach a point where you can remove it from the bones. Do so, and keep the stock as well. Chopped into small pieces and frozen with the giblets (add them in the final half hour of simmering), you have the makings of giblet gravy richly laced with nutritious bits of wild turkey. Combine it with some of the stock you saved and the juices from your baked domestic turkey, and you can produce an abundance of gravy and have the good feeling associated with fully using your wild bird.

Smoky Mountain Stack Cake

This delicacy, so closely associated with festive occasions in the Smokies, has been mentioned repeatedly throughout these pages. That's easily explained, because as a dessert it looms that large in the region's culinary traditions. Here's the way Grandma Minnie prepared her stack cakes, although she "measured" by eye and a lifetime of experience rather than with specifics.

4 cups all-purpose flour

1 teaspoon salt

½ teaspoon baking soda

2 teaspoons baking powder

½ cup shortening

1 cup sugar

1 cup molasses

1 cup milk

3 eggs

Sauce from dried apples, peach butter,
or blackberry jam

Preheat oven to 350°F. Sift dry ingredients except sugar together, and cream in the shortening, then add and mix in sugar a little at a time. Add molasses and blend thoroughly. Then add milk and eggs, beating until smooth. Pour batter a ½-inch deep in greased 9-inch pans. The batter should be sufficient for 7 layers, which for Grandma was the magical number. Bake the thin layers (most ovens will require two "shifts" to do this) to golden brownness, using a toothpick to check that they are done.

After all the baked cake layers have been removed from the oven and cooled, add sauce made from dried apples between each layer and place stack cake in a closed container or the refrigerator. You can also use other fillers, such as peach butter made from dried peaches or blackberry jam, between the layers.

Pumpkin Chiffon Pie

This pie has long been a favorite in my family. Both my mother and Aunt Emma made it, although with slightly different approaches. No late season holiday at our home was complete without "punkin pie," and Mom always prepared at least three or four of them. They disappeared in no time. We used pumpkins grown in our garden, and the time involved in preparing them (cutting up, removing seeds, peeling, and then stewing) was taken for granted.

1 nine-inch pie crust

1 tablespoon gelatin

¼ cup cold water

1¼ cups pumpkin

½ cup milk

½ teaspoon salt, divided

½ teaspoon ground cinnamon

½ teaspoon freshly grated nutmeg

3 eggs, yolks and whites separated

½ cup sugar

Prepare and bake pie shell. Soak gelatin in water and set aside. In a saucepan, combine pumpkin, milk, ¼ teaspoon of the salt, cinnamon, nutmeg, and slightly beaten egg yolks. Cook and stir constantly over hot water using a double boiler until thick. Stir in the soaked gelatin until it is dissolved. Cool.

In a small bowl, whip egg whites and remaining ¼ teaspoon of the salt together until stiff. When the pumpkin mixture begins to set up, stir in sugar and fold in the whipped egg whites. Fill the baked pie shell and chill the pie for several hours. Serve with whipped cream (the real McCoy, if at all possible).

Traditional Pumpkin Pie

This traditional Thanksgiving dish was likewise a fixture with our family, and the fact that Momma would make both chiffon pies and this type, which is more of a standard one, probably says quite a bit about our abundance of cooking pumpkins and enjoyment of them in pies. We always had four or five choices of dessert, but this was one of my favorites. We grew our own cushaws as well, and the "meat" from those or that of candy roasters will work perfectly well in this recipe.

1 cup brown sugar

1 teaspoon ground ginger

1 teaspoon ground cinnamon

¼ teaspoon salt

1 cup stewed pumpkin

2 eggs, slightly beaten

2 cups milk

2 tablespoons butter, melted

Pie pastry

Preheat oven to 425°F. In a large bowl, add the sugar and seasonings to the pumpkin and mix well. Then add the eggs and the milk, and lastly stir in the melted butter. Line a pie plate with a pie pastry, and pour in mixture. Bake for 5 minutes. Then lower the heat to 350°F and bake until the filling is set. The pie should be allowed to cool prior to serving.

Mary Jane Metcalf milks the family cow while Willie Metcalf and
Arnold Thompson watch. Ownership of a milk cow or cows formed
a vital part of contributions to daily diet in the Smokies through
milk, buttermilk, clabber, butter, and sometimes cheese.

Courtesy of the National Park Service.

CHAPTER 24

CHRISTMAS

For most mountain folks in yesteryear, pork furnished the primary meat on family tables, and to an appreciable degree that held true at Christmas as well as other seasons. It was, to be sure, supplemented by game and fish in season. We ate chicken only on special occasions, but when time for Christmas feasting rolled around, just as had been the case at Thanksgiving, nothing but baked hen (actually, multiple hens) would do.

Baked hens from Grandpa's chicken lot, cooked to a lovely brown turn in Grandma's oven, were about as good as eating got. She would make gravy using the giblets, adding three or four boiled, chopped up eggs to the giblets. With a leg or thigh and either a whopping helping of dressing or a brace of cathead biscuits swimming in gravy, I was in pure paradise. The only thing that made it better was being given the privilege of digging into the picked-over carcass to get the little eggs in the making to be found inside. There was a whole line of miniature yolks of diminishing size in the body cavity. It's been even longer since I ate those eggs than it has been since I had a chunk of crackling cornbread fresh from an iron skillet and slathered with butter made in a hand churn. In other words, I've been suffering from serious culinary deprivation for a considerable period of time.

Those may seem strange Christmas recollections to some readers, but that was life as I knew it in boyhood. From an early age I understood the cycle of life in a practical, down-to-earth way that probably not one youngster in a thousand does today. Our Christmas food came from what we raised, cultivated, fed, harvested, preserved, or killed. I'm convinced it meant more to us as a result. I might also note that thanks to the kitchen magic of Grandma Minnie, Momma, and my aunts, it was incredibly delicious. Sure, there were memorable gifts, special moments of various kinds, the joys of caroling and gathering all the greenery and decorations for what was a truly natural Christmas, but looking back nothing enchants me in quite the same way food memories do. When someone mentions "comfort food" to me, I immediately think of foodstuffs connected with Yuletides of my youth.

Momma exhibited great delight with everything connected with the season. She had grown up poor and had a troubled childhood: as an infant, she lost her mother, then she was adopted in less than ideal circumstances, and then she led a peripatetic life, which gave her little chance to establish roots or be loved. She never said much about it, but I suspect that her Christmas experiences as a girl were less than memorable. Indeed, the fact she said so little about them is quite suggestive.

Maybe that explains why she was as excited as any child when Yuletide rolled around. Wide-eyed with excitement, she would shake packages, wonder aloud "Now what could that be?" and on Christmas Day mutter time and again, "I can't believe I'm so lucky. This has to be the best Christmas ever." She also took the family penchant for gag gifts in good stride, laughing heartily at pranks pulled on others—such as Daddy getting a pair of Mickey Mouse underwear or yours truly receiving a primitive fire starter rig from a nephew as a reminder of a time I went camping without any matches. But she was equally good natured when the joke was on her. My favorite moment in that regard was when she received a box full of dried beans with the accompanying description "Smoky Mountain Bubble Bath" from my brother and his family.

She took particular delight in all the cooking connected with Christmas, and her preparations were so extensive, they began with baking on the Saturday following Thanksgiving and continued pretty much unabated until Christmas Day. Then there would follow a week filled with leftovers before she got back into cooking in a big way for our celebratory meal on New Year's Day. Many of the recipes that follow are for desserts, possibly because the family sweet tooth received royal treatment at the Christmas season. But there was no other meal during the entire year, with the possible exception of Thanksgiving Day dinner, that compared when it came to abundance and variety of the dishes on offer Christmas Day.

Orange Slice Cake

I have no idea when the waxy, sugar-crystal-coated candy known as orange slices first came on the market, but it was available loose in jars (like peppermint sticks and a lot of other candy) from my earliest memories. At some point around 1950, someone in the family, quite possibly my aunt Emma, since I always associate this dessert specifically with her, obtained a recipe for a rich cake that incorporated orange slices into what was almost a fruit cake. Since it contained plenty of black walnuts, an ingredient almost sure to provide any dessert with a doctoral degree in deliciousness, it was a huge hit with me. This recipe is the one Mom used.

½ pound (2 sticks) butter, softened

2 cups sugar

6 small, 5 medium, or 4 large eggs

1 teaspoon baking soda

½ cup buttermilk

3 brimming cups all-purpose flour

1 pound dates or yellow raisins, chopped

1 pound candy orange slices, chopped

2 cups black walnut meats

1 can flaked coconut or the equivalent in freshly grated
coconut (the latter makes for a moister cake)

1 cup fresh orange juice

2 cups powdered sugar

Grease and flour a tube pan and set aside. Cream butter and sugar until smooth. Add eggs, one at a time, and beat well after each addition. Dissolve baking soda in buttermilk and add to creamed mixture. Place flour in large bowl and add dates, orange slices, and walnuts. Stir sufficiently to coat each piece.

Add flour mixture and coconut to creamed mixture. This makes a stiff dough that should be mixed with your hands (butter your hands or use rubberized cooks' gloves to avoid the batter sticking to your hands). Put in prepared tube pan and bake at 250°F for 2½ to 3 hours. Combine orange juice and powdered sugar and pour over hot cake as a topping and to make it moister. Allow to cool before serving.

Christmas Fudge

I don't recall Momma ever making fudge except at Christmas, although she may have done so. Also, I don't think Grandma Minnie ever made it, one of the relatively few desserts she didn't produce at holiday time. Yet someone almost always gave us nut-laden fudge at Christmas. If the nuts were English walnuts, the fudge was good; substitute black walnuts, as the recipe below does, and the treat moved several notches up on the taste scale.

½ pound (2 sticks) butter

1 (13-ounce) can evaporated milk

5 cups sugar

2 (12-ounce) packages semi-sweet chocolate morsels

1 (7-ounce) jar marshmallow cream

1 teaspoon vanilla

2 cups chopped black walnuts

Melt butter in a large saucepan and add milk. Stir to blend well, add sugar, stir constantly, and bring to a boil. Boil vigorously for 8 minutes, stirring constantly; remove from heat. Add chocolate morsels and beat until chocolate is melted. Add marshmallow cream and beat until well blended and melted. Add vanilla and chopped nuts; blend well. Pour into a buttered 12-by-7-by-2-inch pan. Cool at least 6 hours before cutting into squares and storing in air-tight containers.

TIP: Do not use any substitutes for the butter—you are already splurging when it comes to calories, and if you are going to slide into a moment of sinful gluttony, it might as well be done right.

Black Walnut Cake

Beulah Sudderth was wonderful neighbor, cherished friend, and sometime house aide to my parents in their later years. This was especially the case in the final decade of Daddy's life when Momma was gone. A key figure in the local African American community, Beulah was a woman of many parts, and anytime I could find an hour or two to sit down with her for conversation on matters such as gardening, cooking, or shared memories of some Black folks who had figured prominently in my boyhood, I always came away feeling better about the world in general. She was one of those rare people with that quality—just being around her lifted your spirits.

You won't find much about the contributions African Americans made to the culinary folklore of the Smokies. That's because the Black presence in the region was always a sparse one and had nothing like the impact it did in the lower-lying regions, especially historic plantations areas, of the South. Yet in the little microcosm of Smokies life in which my family moved and lived, that presence made a significant difference. That was largely because our home was situated squarely between two enclaves of African Americans, both of them small and together not numbering more than a hundred souls, in Swain County. They were our neighbors and we interacted with them in neighborly fashion.

I've already mentioned Aunt Mag's wonderful muskrat stew, and Beulah Sudderth made a black walnut cake Daddy declared was the finest dessert he had ever tasted. After he had been buying Beulah's black walnut cakes for years, I somehow learned what he was paying for them. It was a paltry price indeed, but to Daddy ten dollars for a cake seemed sky-high and definitely in the realms of luxury. When I noted that a comparable cake from a baker would probably cost at least four times that amount, he replied with all the sincerity of a man who had weathered the depths of the Great Depression as a young adult: "I couldn't eat a cake costing that much. It would sour my stomach." My siblings and I accepted that dictate and handled the matter on the sly from that point on—we just secretly paid Beulah a substantial additional amount. It was worth every penny we paid collectively and then some.

The recipe below isn't exactly the one she used. When she died, I had hoped to obtain her recipe from family members, but somehow it never happened. This recipe is close, but it isn't the same. Still, it makes a mighty fine cake, and the flavor of black walnuts was always, in my family, something to whet appetites for whatever treat might be involved.

¼ pound (1 stick) butter

2 cups brown sugar

3 egg yolks, beaten

2 cups all-purpose flour

3 teaspoons baking powder

½ teaspoon salt

⅔ cup milk

1 teaspoon vanilla

1 cup finely chopped black walnuts

3 egg whites, stiffly beaten

Preheat oven to 350°F. Cream butter; add sugar and beat until smooth. Add egg yolks and mix well. Combine flour, baking powder, and salt, and add to creamed mixture alternately with the milk. Add vanilla and walnuts and mix well. Fold in egg whites. Bake in a greased tube pan for 45 minutes or until done.

Butter Frosting

The Black Walnut Cake recipe tends a bit toward dryness, and if you wish, that can be resolved with a simple butter frosting. Here's one Momma made and used on various types of cakes.

¼ pound (1 stick) butter, melted

1 (16-ounce) box powdered sugar

Half-and-half or whole milk

¼ to ½ cup finely chopped black walnuts

Blend butter and powdered sugar. Add enough half-and-half to reach desired consistency. Fold in walnuts, and frost fully cooled cake.

Applesauce Cake

Momma always made her applesauce cakes for Christmas during the Thanksgiving holiday. The ensuing month or so would see them stored in a cool area (usually the unheated downstairs bedroom) and periodically anointed with a few tablespoons of apple cider or a dollop of wine to keep the cakes moist. This combination of aging and moisturizing produced a cake that was, by the time Christmas rolled around and it was sliced, soaked through and through with goodness. A newly cut slice glistened from moisture, and the taste was such it ranks, second only to a stack cake, as my all-time favorite dessert.

½ pound (2 sticks) butter, softened

2 cups sugar

3 cups applesauce

4 cups all-purpose flour

⅓ cup cocoa

4 teaspoons baking soda

1 teaspoon ground cinnamon

2 teaspoons ground allspice

2 cups raisins

2 cups black walnut meats

2 teaspoons vanilla

Pinch of salt

Preheat oven to 350°F. Cream butter and sugar. Add applesauce and remaining ingredients a small amount at a time. Bake for 50 minutes to 1 hour. Check with toothpick to see if cake is done (toothpick will come out dry).

Black Walnut Bars

Throughout the Christmas season there would be, in addition to cakes aplenty, various types of cookies at our house and that of my grandparents. Stored in round tins that had once held things like commercial fruitcakes (for years, at a time when he served as purchasing agent, Daddy got one or more at the plant where he worked every Christmas, and far be it from my frugal mother to let a perfectly good container go to waste), they were available for a quick snack most anytime. At this season of the year I don't even recall the normal strictures such as "you'll ruin your appetite." As was true of about anything containing black walnuts, I loved these bars.

CRUST

¼ pound (1 stick) butter, softened

½ cup packed brown sugar

1 cup all-purpose flour

FILLING

1 cup brown sugar

2 eggs, beaten

¼ teaspoon salt

1 teaspoon vanilla

2 teaspoons all-purpose flour

½ teaspoon baking powder

1½ cups shredded coconut

1 cup chopped black walnuts

Preheat oven to 350°F. Cream butter and brown sugar. Slowly add flour and mix until crumbly. Pat into a 7-by-11-inch baking dish. Bake for 8 to 10 minutes or until golden.

Combine brown sugar, eggs, salt, and vanilla. In separate bowl, add flour and baking powder to coconut and walnuts. Blend into brown sugar and egg mixture and pour over baked crust. Return to oven and bake for an additional 15 to 20 minutes or until done. Cut into bars and place on wire racks to cool.

Russian Tea

Momma always made a big batch, or maybe two or three of them, of this seasonal delight. It was served at family gatherings, to visitors who just happened to drop by, at church functions, and as a refreshing hot drink on a cold winter's day. Grandpa Joe loved the beverage, which he called "Rooshian" tea (and I guarantee he had no idea whatsoever of the geographical connection, or for that matter, that Russia was a country or where it might be situated in the wider world). He would take a lip-scorching hot cup, "sasser and blow" it to cool it down a bit, and then drink with ample evidence of having been transported into a realm of pure bliss.

½ teaspoon whole cloves

1 cup sugar

½ teaspoon ground cinnamon

1 gallon water

1 (16-ounce) can orange juice concentrate

4 tea bags

1 pint boiling water

¾ cup fresh lemon juice

1 tall can pineapple juice

1 quart apple cider (optional)

1½ cups fresh orange juice

In a large pot or Dutch oven, combine cloves, sugar, cinnamon, water, and juice concentrate, adding additional sugar if desired. Bring these ingredients to a boil, and continue boiling for 5 minutes. Meanwhile, steep tea bags in boiling water for 5 minutes. Add steeped tea to cloves mixture, then add lemon juice, pineapple juice, apple cider if desired, and orange juice. Serve hot. *Makes 20 generous helpings, and leftovers can be refrigerated and reheated as desired*

NOTE: The quantities of juice can be varied if you prefer one taste to another.

A GLOSSARY OF SMOKIES FOODSTUFFS AND TERMS

BACON Cured and sometimes smoked meat from the sides of a hog. Also known by a wide array of other names including streaked meat, streak o' lean, fatback, middling meat, and side meat. There are subtle locational differences regarding where the meat came from on a hog's body that an expert might want to argue about, but in essence these various cured cuts were long on fat with just some lean streaks.

BAIT An ample quantity; a synonym for mess, especially a large mess.

BEAN BREAD A Cherokee dish adopted by early residents in the Smokies that usually mixed hominy and beans. Also known as Indian bread.

BEAN STRINGING A social event centering around the preparation (stringing) of green beans to make leather britches.

BEECHNUTS Edible mast of the beech tree.

BIG HOMINY Whole grains of corn prepared as hominy.

BLACK-EYED PEAS A type of field pea distinguished by a black spot (the eye) in its middle.

BOOMER A small red squirrel that despite its diminutive size was sometimes used as table fare.

BOX SUPPER Also known as a poke supper, this was a social occasion fundraiser where prepared meals housed in a box or poke (paper bag) were auctioned off.

BRANCH LETTUCE Also known as bear lettuce or mountain lettuce, a member of the saxifrage family that grows along branches and creeks and was much prized as an early spring vegetable.

BUSHYTAIL A gray squirrel; prized as table fare and the most common table game on the Smokies during the first half of the twentieth century.

BUTTER (FRUIT BUTTER) Used to describe a sweet preparation, usually made with either sugar or molasses combined with various types of fruits, which was used as a spread for biscuits. Among the more common butters were those made from apples, peaches, pears, pumpkins, and candy roasters.

BUTTERNUT Also known as white walnut, a relative of the black walnut, oblong in shape and milder in flavor. Increasingly rare because of disease.

CAN HOUSE OR CANNERY An outside building, usually quite close to a home, where canned goods and possibly other foodstuffs were stored.

CATHEAD OR CATHEAD BISCUIT A large biscuit, presumably the size of a cat's head. It is likely that the description is actually a variation on a "canhead biscuit," since the mouth of a canning jar makes a fine ersatz biscuit cutter.

CHESTNUT BREAD A heavy bread of Cherokee origin made with a flour from chestnuts (sometimes mixed with beans).

CHICKENTOE An edible spring green sometimes known as spring beauty.

CHOWCHOW Sweet relish made from various vegetables and used atop dried beans.

CLAY PEAS A general term used to describe a wide variety of field peas including crowders, black-eyed peas, shelly peas, and others.

COON A raccoon. An animal favored both for hunting and as table fare.

COTTONTAIL A rabbit. Prized game that was always welcome on the table, cottontails were hunted with dogs and trapped using homemade gums.

CRACKLINGS The crisp tidbits left when pork fat is rendered for lard.

CROWDER PEAS *See* clay peas.

CROW'S FOOT An edible spring green also known as pepper root and tooth-wort.

CUSHAW A large winter squash with flesh and taste somewhat similar to that of pumpkins.

DIXIE DEW A store-bought corn syrup that enjoyed great popularity in the Smokies of the 1950s. Its label carried the epitome of advertising genius: "Covers Dixie like the dew and gives a biscuit a college education."

DODGERS Dumplings made from cornmeal dropped in boiling water. Sometimes also used to describe a fried cake of corn of individual serving size.

DOLLOP A modest or moderate amount.

FATBACK *See* bacon.

FIELD PEAS *See* clay peas.

FOUNDER A colloquial term often used in connection with livestock, it describes eating far too much, usually to the point of complete loss of appetite.

FRITTER A pancake, usually made from cornmeal and sometimes having fruit included in the batter.

GARDEN TRUCK Vegetables harvested from a garden.

GINSENG A highly valued plant sometimes used for medicinal purposes but mostly dug for sale to outside markets.

GOSPEL BIRD Chicken.

HEADCHEESE A pâté-like dish prepared with meat from the head and feet of hogs. Sometimes cornmeal was included. It congealed after preparation. More often known as souse or souse meat.

HOECAKE Literally, cornbread cooked on a hoe blade over ashes; more often, small cakes of cornbread.

HOLE UP Store food in the ground (or sometimes, beneath corn shocks) during cold weather.

HOMINY Grains of corn hulled with the use of lye or, sometimes, by boiling.

INDIAN BREAD *See* bean bread.

INDIAN PEACHES Generally any clingstone peach but often used in specific reference to a small type of clingstone with red flesh.

JOHNNYCAKE A cake of cornbread, often baked in a Dutch oven or sometimes atop a rock or board set at the edge of a hearth.

KILT SALAD A salad, mainly associated with spring, of greens and maybe other raw vegetables, such as ramps or onions, topped ("killed") with hot bacon grease.

LARRUPING Exceptionally tasty. "That blackberry cobbler was larruping good."

LEATHER A dried version of any of a number of fruits, notably peaches, persimmons, and pears.

LEATHER BRITCHES Dried green beans that are reconstituted by cooking in water, usually with streaked meat as seasoning.

LIGHT BREAD Bread made with wheat flour; usually refers to store-bought loaf bread.

LITTLE HOMINY Grits.

LOOK YOUR BEANS (OR OTHER FOODSTUFFS) "Looking" beans was precisely that, a careful inspection prior to cooking to make sure that no grit or foreign matter remained.

LYE HOMINY Another description for big hominy.

MAYPOPS Edible fruit of the passionflower; also known as wild apricots.

MERKLES A local name, a variant of miracles, for morel mushrooms.

METHELGIN An alcoholic beverage similar to mead and made with honey.

MIDDLING MEAT Also known as bacon, side meat, fatback, streak o' lean, and streaked meat. Salt-cured pork used extensively in seasoning vegetables.

MOLASSES The colloquial term invariably used in the Smokies to describe sorghum syrup.

MOLASSES BREAD Gingerbread.

MORELS The most easily identifiable of edible mushrooms. Also known as merkles, dry-land trout, and hickory chicken.

MUSH Boiled cornmeal.

OCTOBER BEANS A climbing bean planted in tandem with corn and harvested dry in the fall (hence the name). Also known as cornfield beans and by other names.

PARTRIDGE Colloquialism for ruffed grouse; also known locally as pheasant or mountain pheasant.

PAT A small section, usually from a stick of butter.

PAWPAW A wild fruit that grows on small trees and ripens in autumn. Its taste faintly resembles that of bananas. Sometimes called the mountain banana.

PEA HULLING OR SHELLING OR SHELLING BEE A social gathering where a number of folks would shell the season's crop of field peas while enjoying one another's company and conversation.

PICCALILLI *See* chowchow.

PIE PLANT Rhubarb.

PIE SUPPER Similar to a box supper. Pies would be auctioned off one at a time and the bidder had the privilege of eating some of the pie with the person who made it.

POKE A popular and widespread wild vegetable. The same word is used to describe a paper bag; hence, you could pick a poke of poke.

POLE BEANS Any type of climbing bean.

PONE Cornbread cooked in a round skillet and normally served in slices like a pie. Sometimes corn pone was used to describe a biscuit-sized piece of cornbread.

POSSUM A wild marsupial, the opossum, which was avidly hunted and sometimes eaten. However, because the animal readily and regularly consumes carrion, many Smokies folks would not consume it.

POTHERBS A catchall term used to describe wild greens gathered in the spring.

POT LIKKER Sometimes used to describe the liquid left from cooking various vegetables but also a specific reference to cooked cabbage and streaked meat dishes.

PREACHER MEAT Chicken, especially fried chicken.

PULLY BONE The Y-shaped bone in a chicken breast. After the meat was eaten it was often "pulled" (hence the name) until it broke. Whoever had the longer section got to make a silent wish.

PURSLANE A wild vegetable, also known as pigweed because hogs love to eat it, that regularly appears in gardens and cornfields.

PURT NIGH Pretty near or close to.

PUT UP OR PUT AWAY A catch-all description for preserving food for future use most often connected with canning.

RAMPS A wild leek of mild taste but, when eaten raw, powerful smell. Can be prepared in many ways.

RASH OR RASHER A large quantity usually applied to bacon but also used in nonculinary descriptions.

REDEYE GRAVY The grease left after frying country ham. Usually mixed with coffee or water to make the gravy.

ROASTING EAR PEAS *See* clay peas.

ROASTING EARS Corn in the milk stage and at its peak for being roasted in ashes or, once wood stoves replaced open hearths, cooked in boiling water.

SALLET Cooked vegetables (not a raw salad) such as poke, turnip or mustard greens, creasies, and the like.

SAMP Ground corn soaked in milk.

SASSAFRAS TEA Hot drink made from the roots and root bark of the sassafras plant. Once a popular spring tonic.

SAWMILL GRAVY OR SAWDUST GRAVY A hearty gravy made using cornmeal, lard (or grease from streaked meat), and milk or water. Common breakfast fare in logging camps, hence the name. In modern parlance, sawmill gravy is often used to describe a flour-based gravy with bits of meat in it.

SCRAPPLE Cornmeal cooked with pieces of pork, usually organ meats, and pressed into cakes or large patties that will "set" when cold. It was then sliced to serve, with the slices often being fried for use at breakfast.

SHELLY BEANS A generic term for any type of dried bean removed from its hull and stored in that state.

SHUCK BEANS Same as leather britches.

SIDE MEAT *See* bacon.

SLUMGULLION A stew of mixed ingredients, using whatever foodstuffs were available. Usually associated with hunting or fishing camps.

SMIDGEN A small amount.

SMOKEHOUSE An outbuilding used to store and smoke pork after it had been cured.

SNAP BEANS OR SNAPS Any type of green bean that snapped when broken prior to cooking.

SOAKY Biscuit soaked or dipped in coffee prior to being eaten.

SOCHAN A wild green favored by the Cherokees.

SONKER A deep-dish pie.

SOP To use a piece of bread to gather up pot likker or gravy.

SOPPY Any type of milk gravy.

SOUP BEANS A general term for any type of dried beans, although it was most often applied to pintos, navy, or October beans.

SOUSE MEAT *See* headcheese.

SPECK, NATIVE, OR MOUNTAIN TROUT A salmonid native to the Smokies found in high-elevation streams. Once plentiful, its original range has diminished appreciably, but the fish is still prized fare.

SPRINGHOUSE A structure erected over a spring or the outflow from a spring where meat, dairy products, and other perishables could be stored.

STACK CAKE A tall, round cake made of numerous layers (seven was a favorite number) with sauce made from fruit such as dried apples, peaches, or berry jam between each layer.

STIRABOUT A mixture of leftovers heated together. Similar to *slumgullion*.

STREAKED MEAT *See* bacon.

SUGAR OFF Pour hot maple syrup into snow to make it set. It was then eaten as candy.

SUMAC TEA Made from the berries of sumac and considered a refreshing drink because of its slightly acidic, lemonlike taste.

SWEET BREAD Bread made with molasses or other sweetening; also gingerbread.

SWEETENINGS Any item used to sweeten food, including sugar, molasses, honey, and maple syrup.

SWEET MILK Whole milk.

SYLLABUB A frothy alcoholic beverage featuring brandy and cream that was whipped until it bubbled.

TENDERLOIN Two small but delectable pieces of meat found on the underside of the spine of a hog (or deer); not to be confused (as is often the case) with backstrap, which runs along either side of the animal's spine at the top of the back.

TETCH Touch; a small amount, usually phrased as "just a tetch."

TOE IN *See* hole up.

TOMMYTOES Small tomatoes, almost always from volunteer plants, which have an especially piquant taste and come back year after year as volunteers in garden spots.

TREE MOLASSES OR TREE SUGAR Maple syrup.

TRUCK PATCH Garden.

TURKEY BEAN A bean supposedly first discovered in a turkey's craw with the seed being saved.

TURKEY FOOT MUSTARD A spring green (toothwort).

TURNIP KRAUT Diced turnips pickled like kraut.

VICTUALS OR VITTLES Foodstuffs.

WATERCRESS A type of cress with a peppery taste growing in or at the edge of water.

WHISTLE PIG A groundhog (also known as a woodchuck) prized for eating because of its fat but also considered a real nuisance in gardens, fields, and pastures. They were hunted avidly.

WHITE HOMINY Same as big hominy.

WHITE SOP Milk gravy, especially with a chicken base.

WHITE WALNUTS *See* butternuts.

WILT Used in the same way as "kilt." "We had a wilted salad."

WORK OFF Allow kraut or other types of pickles to ferment. Also used the describe the moonshining process.

YARD BIRDS Usually refers to chickens but also other domestic fowl, including turkeys, ducks, guineas, and geese.

READING AND RESOURCES:
AN ANNOTATED BIBLIOGRAPHY

Maybe it's my former life as a university professor who devoted a fair percentage of his scholarly endeavor to publication of book-length bibliographies, or perhaps it's just an offshoot of being an inveterate bibliophile who has not only read but collected books all his adult life. Whatever the case, I always reserve a warm place in my mind for books that include a bibliography, and if they offer coverage in the form of a bibliographical essay or notes on individual entries, so much the better. Accordingly, in closing this longing look back over the foodstuffs that were a vital part of my raising, it seems appropriate to mention some of my favorite regional cookbooks and their coverage of dishes gracing Appalachian tables in yesteryear and today, list others that putatively deal with the subject, and touch on a selection of general reading material that delves into Smokies food lore in a meaningful fashion.

Throughout virtually all my years not only have I been a hopelessly, happily addicted reader, but I'm the type of bookworm who finds comfort in having works on his favorite subjects close at hand. Accordingly, one of my book-collecting passions has long been cookbooks, and that devotion was reinforced by the realization that getting my wife a cookbook or two for special occasions was always a good move and at least a partial solution to my singular ineptitude when it came to acquiring suitable gifts. Add to those considerations the fact that one of my focal points as a collector has been the literature of the Smokies, and you have a grand melding of food, cooking literature, and a geographical location that is the home of my heart.

Whenever I have discovered a work that falls within the comforting confines of those categories, it immediately takes on a special aura for me. How could it be otherwise given how much I cherish the Smokies and my great fondness for the culinary arts as practiced in that region? I've never counted but my total holding of cookbooks probably is in the area of five hundred volumes (not only were such works always a suitable and welcome gift for my wife, I can't deny a degree of selfishness in that I also enjoyed the books, not only for the pleasure they provided in reading but also in what they brought to the family table). Add another thousand volumes or so dealing with southern Appalachia and you begin to get some inkling of what many might consider an obsession with books.

Yet in the midst of my obsession it seems that when Smokies foods are the subject of moment, disappointment is a constant companion. Maybe I'm too parochial, but time and again books with titles suggesting they will carry me lovingly to the folkways and foodways of the Smokies turn out to be exercises in hype, works that mislead, or what is sometimes called "bait and switch" in the world of advertising. I receive the latest book, eagerly turn to its pages, and discover that the word *charlatan* would not be out of place. Either the author or publisher (or both) apparently think that merely throwing "mountain" into the mix when it comes to cooking is somehow magical. What they fail to realize is that historically regional variations, delightful distinctions, and differing food traditions existed right alongside shared culinary practices. For example, daily fare in Kentucky or West Virginia coal-mining country wasn't necessarily the same as that consumed by residents of the Great Smokies of North Carolina and Tennessee. For all that there were similarities, the regions didn't grow exactly the same crops, rely on the same herbs, have the same food rituals, or employ precisely the same methods of cultivation and preservation. To imply that culinary uniformity reigns supreme through the southern Appalachians, and it happens with many of the books listed below, is to do an injustice.

There are certainly hundreds, and possibly even a few thousand, of cookbooks dealing with the somewhat vaguely defined region known as the southern Appalachians. In the sense of demonstrating a deep understanding of and real appreciation for the distinctiveness of the specific geographic region known to cartographers as the Smokies, most of the works fall well wide of the mark. For that reason alone, those that do carry the tone of authenticity, credentials that cry out, page after page, "been there, cooked that, and eaten that," are culinary gems to be treasured. A cross sign (†) before a title in the list that follows indicates that I feel the work is at least somewhat true to Smokies fixings as I have known them.

Without exception the Smokies-related cookbooks that rank as my favorites combine recipes with narrative material. That approach to me seems the preferred one for regional cookbooks, because the dining is only part of the overall picture. Traditions, how food is grown or procured, meals as a part of life, holiday dining, and a whole host of related matters figure in culinary considerations as part of a culture. I've taken a similar approach in previous cookbooks of my own, and those listed below that are preceded by an asterisk (*) offer the pleasing combination of recipes and commentary. Some of these works are readily available on either the in-print or out-of-print market; others are rather difficult to obtain. Over the years, all have given me, in varying degrees, gustatory pleasure, insight, and some joyous armchair adventure while pondering comestibles.

In the listings below I also offer thoughts on the nature of the work or my assessment of its importance in the general field of cookbooks dealing with the Smokies specifically or southern Appalachia. Some of these evaluations may seem overly critical, but keep in mind that the books are being viewed primarily from a Smokies perspective as opposed to the more general and geographically amorphous one of Appalachia.

In addition to the books covered here, there are untold numbers more that fall into a category that might be loosely defined as fundraisers, family cookbooks, or "front porchers." The fundraisers come from church circles, civic groups, women's clubs, chambers of commerce, and others. Many of these contain recipes for fine traditional fare of a local nature, and if the sponsoring organization comes from the Smokies, in all likelihood a goodly portion of the coverage will have a local flavor. Family cookbooks, often just stapled or comb-bound pages printed from typescript, are elusive but likely to contain a few absolute jewels. I know such is the case for the little *The Casada Family Cooks*, which was an outgrowth of reunions of my own family. Then there are what I style front porchers because they offer a collection of recipes for standard fare or menu items associated with noted lodges, venerable retreats, bed-and-breakfast establishments, or hotels where rocking chairs are about as close as the guests get to actual kitchen doings. Most such hostelries found in the Smokies have front porches equipped with rocking chairs where you can ruminate, gently allow your vittles to settle after a fine supper, or maybe enjoy a soothing libation.

† A cookbook that is at least somewhat reminiscent of Smokies cooking as I have known it.

* A cookbook combining narrative material or commentary with the recipes.

†*Sam Beall, *The Foothills Cuisine of Blackberry Farm*, 2012. As perhaps might be expected from an establishment that caters to folks who can spend a great deal of money for a three-day stay at a plush retreat nestled tight against the park's boundary on the Tennessee side, this book belongs more to an end table in a high-dollar home than the kitchen counter of average Smokies folks. It's beautifully done, coffee-table size, lavish in every way, and the author grew up in the Smokies. Yet the title of one recipe alone, "Sumac-dusted Brook Trout," immediately tells this native of the Smokies that there are some problems with high-country authenticity. No self-respecting son or daughter of the region who knows and speaks its vernacular will use the term "brook trout." Call 'em specks, speckled trout, natives, or my favorite, mountain trout, and

you are on solid ground. Brook trout are something swimming in streams up Maine way or in Labrador. Most of the recipes here feature ingredients true to regional food roots, but with the exception of a few offerings, such as hoecakes and bread-and-butter pickles, they carry strong overtones of culinary schools, not Smokies kitchens (it will be a day when trout all face downstream and become bottom-feeders like catfish when you find an array of bottles of Châteauneuf-du-Pape in a mountain kitchen). I actually love the book. It's just not redolent of the Smokies, despite the geographical setting and recipe ingredients.

†Jean Boone Benfield, *Mountain Born: A Recollection of Life and Language in Western North Carolina*, 2009. All of part 2 in this work (pages 73–111), with the simple title of "Vittles," deals with food. It involves reminiscences, not recipes, and the author's coverage ranges widely. Although she grew up just outside the Smokies in Buncombe County, she's quite close to my age, and her food-related recollections meld rather closely with mine.

†*Carolyn G. Bryan, *Appalachian Kinfolks Cookbook*, 1990. Contributions from a widespread family with members spread all up and down the spine of the Appalachians. While a decidedly mixed bag, recipe-wise, there are delightful little tidbits of information scattered throughout the book.

†*Cades Cove Preservation Association, *Recipes, Remedies, and Rumors*, 2 vols., n.d. A massive collection, running well over six hundred pages, of a little bit of everything. Recipes take center stage, and many of them come from old-time mountain cooks descended from Cades Cove families or who, in some instances, were actually born in this little piece of mountain paradise.

*Sam Carson and A. W. Vick, *Hillbilly Cookin' 2: More Recipes, More Sayings*, 1972. This is one of many short works designed more with the intention of catching the attention of flatlanders and extracting cash from them than paying meaningful tribute to enduring food folkways. I find the gratuitous over-indulgence in "mountain talk" galling as well as demeaning, but the approach evidently sells books to tourists. That annoyance being duly noted, some of the snippets of information on folk remedies, adages, and mountain lore are of interest. There are scattered useful recipes as well, and they have the undeniable virtue of simplicity.

†*Bonnie Lou Cochran, *Ways of Old: Growing Up in the Needmore/Hightower Community, Bryson City, N.C.*, 2006. If you want a genuine feel for growing up in a rural setting in the Smokies, this book is a dandy. A goodly portion of its contents revolves around food for the simple reason that farm life in the region and eking out an existence loomed large for folks living there. The author, who is a few years younger than me, isn't a trained writer. Nonetheless, her account exudes authenticity from the first page to the last. There are a few recipes, but accounts of things such as hog butchering, canning, the role of corn in mountain life, and tales of day-to-day existence are what distinguish this book.

Her description of making butter and buttermilk is as succinct and spot-on as one could wish, and she places dairy products from the milk cow or two that most everyone owned squarely in their important place in Smokies diet.

†*Judy Alexander Coker, *Cataloochee Cooking*, 2002. Cataloochee Ranch, with its rich history and exquisite geographical setting, is rightly renowned for the food served to guests. In this book, a daughter of the founding husband-and-wife team, who is a woman deeply imbued with traditions of the Smokies in her own right, shares not only a panoply of scrumptious recipes but all sorts of family history, interesting background information, and even a bit of folk medicine. I highly recommend this book and particularly like the chapter on "Wild Game and Food from the Woods."

†*Joseph E. Dabney, *Smokehouse Ham, Spoon Bread, and Scuppernong Wine: The Folklore and Art of Southern Appalachian Cooking*, 1998. A big book, at upwards of five hundred pages, this is a work of major importance. It won all sorts of recognition when it first appeared, including the prestigious James Beard Cookbook of the Year Award, and Dabney clearly spent a great deal of time interviewing traditional mountain cooks. The book is liberally laced with scores of quotations from books and interviewees, and Dabney leaves no doubt whatsoever of his mastery of the subject material. Unlike a great many "Appalachian" cookbooks that focus on coal-mining country, the Blue Ridge region of Virginia, or foothills regions, this one includes plenty from the Smokies for readers to sample and savor. Essential.

*Nanette Davidson, *The Folk School Cookbook: A Collection of Seasonal Favorites from John C. Campbell Folk School*, 2018. While most of the recipes go a step, or in some cases several steps, beyond the straightforward simplicity that was actually a key ingredient of mountain cooking, this is a lovely book from an aesthetic standpoint and the recipes are appealing. They just aren't, with relatively few exceptions, traditional Smokies fare.

*Durwood Dunn, *Cades Cove: The Life and Death of a Southern Appalachian Community, 1818–1937*, 1988. This work is a first-rate study of arguably the best-known of all Smokies settlements. While food does not figure prominently in its coverage, the reader is given a fine view of daily life. It should be noted, however, that existence in Cades Cove was not totally reflective of how the average farmer of the region lived. The land there was far more fertile, level, and more generally amenable to agriculture than that found on the typical mountain farm. As a result, those living in Cades Cove produced such an abundance of food its residents could almost be described as enjoying the comparative luxury of a farm economy as opposed to hardscrabble living off the land. Annually a train of wagons left the isolated valley and made its way to Knoxville laden with produce. Folks in Cataloochee also ate quite a bit of beef, with cattle thriving thanks to the gentle slopes and limestone underlying the valley. That was something that was decidedly uncommon in the Smokies.

Louise and Bill Dwyer, *Southern Appalachian Mountain Cookin': Authentic Ol' Mountain Family Recipes*, 1974. While it contains a goodly number of recipes that could be deemed authentic, this cookbook is a prime example of the sort of concoctions conjured up to capture flatlander dollars rather than reflect the verities of mountain cooking. I find the ill-conceived attempt to render "mountain talk" particularly repugnant. While I cherish (and use) the Smokies vernacular constantly, you won't find locals calling a creek a "crick," or as this book does, coining the word "dumperlin's" for dumplings or "breeches" for leather britches beans. A note in the front indicating that one of the authors is Yale educated probably says enough. There are those who are *in* the Smokies and those who are *of* the Smokies. I have little doubt that the authors, if they have actual connections to the region at all, fit in the former category.

†Georgann Eubanks, *The Month of Their Ripening: North Carolina Heritage Foods through the Year*, 2018. This book offers a detailed essay on a representative Tar Heel food for each month of the year. While the snow cream start with January may be a bit of a stretch, the rest of the chapters are well chosen, and solid research combined with sprightly writing make for an interesting read. Four of the chapters—on ramps, serviceberries, apples, and persimmons—cover foodstuffs of longstanding use and (except for serviceberries) importance in Smokies diet. There's also a chapter on scuppernongs, but it deals with cultivated varieties primarily associated with the lower Piedmont and the eastern portions of the state rather than wild mountain grapes.

†*Sidney Saylor Farr, *More Than Moonshine: Appalachian Recipes and Recollections*, 1983. A minor classic by an individual who has been well to the forefront of Appalachian studies and the upsurge in interest in the region, this book is part anecdote, part recipes, and all pure pleasure. It has some gaps—there is little information on fish and game, for example—and the author's roots lie in Kentucky rather than the Smokies. But the book has the clarion bell of authority ringing from every page. Farr was a woman who truly had "been there and done that" as far as the contents go, and I rejoice in the fact that they show she is unabashedly proud of her roots. Also useful, although it is an autobiography rather than a cookbook, is her *My Appalachia: A Memoir* (2007). Appreciable portions of the book's coverage deal with food lore. Highly recommended.

Food Favorites of the Great Smoky Mountains Park Families, 1992. A short, spiral-bound work compiled by the Park Women's Organization of the GSMNP (presumably wives of men employed by the park), this cookbook is included primarily because of the geographical location of the contributors as opposed to the contents being focused on the Smokies.

†Susan Freinkel, *American Chestnut: The Life, Death, and Rebirth of a Perfect Tree*, 2007. While, at least for the present, the "rebirth" portion of this book's subtitle remains a bit optimistic, we can at least see a glimmer of the wondrous chestnut's resurrection. This carefully researched and well-written

study devotes considerable (and justifiable) attention to the American chestnut as a food source.

†*Patsy Moore Ginns, *Snowbird Gravy and Dishpan Pie: Mountain People Recall*, 1982. This is a collection of interviews Ginns conducted with a number of old-timers, almost all of whom were born in the latter part of the nineteenth century. A goodly number of the accounts deal with food. None of the interviewees lived in the Smokies, but all were from quite close by, either dwelling in northwestern North Carolina or in the state's far southwestern counties of Cherokee and Clay. Ginns wrote a companion book taking the same approach, *Rough Weather Makes Good Timber: Carolinians Recall* (1977), with most of those interviewed living in North Carolina's piedmont counties.

Joseph S. Hall, *Smoky Mountain Folks and Their Lore*, 1960. A tireless field researcher who focused on linguistics, Hall made repeated trips to the Smokies and recorded conversation with scores of folks. His research is *the* key underlying element in Michael Montgomery and Joseph S. Hall, *Dictionary of Smoky Mountain English* (2004). Though not a cookbook, this work is a delight and full of culinary insight on Smokies ways.

†Paul B. Hamel and Mary U. Chiltoskey, *Cherokee Plants: Their Uses—A Four Hundred Year History*, 1975. An obscure but important work that offers an insightful look at the way plants and knowledge thereof were woven into the entire existence of the Cherokees. The heart of the book is an alphabetical listing of plants by their common and then scientific name. Each entry includes brief information on the uses for the plant. Most of the coverage deals with those having medicinal or consumptive uses.

†*Ila Hatter, ed., *Roadside Rambles: A Collection of Wild Food Recipes*, 2001. While the recipes and information in this most useful little work aren't focused specifically on the Smokies, the editor lives there, virtually all the edibles from nature are found there, and the contents form a fine reminder of just how close to nature the people of the region have always been. For generations they depended in appreciable measure on nature's wild bounty for sustenance as well as medical uses, and Hatter's work is a fine reflection of their folkways.

†*Rose Houk, *Food and Recipes of the Smokies*, 1996. Written for and published by the Great Smoky Mountains Natural History Association, probably as a work-for-hire project since the author is a professional freelancer, this cookbook shows the author's normal competence and care. I strongly suspect, although I don't know it for a fact, that Houk is not a native of the Smokies. There are hints in that regard here and there, but there's no question she has done her research, interviewed cooks who know their stuff, and provided a workmanlike volume. Many of the recipes come from other cookbooks.

†*Sue Hyde, *Blue Willow Dishes: Recipes and Remembrances*, n.d.; *Gone Full Circle: More Recipes and Remembrances*, n.d.; and *From the Kitchen; From the Heart*, n.d. These three self-published books have some of the problems

inherent to that genre in terms of spelling, style, and the like, but the "From the Heart" portion of the third listing's title pretty well says it all. These are tales and tastes from a Swain County lass who came from a poor but proud background, and like all of her family, has done wonderfully well. There are literally hundreds of recipes, and a goodly portion of them are redolent of the Smokies. For years the author oversaw day-to-day operations at the bed-and-breakfast establishment that has, over time, been variously known as the Calhoun Hotel, Calhoun Country Inn, Historic Calhoun House, and other names, all of them associated with the Calhoun family who "moved to town" from Hazel Creek in the aftermath of the park's creation and Fontana Lake's flooding to start over. One of the key figures was venerable Granville Calhoun, often known as the Squire of Hazel Creek. The author's mother worked there, and in many ways the family's acquisition of the business is a tribute to her. These books are redolent of mountain life and mountain food in every way, although I'm unabashedly partial inasmuch as I've known the author virtually all her life.

†Alan and Karen Singer Jabbour, *Decoration Day in the Mountains: Traditions of Cemetery Decoration in the Southern Appalachians*, 2010. While certainly not a cookbook, this work is of note because "dinner on the grounds" and traditional foods were an integral and important part of Decoration Day. Since the practice continues to be a cultural stronghold in the Smokies, especially in connection with the numerous cemeteries scattered within the park along Fontana Lake's North Shore, the authors rightly gave this aspect of cemetery maintenance and reverence for ancestors appreciable coverage.

*Horace Kephart, *Camping and Woodcraft*, 1916. I'm no fan of Kephart's famed *Our Southern Highlanders*. To me appreciable portions of the book are a travesty in stereotyping aimed at selling books rather than sharing the realities of early twentieth-century life in the Smokies. I consider it a monumental shame that such a large portion of the general reading public view Kephart's depiction of mountain life as the essence of accuracy. Increasingly, serious students of the region agree with my view, although Kephart still has far more devoted disciples than insightful critics. Such considerations aside, the man knew cooking, especially when undertaken in an outdoor setting, and since an appreciable portion of the material in this book came from his experiences during the first decade he spent in the Smokies, it merits serious attention. So does a slender little volume he wrote earlier, *Camp Cookery* (1910).

†*Walter N. Lambert, *Kinfolks and Custard Pie: Recollections and Recipes from an East Tennessean*, 1988. This is a wonderful book by a professional chef who hasn't for a moment forgotten his roots. He's funny, slightly irreverent, and knowledgeable. Country as cornbread, down to earth, and genuine as blackstrap molasses, this book is an absolute must have for anyone who wants to understand the folkways underlying Smokies fixings. I disagree with

Lambert on a few points, such as his definition of pork tenderloin, but his work ranks right in the top echelons of my list of books on the food folklore of the high country. Indispensable.

†*Jan J. Love, *Farms, Gardens, and Countryside Trails of Western North Carolina*, (2002). You won't find a lot of recipes in this work, although they are scattered as sidebars here and there. It is essentially a guide, covering hundreds of destinations, although only a few of its two-hundred-plus pages touch on the Smokies. That's arguably a hidden blessing, because it suggests the region hasn't become quite as commercialized as other parts of western North Carolina.

*Ronni Lundy, ed., *Foods of the Mountain South: Cornbread Nation 3*, 2005. As is so often the case with cookbooks with titles including words or phrases like "Mountain South," "Mountain," "Southern Appalachian," and the like, the region that should be considered *the* heart of Appalachia and regional cookery, the Smokies, is to a large measure ignored in this work's pages. A quick look-see at the list of more than forty contributors does not reveal a single one with direct links to (i.e., living in or a native of) the Smokies, although Fred Sauceman comes close. There are a number of poems, and this is really a collection of food-related essays, many esoteric or even exotic, rather than a ladle in hand or seat at the table work on food. The book was, to me, a disappointment, although there are a few dandy pieces such as John Edge's treatment of fried pies and Coleen Anderson's peek at pawpaws.

†*Ronni Lundy, *Victuals*, 2016. Although this work, like *Cornbread Nation 3*, gives the Smokies rather short shrift, it is a marvelous cookbook. Superbly illustrated and with lots of eminently practical recipes that somehow seem to be overlooked all too often (mashed potatoes, greens, tomato gravy, pie crust, and brown sugar pie are but a few of many examples), this effort touches most of the key bases, and a solid indication of its merits is that it won, among numerous awards, the coveted James Beard Foundation Book of the Year. Some recipes don't exactly fit my idea of mountain vittles (for example, "Shelley Cooper's Specked Butter Bean Cassoulet with Rabbit Confit"), and Lundy just skirts around the edges of the Smokies or covers the area's restaurants rather than venturing into the true heart of Appalachia, its home kitchens and fine mountain cooks with generations of experience behind them. There's a bit too much of the fancified air of the upscale restaurant scene for this hardened hillbilly, but maybe for Lundy that's a hidden blessing. She has kitchens to visit and the minds of old-time mountain cooks still waiting to be picked, and she writes in a relaxed, chatty manner I find most appealing.

†Margaret McCaulley, *A Cades Cove Childhood: Remembered by J. C. McCaulley*, 2008. An interesting memoir of growing up in Cades Cove that includes a fair amount of food-related material as a part of lifestyles there in the immediate prepark era.

†*Rick McDaniel, *An Irresistible History of Southern Food: Four Centuries of Black-eyed Peas, Collard Greens, and Whole Hog Barbecue*, 2011. Most cookbooks where the word "Southern" or its derivatives appear in the title send up a red flag. They are more likely to focus on plantation foods, African American influences, and the coastal and red clay regions of the Old South than the mountains in general and the Smokies in particular. This work is no exception, but it is well illustrated and far better written than average, contains fine chapters on pork and "The Gospel Bird" (chicken), and a usual overview of regional culinary history. As is so often the case, Scots-Irish influences, which along with those of the Cherokees loomed large indeed in the Smokies, get somewhat short shrift.

†Zell Miller, *The Mountains within Me*, 1985. Zell Miller grew up in the mountains of North Georgia, and as the title of this book suggests, took immense pride in his roots. He rose to prominence as the governor of Georgia, a senator, and for his ultimate disenchantment with the Democratic Party. You won't find recipes in this book, and the author readily acknowledges his mother was an indifferent cook, but he touches on the basic items of diet as they were in his youth quite nicely. There are a few differences with the Smokies—among them his description of cathead biscuits, his understanding of the exact way to determine whether a persimmon is ripe, and where the tenderloins are located in a pig. The book is a joy to read and the author's life story an uplifting one.

†*Patricia B. Mitchell, *Southern Mountain Cooking*, 2000. By one of those strange strokes of serendipity that we encounter in life from time to time, the author of this work grew up in my wife's hometown and was close to the same age. However, I had no idea she was not only a cookbook author but the genius behind an impressive self-publishing cottage industry that has seen the production of dozens of thirty-six page works with specific culinary themes. This book offers roughly four dozen recipes along with anecdotes, history, and more. While its focus isn't just the Smokies but exactly what the title suggests, most of the recipes are true to the foods of the region where I grew up. Other books by Mitchell that link closely to the Smokies include *Apple Country Cooking* (1989), *Sweet 'n' Slow: Apple Butter, Molasses, and Sorghum Recipes* (1988), and *True Grist: Buckwheat Flour and Cornmeal Recipes* (1988).

†Larry G. Morgan, *Mountain Born, Mountain Molded*, 2002. The author grew up in the remote Macon County community of Nantahala in the 1940s and 1950s. Good-natured and filled with quiet but obvious pride of "a little boy who didn't know he was poor" (as was true of a lot of us in that time and place), the coverage is arguably overwrought in its depiction of food as being "Simple, Same, and Plentiful," and the treatment of canning and meals doesn't reflect what I experienced as a lad growing up at almost exactly the same time and not thirty miles away. Our food may have been simple and plentiful, but there

was ample variety, ingenuity when it came to preparation, and sameness usually reflected consistently fine fare rather than the taste bud dulling Morgan implies.

Mountain Makin's in the Smokies: A Cookbook, 1957. A short but most useful effort published by the Great Smoky Mountains Natural History Association, presumably as a fundraiser.

†Bonnie Trentham Myers (with Lynda Myers Boyer), *Best Yet Life and Lore of the Smokies: An Anecdotal Encyclopedia of Smoky Mountain People*, 2002. An interesting approach, with entries covering a little bit of everything connected with Smokies folkways. The author was born and grew up in the Fighting Creek Gap area near Gatlinburg and the park's Sugarlands Visitor Center. Her thoughts ring as true as a church bell on a quiet Sunday morning and no punches are pulled. She roundly condemns misrepresentations of area residents as rubes and worthless rustics, and while admitting there is a modicum of truth in some stereotypes, condemns mythmaking. She speaks passionately of "strong people who lived worthy lives of substance and meaning" instead of the "image [Horace Kephart] painted of us as 'wretched backward creatures living in depravity and degradation.'" Her coverage of food traditions effectively counters Kephart's descriptions.

†*Earlene Rather O'Dell, *The Flavour of Home: A Southern Appalachian Family Remembers*, 2000. Set primarily in northeast Tennessee (the author grew up in Bristol), this book combines specific recipes with family lore, anecdotes, and heartwarming commentary on mountain life. The recipes form an interesting mix of the traditional with preparation techniques and types of dishes that would have been unknown in the Smokies until the final third of the twentieth century. You'll find mush bread and berry dumplings just pages away from seafood dishes featuring oysters and scallops along with pastry puffs and soufflés. I just wish the person responsible for the Anglicized spelling of *flavor* in the title had a clue.

†*Duane Oliver, *Cooking on Hazel Creek*, 1990; *Cooking and Living along the River*, 2002; and *North Shore Cookbook*, 2011. Like all of Oliver's works, his cookbooks are cheaply done publications that appear to have been reproduced directly from typescript. That's a shame. Perhaps publishers rejected them, which could have been a distinct possibility with the cookbooks, but what is unquestionably his most important effort, *Hazel Creek from Then Till Now* (1990), deserved commercial publication. It has some fairly significant problems, but most of those could have been rectified to an appreciable degree by insightful editorial guidance, some fact-checking, and proofreading assistance. I suspect, however, that he just decided to go the self-publishing route. Oliver grew up in the dam and logging boomtowns of Fontana, Judson, and Proctor, now under the waters of Fontana Lake or within the bosom of the park, and it is his sharing of food traditions and historical food lore, as opposed to recipes,

that is of significance. I hardly think "Lasagna Florentine," or for that matter chili, béchamel, yogurt, salmon, macadamia nuts, "Welch [sic] rabbit," schnitzel, or an entire section devoted to pasta in his second cookbook fit the mold of Smokies cooking. And how so much as mention of a TV dinner (literally) finds its way into a cookbook is beyond my ken. I have no idea why Oliver strayed so far from his culinary roots with the recipes, but half or more of them have no meaningful connection whatsoever to the Smokies, never mind that the introduction to one of them claims it is devoted specifically and exclusively to the region along Fontana Lake's North Shore. Still, thanks to their narrative material, these are works deserving of a modicum of attention, although I think Joe Dabney, a culinary hero of mine, is far too uncritical in the considerable credit he accords Oliver when it comes to culinary knowledge.

†Ted Olson, *Blue Ridge Folklife*, 1998. A volume in the University of Mississippi Press's Folklife in the South Series, this book does not address the Smokies thanks to a companion volume on *Great Smoky Mountain Folklife* (see below) by Michael Ann Williams. However, it merits inclusion because an appreciable portion of the material on food folkways (mostly on pages 156–69) is applicable to the ways of residents of the Smokies.

†Linda Garland Page and Eliot Wigginton, eds., *Aunt Arie: A Foxfire Portrait*, 1983. A portrait of "Aunt" (an honorific given exclusively to women who are widely revered in a community) Arie Carpenter, a beguiling woman brimming with life and beloved by all, mostly told in her own words, this book is a pure delight with much of it devoted to food traditions. Who can fail to be intrigued by her statement "I'd a heap rather cook as t' eat" or resist the toothsome appeal of a Sunday menu at her house featuring "souse and sausage, chicken and dumplings, leather britches, hominy, cabbage cooked in a frying pan in the broth from making souse, potatoes cooked in a Dutch oven, chow-chow, bread, egg custards, peach cobbler"? Aunt Arie resided in the Coweeta area of Macon County, North Carolina, just outside the Smokies proper, and to read her story, for me, is to envision a woman who was a composite of a number of those I knew as a youngster. What a treat it would have been to plunder around her kitchen, helping out (which she encouraged Foxfire students to do) and then sit down to a true mountain meal.

†*Linda Garland Page and Eliot Wigginton, eds., *The Foxfire Book of Appalachian Cookery*, 1984. The home stomping grounds of the Foxfire program in Rabun Gap, Georgia, lie outside the confines of the Smokies, but not by much. This work, as is true of all the long-running Foxfire collection, is a solid reflection of my highland homeland. While it contains a number of fine recipes, and I'm particularly partial to the sections on game and fish, it is the narrative material that is most useful. Not far behind are the numerous photographs and diagrams. By careful perusal of these pages, you will come away with a solid

feel for traditional approaches to mountain cooking. Along the way you'll meet a fetching cast of cooks and characters.

†*John Parris, *Mountain Cooking*, 1978. For well over four decades this writer's column, "Roaming the Mountains," graced the pages of the *Asheville Citizen-Times* three times a week. It ranged widely across all aspects of mountain culture, but foodways ranked well toward the top of Parris's interests. Much of this work (the first 250 pages), as is true in their entirety for his other books, contains pieces that originally appeared as newspaper columns. The remainder of the work is composed of scores of recipes, most of which feature the Smokies way of cooking (Parris was a native of Jackson County, on the edge of the Smokies proper). This is a work of considerable significance, which no one interested in food folkways of the Smokies can afford to overlook. His other collections of columns, *Roaming the Mountains* (1955); *My Mountains, My People* (1957); *Mountain Bred* (1967); and *These Storied Mountains* (1972), all contain appreciable coverage of mountain food traditions. To me, Parris captured the overall mountain way of life about as well as anyone has to this point in time.

†*Willadeene Parton, *All-Day Singing and Dinner on the Ground*, 1997. Written by an older sister of famed singer Dolly Parton, this book is about as down-to-earth, authentic Smokies as is available in the cookbook field. It is composed primarily of recipes, but the narrative portion is informative and entertaining, with the coverage of Easter, hunting season, Thanksgiving, and Christmas being especially well done. Where many so-called Smokies cookbooks are what folks where I grew up would have called "off-putting" (a nice way of saying offensive), this one brings delight and promise of many a good dinner in its pages. I don't know how I overlooked it for a full two decades after its publication, but it is redolent of my hillbilly homeland in every page and virtually every recipe. Essential.

†Elizabeth Powers with Mark Hannah, *Cataloochee—Lost Settlement of the Smokies: The History, Social Customs, and Natural History*, 1982. This is an obscure work of considerable importance and one that cries out for reprinting since it is virtually impossible to find. Powers describes herself as "the transmitter of the flame," while Mark Hannah was born and raised in Cataloochee and retained his connections even after the coming of the park, thanks to being an early ranger. Chapter 19, "Plenty (Cataloochee Cooking)," focuses specifically on, in the words of Hannah's father, the manner in which "we made what we eat, and we eat what we made." But other portions of the book reflect a vanished way of life in a place that was, along with Cades Cove on the Tennessee side of the Smokies, truly deserving of mountain poet Leroy Sossamon's description of the Smokies as "the backside of heaven."

†*John F. Rehder, *Appalachian Folkways*, 2004. A chapter of this scholarly work is devoted to "Foodways." The author was a trained academic geographer,

and in most ways his coverage, which includes a few recipes, is interesting and instructive. However, it offers some information that is perplexing in the extreme. The statement that sourwood trees grow in an "ecological niche" in the mountains "at about 3,000 to 5,000 feet" is, simply put, dead wrong. Sourwoods are as common as pig tracks throughout the Smokies at much lower elevations and can be found as far south as northern Florida. That in turn makes his coverage of another Smokies sweetener, syrup, suspect. Rehder is adamant that molasses is in effect a rank stranger to the mountains, maintaining it is made from sugarcane, while sorghum cane produces only syrup. I'm not about to delve into etymological minutiae, but I'll stand my ground when it comes to stating that folks in my homeland consistently used the word *molasses* to describe any sorghum syrup that was dark. Beyond that, the various entries on molasses found in the ultimate authority on mountain talk, Joe Hall and Michael Montgomery's *Dictionary of Smoky Mountain English*, support my perspective. Certainly folks in the Smokies, in their everyday mode of expression, have long thought otherwise as regards Rehder's statement, "There is no such thing as 'sorghum molasses.'"

†Gladys Oliver Ridings, *Cades Cove and Parts of the Great Smoky Mountains*, 1983. This is primarily a family history focused on the Oliver clan, although there is considerable material on members of the Walker and Stinnett families as well. While the Cades Cove community figures prominently, so does life in Little Greenbrier. There are scattered food references and one intriguing list of "Foods Grown and Prepared on a Farm," which includes some dishes I've never seen mentioned elsewhere, such as "Fried Cucumber," "Fried Dried Beans," and "Popcorn in Sweet Milk."

†*Gladys Trentham Russell, *Call Me Hillbilly*, 1974. This short memoir, liberally spiced with vintage photographs, rings as true as a whippoorwill's call in a remote hollow at daybreak. She offers delightful food memories, and the way in which she unabashedly crowns herself with the term "hillbilly," proud of the moniker and unafraid of letting others know as much, tickles my fancy.

†Gladys Trentham Russell, *It Happened in the Smokies*, 1988. A literary potpourri embracing "a mountaineer's memories of happenings in the Smoky Mountains in Pre-Park Days." A goodly number of the author's memories focus on food, and they are as down-to-earth and authentic as anything you'll find in print. Words such as "I don't recall that we even owned a cookbook," description of her favorite snack as "a green onion from the garden and a piece of cold cornbread," or commenting that a rainy summer day "put molasses on your feet" tell the tale of a woman whose final words in this slender work speak volumes: "Grateful I'm still a mountaineer." Russell's books are pure treasures thanks to their genuineness and the manner in which her love of place graces every page.

†*Fred W. Sauceman, *The Place Setting: Timeless Tastes of the Mountain South, from Bright Hope to Frog Level*, 2006. This collection of food memories, almost five dozen in all, focuses on food festivals, restaurants, and a few timeless regional traditions. Only a handful of the pieces focus specifically on the Smokies, but a good many of them deal with food subjects of lasting significance to the region. There are just over a dozen actual recipes, but the pages provide an unfolding story of gustatory enjoyment in fine, readable fashion.

Pearlie B. Scott, *Great Smoky Mountains Cookbook*, 2000. You don't have to dig very deeply in this work to realize that its title is well wide of the mark. While it contains numerous recipes that could have come out of the Smokies, when the book opens with a section devoted to beef, you know it is "off." Smokies folks, at least in yesteryear, very rarely ate beef. Then there are recipes for salmon, tuna, lots of dishes containing rice, Amish desserts, and more. In other words, either the author or the publisher used the title to sell books as opposed to offering a reflection of its actual contents.

†*Susi Gott Seguret, *Appalachian Appetite: Recipes from the Heart of America*, 2016. Beautifully illustrated and with ample information on foodstuffs near and dear to Smokies folks, this is a book I love yet simultaneously find troubling. There are grand links of mountain music and table makings, a one-page listing of "Appalachian Ingredients," which is something of a stroke of genius when it comes to wild foods, and a fine literary style. On the other hand, the recipes are, with relatively few exceptions, quite complicated and associated more with skilled chefs than with kitchen cook stoves and down-to-earth eating. When you have information on preparing leather britches just six pages removed from "Carolina Bison Sirloin with Red Wine Butter and Stuffed Ulster Baked Potato," perhaps you get the picture. Just the name of the latter recipe would have given Grandma Minnie the vapors.

*Ferne Shelton, *Southern Appalachian Mountain Cookbook*, 1964. A collection of 175 recipes and remedies (only a few of the latter) from "the Blue Ridge and Great Smoky Mountains." There is considerable emphasis on sweets with minimal coverage of meat. The author was a prolific producer of small cookbooks and related items on remedies, beauty secrets, and the like. All ran to thirty-two pages and were designed to be mailed in the same manner as an oversized post card. A few of the recipes—"Raspberry Shrub," "Rhubarb Nectar," and "Sweet Potato Cobber," for example—are unusual yet seem well suited to a Smokies kitchen. Most are a stretch.

"Sis and Jake," *Ma's Cookin': Mountain Recipes*, 1966. This work is yet another disgusting exercise in stereotyping (the rear cover shows a barefooted hillbilly leaning against a tree, passed out, with his jug of moonshine at his side). As someone who is well educated yet proudly wears the badge of being a son of the Smokies, resort to this kind of stuff for nothing but the crassest of monetary reasons irritates the dickens out of me. There are several useful recipes, although both the place of publication and internal evidence suggest the mountains of this book may well be the Ozarks rather than the Smokies. There are, however, based on my years of personal observation and detailed conversations with native Ozarkians, many similarities between the two regions.

†*Janet F. Smart, *Cooking with Family: Recipes and Remembrances*, 2017. Although she lives in West Virginia, judging by her comments, an introductory poem entitled "I Am from Appalachia," and the general thrust of her thoughts on cooking and life, Smart could well be a daughter of the Smokies. Her recipes are straightforward, scrumptious (at least the ones I've tried), and in some senses a refreshing break from the preponderance of regional cookbooks focused on restaurant cooking and haute cuisine that, for inexplicable reasons, has decided to take refuge in words such as *mountain* and *Appalachia*. The grouping of tidbits of wisdom—"Food Substitutions," "Conversions," "Cooking Tips," and "Food Traditions and Superstitions"—at book's end are a literary lagniappe of the first water.

†*Mark F. Sohn, *Appalachian Home Cooking: History, Culture, and Recipes*, 2005. This probably should be considered Sohn's most important piece of culinary writing, and the concept suggested by the book's subtitle exactly fits my vision of what a truly informative cookbook should cover. He takes a lot of interesting approaches, such as listing what he thinks are the most common Appalachian foods, devoting an entire chapter to breakfast, and offering extensive narrative coverage of all aspects of regional food folkways before getting to the section (a bit under half the book) containing recipes. As would be expected from an author who spent most of his career at Pikeville College, the book is, as seems somehow to be the case with a surprising percentage of all the cookbooks covering Appalachia, somewhat Kentucky-centric. The wild foods coverage is also somewhat sparse. Still, its general thrust incorporates the foodways I have known, and the book forms a most worthy addition to any shelf devoted to works on mountain cookery.

†*Mark F. Sohn, *Mountain Cooking: A Gathering of the Best Recipes from the Smokies to the Blue Ridge*, 1996. Just because a cookbook is published by a big-time New York outfit (this one by St. Martin's Press) doesn't mean its contents are in any way special. Often such works are more fluff and folderol than fine eating, but this effort is the real deal. As John Egerton rightly states in the work's foreword, this book contains "a wealth of information about food in the Appalachian mountain region, a virtual encyclopedia . . . that will be of immeasurable value to every cook and student of culture who cares about the region and its people." My gut feeling is that there's far more Blue Ridge and eastern Kentucky in these pages than Smokies (Sohn incorporates parts of nine states in his definition of Appalachia), but food variations in these particular

geographical subregions, while real, aren't usually all that dramatic. The author is a professional chef and TV cooking host, and his narrative material is more useful than the recipes—and many of them are jewels. He pays a considerable attention to low-calorie counts and fat-free alternatives, concerns that were of no import in the Smokies of yesteryear.

†*David A. Taylor, *Ginseng, the Divine Root*, 2006. Although Smokies folks occasionally used ginseng as a tonic or for other medicinal purposes, the fact that it was highly prized as a marketable commodity and could bring welcome infusions of cash money during "sanging season" meant it was primarily viewed as a cash crop from nature. This work is an extensive history of the plant and includes a chapter on its modern use as a foodstuff and a few recipes.

†*Mary Ulmer and Samuel E. Beck, eds., *Cherokee Cooklore: Preparing Cherokee Foods*, 1951. To my knowledge this is the only cookbook ever published that deals exclusively with Cherokee foods. It's short, and over half of its pages are devoted to photographs of Cherokees preparing various foods. But the recipes are genuine, with the names even being given in the Cherokee language using both the twenty-six-character alphabet and the considerably more complex one developed by Sequoyah.

†*Betsy Tice White, *Mountain Folk, Mountain Food: Down-Home Wisdom, Plain Tales, and Recipe Secrets from Appalachia*, 1997. There are far more tidbits of wisdom than recipes (only nineteen of these) in the pages of this book, but the offerings are worthwhile. Two recipes, the coverage of molasses pie and persimmon pudding, satisfy the sweet tooth and are worthy of every Smokies cook's attention.

†Cleo Hicks Williams, *Gratitude for Shoes: Growing Up Poor in the Smokies*, 2005. Although the subtitle of this book is geographically inaccurate (the author grew up on Junaluska Creek in Cherokee County, which lies a good many miles outside the Smokies), and the author's rendering of words into mountain talk is overwrought, the fact remains that her obscure work is in many ways a gem. It is chock-full of insight and remembrances of foodways from her youth (she was born in 1934), and the fifty-plus-page section entitled "Living Simply—Simply Living" covers key considerations such as corn, chickens, hogs, wild foods, cooking on a wood-burning stove, and "Eatin'." Every iota of reminiscence, every mention of a particular food or way of preparing it, right down to "Dad said a dang possum's too naisty [*sic*] to eat," rings true.

†Michael Ann Williams, *Great Smoky Mountains Folklife*, 1995. A volume in the Folklife in the South Series, this work devotes chapter 5 to "Food, Drink, and Medicine." The author makes a key point in suggesting that "food still plays an important role in defining the past," and her general overview of the role of food in Smokies life is nicely done. It's a reasonable place to start for anyone wanting a basic grasp of Smokies foodways.

INDEX TO RECIPES

GENERAL INDEX